Physics'
Assimilation
and
Purpose

Physics'
Assimilation
and
Purpose

Fundamentals and uses of
measurement, theory, and observation.

Philip Henderson

Calluna Publishing, UK

https://www.philipjameshenderson.co.uk/
mail@philipjameshenderson.co.uk
https://www.linkedin.com/in/philip-henderson-b8439372/

Second edition, with answers to all questions[1]:

Hardback: April 2026 (ISBN 978-1-9191987-0-5)
Paperback: April 2026 (ISBN 978-1-9191987-1-2)

British Library Cataloguing in Publication data – data available

---

[1]Without answers, independently published:
Hardback, first edition, January 2025 (ISBN 979-8839647756)
Paperback, first edition, January 2025 (ISBN 979-8839640566)

Preface

Starting small, but seeking profound enlightenment, this book expounds the methodology and usage of the physical revelation of Nature. For physicists of up to first-year undergraduacy, and with interests spanning experiment[1], theory[1], and the liberal arts, the book acts as an explanatory companion to the handling of data, and other topics ranging from mechanics, waves, and electricity to the exotica of photonics, healthcare[1], and the stars[1].

With an accessible style that includes margin notes, examples, and multiple-choice questions, the content is holistic throughout, occasionally mathematical, and fully referenced to help instil best practice, thought, and understanding. And, with a profusion of guidelines, applications, and tips, as well as pointers on active areas of research[1], the curious may be eased deeper into the subject.

---

[1]Note that easy access to these and other specialist topics is via a preliminary index.

Introduction

The Scientific Method, and This Text

Regardless of our awareness, we exist within a universe whose evolving structure continuously yields to our destiny. Physics, however, allows us to take control. Rooted upon perception of Nature, and with origins in a miscellany of disparate disciplines – that include philosophy, mathematics, religion, and intuition – physics has come to elucidate the interactions of matter ranging from subatomic entities to the largest bodies in space; and *inter alia* has eased applications of motion, and the practising of communication, medicine, and astronomy.

At the heart of physics is a fundamental inter-connective methodology that unlocks the simplicity, symmetry, and beauty of Nature. Indeed, the grail of many physicists is the establishment of a unified and comprehensive explicative theory. Although far from complete, our present discourses on particles, energy, and physical interactions include the conceptual unification of electricity and magnetism by Maxwell (1865), and major strides towards understanding mass and gravitation by Newton (1687) and Einstein (1916). Nonetheless, advances in physics require a cautionary approach. Time, for example, has been debated since antiquity yet, in physics, is merely a descriptor of change – after all, without change, physical systems would not age, there would be no clocks, and the concept of time would have no meaning. So, whilst we are concerned with the physics of Nature, we must remain acutely aware of the nature of physics.

Whereas physics is but a representation of Nature, its practice contributes to the growth of knowledge accelerated by both innate human desire and rigorous scientific doctrine. With the latter having origins in experimental principles established by al-Haytham (*c.*1016), first modern investigative procedure formulated by Bacon (1620), consolidative works by Galileo (1638), and deeper philosophy of Newton (1687), successful physicists follow a maturing tradition known as the scientific method:

Introduction

The Scientific Method	
Scrutiny	Since antiquity, the curious have sought to make sense of the universe. Postulates are propounded. Concepts are originated.
Measurements and records	Empiricists observe and measure. Data are recorded. Manual and electronic techniques are used for visualisation. A good sketch or graph can, indeed, paint a thousand words.
Theory	Theoreticians engage the language of mathematics to predict outcomes, and explain recorded data.
Establishment of physical laws, and growth of knowledge	Empiricism and theory are used to test postulates and concepts. Substantiation increases our knowledge of Nature, whilst the establishment of physical laws provides a universal, timeless predictive power that is often juxtaposed by the brevity of a simple formula and concise description.
Dissemination	Scientific works are communicated to the wider community through the principal languages of English and mathematics. Good publication requires novel works packaged as a balanced mixture of text, formulae, and diagrams.
New scrutiny, review, and acceptance of change	New topics are continuously identified and advanced through the same scientific method, whilst existing ones are subjected to confirmation or refutation. Scientists must be eager to renew their understanding in the light of new information.

This text now unlocks the method's best-practice by addressing physics' inter-connective content tabulated here in terms of Chapters and use:

#	Title	Use
1	Data	
2	Particles, Kinematics, and Mass	
3	Newtonian Force; Momentum and Energy	
4	Energetic propagation	Medical imaging via ultrasound
5	Interactions and Unification	Medical imaging via magnetic resonance
6	Electronics and Photonics	►Semiconductors ►Communication ►Medical imaging via endoscopes ►Medical imaging via X-rays ►Medical imaging via gamma rays
7	Space and Time	►Astronomy ►Cosmology

Dedication

To all enlivened by Nature:

my students
those with boundless patience
and everyone with indomitable spirit[1]

[1] In particular, a collective debt of gratitude follows my late father-in-law, Masood Hasan's wish (2014) for the present works to be published, and for the indefatigable evocation of that wish by both his daughter and grand-daughter – my wife Naveed Henderson and funky daughter Maliha Henderson.

Epigraph

Do not undertake a scientific career in quest of fame or money.

There are easier and better ways to reach them.

Undertake it only if nothing else will satisfy you;
for nothing else is probably what you will receive.

Your reward will be the widening of the horizon as you climb.

And if you achieve that reward you will ask no other.

Cecilia Payne-Gaposchkin:
An Autobiography and Other Recollections (1996)

Contents

Contents

Contents

Contents

Symbols and Terms

Scalar – A quantity without regard to spatial direction whose representation has a single number that could be positive or negative dependent on type:

Roman scalars:
a ....width, constant
A ....area
b ....baseline length, constant, rational number
c ....axial intercept of a straight line
c ....299 792 458 m s^{-1} definition of speed of light in free space
d ....diameter of detector, distance, number of dynodes
D ....distance from emitting surface, distance to a star
e ....1.602 176 634 × 10^{-19} C definition of electronic charge, extension
E ....energy
f ....frequency
g ....about 9.8 m s^{-2}, magnitude of the Earth's near-surface gravitational acceleration
G ....6.674 30(15) × 10^{-11} m^3 kg^{-1} s^{-2} gravitational constant
h ....6.626 070 15 × 10^{-34} J s definition of Planck's constant, height
I ....(absolute) intensity of light, electric current
k ....constant of Coulomb's law, stiffness, thermal conductivity
K ....kinetic energy
l ....luminosity
L ....distance, length
m ....gradient of a straight line, mass, integer
M ....total mass
n ....order of magnitude, refractive index, integer
N ....number of electrons, number of rulings in a diffraction grating
p ....pressure, integer
P ....power
q ....charge
Q ....heat
r ....distance, radius
R ....electric resistance, radius
t ....thickness, time
T ....temperature, temporal period (often referred to simply as period)
U ....potential energy
v ....speed in a medium
V ....voltage, volume
W ....work done
x, y, z ......components of position (also see *Cartesian vector formalism*)

Symbols and Terms

Greek scalars:
α .... fraction of light intensity absorbed per unit length of propagation
ε_0 .... 8.854 187 8128(13) $\times$ 10^{-12} kg^{-1} m^{-3} s^4 A^2 permittivity of
            free space
θ .... (geometric) angle
λ .... wavelength (spatial period) of light in a medium
λ_0 .... wavelength (spatial period) of light in free space
μ .... unit-less constant pertaining to static friction
μ_0 .... 1.256 637 062 12(19) $\times$ 10^{-6} kg m s^{-2} A^{-2} permeability of
            free space
π .... 3.141 592 654 ... pi
ρ .... density
φ .... phase angle
Φ .... work function

Vectors (quantities that encode spatial direction, and that may contain multiple
unit vectors, and multiple scalar components):
a .... acceleration
ā .... average acceleration
B .... magnetic field
E .... electric field
F .... force
p .... momentum of particle
P .... momentum of body
r .... position
v .... velocity
v̄ .... average velocity
W .... weight
Note 1: See ***Cartesian vector formalism*** opposite for a rigorous representation.
Note 2: All may be converted into a single positive scalar via the evaluation of
magnitude – e.g. $|\mathbf{W}|$ = magnitude of weight.

Symbols and Terms

Cartesian vector formalism (a specific representation of all vector quantities via a combination of positive or negative scalars, and the mutually perpendicular positive unit vectors $\mathbf{i}$, $\mathbf{j}$, and $\mathbf{k}$ – included here are just two examples concerning acceleration $\mathbf{a}$ and position $\mathbf{r}$):

Example 1: A 3D Cartesian representation of acceleration $\mathbf{a}$ as $\mathbf{a} = a_x\mathbf{i} + a_y\mathbf{j} + a_z\mathbf{k}$ for some scalars a_x, a_y, and a_z, where:

a_x ....is the component of acceleration associated with $\mathbf{i}$
a_y ....is the component of acceleration associated with $\mathbf{j}$
a_z ....is the component of acceleration associated with $\mathbf{k}$

Example 2: A 3D Cartesian representation of position $\mathbf{r}$ as $\mathbf{r} = x\mathbf{i} + y\mathbf{j} + z\mathbf{k}$ for some scalars x, y, and z, where:

x ....is the component of position associated with $\mathbf{i}$
y ....is the component of position associated with $\mathbf{j}$
z ....is the component of position associated with $\mathbf{k}$

Note: Associated values of such components may be referred to as Cartesian coordinates.

Rotational formalism (although, here, subject to scalar representation, the associated sign may conveniently indicate the rotational sense – hence the loose use of vector terminology):

r ....radius (positive)
θ ....angular position (positive or negative)
s ....arc displacement (positive or negative)
ω ....angular velocity (positive or negative)
$v_{\text{tangential}}$ ...tangential velocity (positive or negative)
$a_{\text{centripetal}}$ ...centripetal acceleration (positive)

Note 1: Where 'positive or negative' is stated, the positive option indicates anticlockwise rotation, and the negative option indicates the opposite.

Note 2: Centripetal acceleration, however, is always directed towards the rotational centre.

Note 3: The quantities r and θ may be referred to as polar coordinates.

Symbols and Terms

Other nomenclature:

|vector| .... vector's magnitude

|scalar| .... scalar's absolute value and magnitude

[value 1, value 2] ..... the range of values from 1 to 2

a.k.a. .... also known as

AC .... alternating current

ADC .... analogue to digital converter

AM .... amplitude modulation/modulated

c. .... *circa*

classical .... pertaining to older treatments, likely excluding relativistic/quantum physics

CNO-cycle .... carbon-nitrogen-oxygen-cycle

d .... calculus derivative

D .... dimension (as in, for example, 1D, 2D, or 3D)

DC .... direct current

∂ .... calculus partial derivative

Δ .... delta, change in some quantity

e.g. .... for example

eV .... electron-volt

etc .... *et cetera*

EPR .... electronic paramagnetic resonance (i.e. inter-atomic resonance of net electronic spins)

FM .... frequency modulation/modulated

i.e. .... that is

NMR .... nuclear magnetic resonance (i.e. inter-atomic resonance of net nuclear spins)

QCD .... quantum chromodynamics

QED .... quantum electrodynamics

$\hat{\mathbf{r}}$ .... unit vector acting from one position to another

SHM .... simple harmonic motion

SI .... Système International (International System)

vector.vector .... vector dot product (e.g. $\mathbf{F}_{net}.\mathbf{dr}$)

vector × vector .... vector cross product (e.g. $\mathbf{v} \times \mathbf{B}$)

Wi-Fi .... Wireless network protocol, brand name

Chapter 1   Data

Whether observed or calculated, the **handling** of physical quantities calls for clarity, consistency, and accuracy of representation. Ongoing discussions will encompass two main types of quantity known as **scalars** and **vectors**, and will cover best-handling practices for their representation's features of **sign**, magnitude, and spatial direction:

1.1   Magnitude and subsumed unit

Notably having a different **form of calculation** for scalars and vectors, magnitude refers to the overall size of any quantity of physical significance and, in many cases, subsumes a positive multiplicative entity called a unit†:

But quantities of units may be compared only if they are of the same type. Thus, for example, one second and one year may be compared since both concern time; nonetheless it is notable that, despite the common multiplier of one, different magnitudes ensue due to the different sizes of unit.

Furthermore, the **analysis of units** allows an understanding, and even prediction, of inter-quantity relationship.

Due to such key overall importance, a quantity's units must be expressed wherever applicable††.

Such **handling** is but one exemplification of the physicists' representation of Nature.

Scalars may be positive or negative, but are not assigned spatial direction.

Vectors include aspects of scalars plus the encoding of spatial direction in up to typically three dimensions (although more may be defined in advanced treatments).

Notes on **sign**:
►A positive representation does not need a + sign, although one may be included for emphasis.
►A negative representation, however, must have a – sign.
►Representations that are both positive and negative should be examined for physical meaning – e.g. the solutions to a square root.

Form of calculation:
►For scalars, this is the absolute value.
►For vectors, this involves a spatially independent theorem, such as that of Pythagoras (*c.*530BC).

†Applying to most defined quantities, such units notably have intrinsic size.

Analysis of units: Referred to as dimensional analysis, examples are numerous and often complex, but consider simply that distance is the product of speed and time.

††Theoreticians, however, may normalise unit-based content for ease of handling.

1D, 2D, or 3D refer to the dimensionality of the system – 1D is a line, 2D is a surface, and 3D is a volume. (And further dimensions may be defined in advanced treatments.)

For *vectors* this text uses bold font (e.g. **F**). But, for clarity of written form, it is better to use a superposed right-pointing arrow (e.g. $\vec{F}$). Force is a common example.

For *scalars* this text uses italic font (e.g. t). But they should appear normally (e.g. t) in written form. The scalar $t = +\,3$ seconds, for example, has units (Section 1.1) of time and, notably, is positive. But some scalars can also be negative, such as electric charge.

The *components* of a vector are scalars that represent size with respect to some defined direction. And the values of such components may be plotted on an axis and called coordinates.

Cartesian geometry is quantified by a set of Cartesian axes – mutually perpendicular lines that provide a definition of the dimensionality in space, and where each carries a spatially uniform scale with uniformly incrementing values.

Unit vectors are vectors of unitary magnitude.

†Of course, any Cartesian vector component – whether of position, force, *etc* – may plotted on its associated Cartesian axis.

1.2 Spatial direction; vectors versus scalars

Spatial direction often involves up to three dimensions – *1D, 2D, or 3D*. In Section 1.1 it was asserted that *vectors* encode spatial direction whilst *scalars* do not. A related distinction is that vectors often include up to three scalars depending on the dimensionality of their representation. These scalars are referred to as *components*, and are often defined in so-called *Cartesian geometry* as Cartesian components. For example, the Cartesian 3D position vector $\mathbf{r} = x\mathbf{i} + y\mathbf{j} + z\mathbf{k}$ has the Cartesian components x, y, and z that, with reference to Figures 1.1 and 1.2:

►Are associated with mutually perpendicular directions via multiplicative association with mutually perpendicular *unit vectors* **i**, **j**, and **k**.

►Have sizes that may be plotted on x, y, and z Cartesian axes configured to increase in the sense of the respective unit vector†.

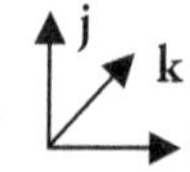

Figure 1.1: Mutually perpendicular unit vectors **i**, **j**, and **k**

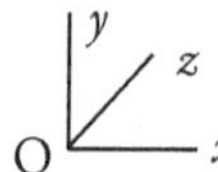

Figure 1.2: Associated positive Cartesian axes x, y, and z

Some notes on Figures 1.1 and 1.2:

►Unit vector **k** and its depicted z-axis project together out of the plane of the page.

►While positive vector components would lie on the depicted positive axes, negative ones would project opposite to the origin O.

►Any specific value of x, y, or z (positive or negative) represents one positional coordinate.

Cartesian vector treatments with up to three mutually perpendicular unit vectors, up to three associated Cartesian axes, and up to three components or coordinates provide for many typical applications.

But cases of simplest analysis are to be had from choosing Cartesian axes of both fewest number and maximum alignment to the vectors of interest, where it is notable that any instantaneous alignment with only one axis will result in vector components of zero value along all others†.

†Of course, such alignments are not necessarily fixed, and the instantaneous direction of any vector can change with time.

Indeed, 1D Cartesian geometry offers treatments of minimum dimensionality and simplest application, where:
► Just a single axis is involved.
► Over all values of time, there is mutual alignment, by necessity, of all vectors of interest.
► Each vector has a single instantaneous component or coordinate.

As an example, Figure 1.3 illustrates a Cartesian 1D force vector $\mathbf{F} = F_x\mathbf{i} = (2\,\text{N})\mathbf{i}$, where the component $F_x = 2\,\text{N}$, being positive, is consistent with $\mathbf{F}$ and $\mathbf{i}$ having the same direction, and N is the unit (Section 1.1) of force.

Figure 1.3: 1D force vector $\mathbf{F} = F_x\mathbf{i} = (2\,\text{N})\mathbf{i} = 2\mathbf{i}\,\text{N}$, and its plotting on an associated Cartesian F_x axis

1.3   SI system of units

For consistency and clarity, many physicists follow the so-called SI system of units by handling physical quantities (Section 1.1) according to the base system of the SI Brochure (2019). Such handling is shown in Table 1.1††.

††Following Section 1.1, note that:
► The base units of the SI system may be used to derive the units of all other physical quantities.
► But there is an over-sufficiency of such base units, whose unhelpful redundancy unnecessarily complicates applications of dimensional analysis between physical quantities.

Base quantity	Base unit	Symbol	Note
mass	kilogram	kg	
length	metre	m	
time	second	s	According to convention, the symbols for kelvin and amp are written in upper case.
temperature	kelvin	K	
electric current	amp (or ampère)	A	
amount of substance	mole	mol	
luminous intensity	candela	cd	

Table 1.1: SI base quantities and units

As shown in Table 1.2, the SI system also specifies a range of prefixes for the representation of physical quantities:

Prefix	Symbol	Scientific notation	Arithmetic notation	Examples of quantities	Notes
yotta	Y	10^{24}		(rarely used)	unit symbols conventionally in upper case
zeta	Z	10^{21}		(rarely used)	
exa	E	10^{18}		exawatt (EW)	
peta	P	10^{15}		petawatt (PW)	
tera	T	10^{12}		terawatt (TW)	
giga	G	10^{9}		gigawatt (GW)	
mega	M	10^{6}	1 000 000	megabyte (Mb)	
kilo	k	10^{3}	1 000	kilogram (kg)	unit symbols conventionally in lower case
hecto	h	10^{2}	100	(rarely used)	
deka	da	10^{1}	10	(rarely used)	
deci	d	10^{-1}	0.1	decibel (dB)	
centi	c	10^{-2}	0.01	centimetre (cm)	
milli	m	10^{-3}	0.001	millimetre (mm)	
micro	μ	10^{-6}	0.000 001	micron (μm)	
nano	n	10^{-9}		nanometre (nm)	
pico	p	10^{-12}		picometre (pm)	
femto	f	10^{-15}		femtosecond (fs)	
atto	a	10^{-18}		attosecond (as)	
zepto	z	10^{-21}		(rarely used)	
yocto	y	10^{-24}		(rarely used)	

Table 1.2: SI prefixes, and examples of not-necessarily-SI quantities

Thus, the kg from Table 1.1 is actually a prefixed SI base unit, equivalently 10^3 grams.

1.4   Scientific notation

As exemplified in Table 1.2, scientific notation involves powers of 10, whilst arithmetic notation does not. Scientific notation combined with an arithmetic multiplier – e.g. 2×10^3 – is the most general notation: First, for the very large and the very small, arithmetic notations would have too many zeroes to assimilate. And, second, no SI prefixes are defined beyond $10^{\pm 24}$†.

    Tables 1.3-1.5 use scientific notation to give real examples of mass, length, and time ranging from the very big to the very small:

†In Table 1.2, for example, arithmetic notations are deliberately restricted to within $10^{\pm 6}$, and the yotta and yocto are the extreme SI prefixes.

known universe	1×10^{53}
Sun – our local star	2×10^{30}
Earth – one of the Sun's planets	6×10^{24}
Moon – the Earth's natural satellite	7×10^{22}
strand of hair	1×10^{-6}
molecule of penicillin†	5×10^{-17}
proton, atom of hydrogen†	2×10^{-27}
electron†	9×10^{-31}

Table 1.3: Approximate masses in kilograms

distance to the furthest *galaxies*	1×10^{26}
distance to the next galaxy – Andromeda	2×10^{22}
radius of our galaxy – the Milky Way	5×10^{20}
distance to the next star – Proxima Centauri	4×10^{16}
distance to Pluto – an outlying so-called dwarf planet of the Sun	5×10^{12}
distance to the Sun	1×10^{11}
radius of the Earth	6×10^{6}
height of mount Everest	9×10^{3}
thickness of a sheet of paper	1×10^{-4}
length of a virus	1×10^{-8}
radius of an atom of hydrogen†	5×10^{-11}
radius of a proton†	8×10^{-14}

Table 1.4: Approximate lengths in metres

minimum lifetime of a proton†	3×10^{41}
estimated age of the universe	4×10^{17}
duration of humankind	4×10^{12}
human life expectancy	2×10^{9}
duration of a day	9×10^{4}
lifetime of a *muon*	2×10^{-6}
duration of the shortest laser pulse	4×10^{-18}
predicted lifetime of a top quark†	5×10^{-25}
the *Planck time*	5×10^{-44}

Table 1.5: Approximate times in seconds

1.5   Order of magnitude

Taking n to be an integer:

▶ 10^n has an order of magnitude defined as n.

▶ $m \times 10^n$ has a nearest order of magnitude that is still taken as n when $1 \leq m < 5$, but as $n + 1$ when $5 \leq m < 10$††.

†Notes:
▶Quarks are inferred from the fleeting products of artificial high-energy particle collisions, and, of which, there are six named types: top, bottom, charm, strange, up, and down.
▶The existence of protons is taken as due to enduring interdependent mutual binding between up and down quarks.
▶Atoms comprise at least one proton/electron pair, and possibly also entities known as neutrons; furthermore they are chemistry's basic building blocks, about 10^{-10} m in size, of which the subject's periodic table incorporates 118 known elements.
▶Molecules comprise two or more atoms which have mutually bound together, and which are the smallest possible amount of a recognisable chemical substance or compound.

A *galaxy* is a localised but vast body of matter and energy, with billions of stars, bound by its own gravity.

A *muon* is a massive, unstable, and normally extra-atomic form of electron.

The *Planck time*, according to the big bang model of cosmology (see Section 7.8), is the age of the universe at which the known laws of physics become valid.

††Order of magnitude calculations may be appropriate when values are very large or very small, and not well known.

1.6   SI standards

Precise standards for the SI base units (Section 1.3) enable calibration of sophisticated instrumentation for the most accurate measurements of physical quantities. A few examples:

► The SI second is based on a caesium atomic clock, being the time for the clock to undergo 9 192 631 770 periods of transition†.

► The SI metre is the distance travelled by light in *free space* in $(299\ 792\ 458)^{-1}$ of an SI second.

► The SI kilogram has a complex definition requiring additional knowledge of the so-called Planck's constant (see Section 6.9).

1.7   Conversion and derivation of units

To prevent clerical errors, measurement data should be recorded immediately and in the same form as provided by the instrumentation. Then, for consistency and clarity, that data should be converted to SI units (Section 1.3) before subsequent calculation††.

The process of unit conversion follows the rules of arithmetic. For example, before summing 206 mA and 0.523 A, the 206 mA is first converted to 0.206 A, noting that the mA is exactly 0.001 A. The sum thus becomes $(0.206 + 0.523)$ A, giving the result 0.729 A. Commonly required unit conversions include hours to seconds, kilometres per hour to $\mathrm{m\,s^{-1}}$, and $\mathrm{g\,cm^{-3}}$ to $\mathrm{kg\,m^{-3}}$ (where the unit g is the gram)†††.

Since units follow the rules of arithmetic, formulae which derive a new quantity from two or more other quantities also derive the units of the new quantity. Table 1.6 gives a few simple examples showing the derived SI units.

†Notes:
► Caesium is a type of atom (Section 1.4).
► As a clock, caesium atoms are isolated and undergo naturally very small, but temporally very regular, so-called hyperfine, transitions in electronic energy levels.

Free space is an idealised concept for the complete absence of matter – i.e. a perfect vacuum.

††Notes:
► Such SI units are preferably base, but could be derived (see next but one paragraph).
► New data may also benefit from conversion into scientific notation (Section 1.4). Electrical meters, for instance, may display current in mA rather than in the SI base unit A.

†††Beware of nomenclatures such as $\mathrm{cm^{-3}}$. The prefix centi (Section 1.3) is part of the unit so that, for example, $\mathrm{cm^{-3}} = (\mathrm{cm})^{-3} = (10^{-2}\ \mathrm{m})^{-3} = 10^{6}\ \mathrm{m^{-3}}$.

Considered quantity	Derived nomenclature	
	Quantity	SI base units
length × width	area	m^2
area × height	volume	m^3
mass / volume	density	$kg\ m^{-3}$
distance / time	speed	$m\ s^{-1}$

Table 1.6: Some simple derived quantities and units

Further examples are given in Table 1.7, involving new unit nomenclatures.

Considered quantity	Derived nomenclature			
	Quantity	SI base units	New unit symbol and name	
electric current × time	charge	$A\ s$	C	coulomb
mass × acceleration	force	$kg\ m\ s^{-2}$	N	newton
force × distance	energy	$kg\ m^2\ s^{-2}$	J	joule
force / area	pressure	$kg\ m^{-1}\ s^{-2}$	Pa	pascal
energy / time	power	$kg\ m^2\ s^{-3}$	W	watt
$(time)^{-1}$	frequency	s^{-1}	Hz	hertz

Table 1.7: Some derived quantities with their own unit symbols and names

1.8   Significant figures

By helping to indicate the accuracy of a represented quantity, the concept of significant figures is fundamental – the greater the number, the greater the accuracy†.

For example, the three arithmetically identical representations, 3.4 cm, 0.034 m, and 3.4×10^{-2} m all have two significant figures, and hence are also physically identical††.

But how is this number of significant figures recognised? The answer lies in the following rules:

►Taken as not significant are zeroes to the left of the first non-zero figure, and powers of ten.

►But taken as significant are all other figures†††.

1.9   Decimal places and rounding

If there is a decimal point in a quantity's representation, the number of figures to its right is the number of decimal places. This number is

†Of course, it is essential that all quoted figures are significant. Physicists should always justify the accuracy of their representations.

††Thus, accordingly, 3.4 cm = 0.034 m = 3.4×10^{-2} m is a physically correct relation.

†††Examples:
►The following three representations are physically identical and each has three significant figures: 3.40 cm, 0.0340 m, and 3.40×10^{-2} m.
►0.003040 m has four significant figures.

not fundamental because it can change if the representation is changed, such as a change from arithmetic to scientific notation, or a change of unit†.

A quantity's representation can be rounded only if it has decimal places. Such rounding is applied to one or more decimal places from the right, resulting in a representation with fewer decimal places. With the process best illustrated by example, please refer to Table 1.8.

†For example, the representations,
3.4 cm and 0.034 m,
respectively have 1 and 3 decimal places, but are still both arithmetically and physically identical.

Process to be applied	Immediate retention	Figures to be rounded	The leftmost figure to be rounded taken as units, and associated rule		Result
Rounding of 3.426 cm to two significant figures.	3.4 cm	26	2.6	If < 5, do nothing to the immediate retention.	3.4 cm
Rounding of 3.426 cm to three significant figures.	3.42 cm	6	6	If ≥ 5, add 1 to the immediate retention's rightmost figure.	3.43 cm

Table 1.8: Exemplified process of rounding

Here are two cases to be wary of:

►All figures to be rounded must be considered simultaneously, and not rounded successively (figure by figure) from the right. E.g. 3.449 cm rounded to two significant figures is 3.4 cm, not 3.5 cm.

►Scientific notation (Section 1.4) must be applied when there are insufficient decimal places. E.g. 342 m rounded to two significant figures could be written as 3.4×10^2 m or 0.34×10^3 m, but there is an infinite number of other solutions.

1.10 Concepts of error and exactness

Accuracy may be specified more precisely than the number of significant figures (Section 1.8) via the concept of error††.

As a quantity's represented value is likely to be inexact, its likely maximum **deviation** from the true value is a key quantification. But how

††This concept of error is specifically not in the sense of mistake, but as a consequence of an abundance of mechanisms that prevent perfect knowledge. For example, in the act of measurement, error mechanisms encompass the performance of any instrumentation and human reading ability.

Deviation is calculated as the magnitude of the difference between any two values of the same type of quantity – e.g. $|L_2 - L_1|$ for some quantity L. Note that, whilst such deviation is calculated/quoted positively, a ± sign generally needs to be included when used as part of a quantity's representation.

does such quantification relate to the number of known significant figures and, more generally, to the concept of error?

Take, for example, the representation 3.4 cm. This has two significant figures, three units, and four tenths of centimetres. But, what of the unstated number of hundredths? In fact, seen as equivalent, when rounded (Section 1.9) to two significant figures, are all representations ranging from 3.35 cm to slightly less than 3.45 cm. The representation 3.4 cm thus has an implicit maximum deviation of 5 in the second decimal place. Accordingly, the representation may be better written as 3.40 cm ± 0.05 cm, where a 0 has been appended to the 3.4 for notationally consistent decimal places, and the 0.05 cm term is referred to as the error†.

However, the ± notation of the representation may be avoided via the more succinct form 3.40(5) cm, wherein the figure in brackets is read as referring to the error in the figure immediately to its left.

Often error is known well enough to be quoted to only one significant figure as a final result. Nonetheless, carefully controlled examples exist where more than one significant figure is justified††.

Some further useful definitions:
►Assuming error is quantified to subsume all known contributions, it represents the best estimate of the maximum deviation from the true value, and is referred to as absolute error.
►So-called relative error is the absolute error divided by the magnitude of the represented value†††.
►Multiplying relative error by 100% gives the % relative error.

Now consider the concept of exactness. If a represented value is claimed as exact, it must deviate by zero from the true value, and should have an infinite number of significant figures.

†Note that error is always quoted positively, but a ± sign generally needs to be included when used as part of a quantity's representation.

††For example:
►3.040(13) cm would be equivalent to 3.040 cm ± 0.013 cm.
►The currently accepted value for the permittivity of free space is $8.854\,187\,8128(13) \times 10^{-12}$ $kg^{-1}\,m^{-3}\,s^4\,A^2$.

†††Notes on calculating relative error:
►The magnitude is used to ensure a positive result, even when the represented value is negative.
►Since the units within the numerator and denominator must be same, they cancel in the ratio, leaving a result without units.

†*Specifically:*
►Unit conversion can be exact by definition. For example, one litre (L) is exactly one thousand cubic centimetres.
►Despite the notational conflict with significant figures, physicists may highlight the exactness of integers (including zero) by omitting the decimal point – e.g. 1 L = 1000 cm³.
►Counting may be claimed as exact because a claim of there being seven apples in a box could reasonably be true.

Systematic error is likely to be present when repeated measurements are consistently bigger or smaller than the true value. Systematic errors cannot be reduced statistically.

Random error is inaccuracy that applies even when all systematic error is removed. Because it is random, its contribution to the absolute error can be reduced by some form of statistical averaging, assuming that repeated measurement is possible.

A ***single*** measurement may be inevitable if, for example, a rapidly changing measurand, or some instrument limitation prevents repeated measurement.

††Reading error is reflected in human ability to read an instrument.

This seems unrealistic, but there are cases where exactness has physical validity, such as in unit conversions, integers, and counting†.

A further case is the recurrent decimal, although this is of questionable physical use. A recurrent decimal has a decimal figure, or group of decimal figures, that repeats indefinitely. With the overscore being one of numerous notations for highlighting the indefinite recurrence, Table 1.9 gives two examples.

$\frac{1}{3} = 0.\overline{3}$	$\frac{1}{7} = 0.\overline{142857}$

Table 1.9: Examples of recurrent decimal

1.11 Error in measurement

Measurements are likely to be affected by both ***systematic error*** and ***random error***. All such error is unwelcome because it contributes to the estimation of the absolute error (Section 1.10) in a represented value.

The biased nature of systematic error could be due to *inter alia* badly arranged apparatus and badly specified/calibrated instrumentation. It is important that all such systematic deficiencies are identified and eliminated prior to measurement.

What, then, ideally remains is random error such that, over a sufficiently large number of repeated measurements, an expectation exists for there to be roughly equal spreads thereof that are larger and smaller than the true value. Tightly controlled measurement practices will reduce the spreads, and converge on the true value.

First consider a ***single*** measurement. Being the least accurate empirical approach to physical quantification, that single measurement has to be used to represent the quantity's value. And an estimate must be made of the absolute error, which must be at least that of the associated reading error††:

►On *analogue* scales, reading error is related to the smallest graduated increment – for example, in a rule marked down to millimetres, the smallest increment is 1 mm. Equivalence of the reading error to such an increment is the simplest possibility. But there could be a claim of a smaller error via interpolation, or a larger one if constrained by human factors†.

►On electronic *digital* scales there should be no human factors, and the reading error is simply the smallest digital increment. Suppose such a scale highlights 27 mA, with adjacent possibilities of 26 mA and 28 mA, then the smallest increment and reading error is 1 mA.

►But implicit in the above examples is that the scale is set up to measure accurately what is intended, as well as being intrinsically accurate to its smallest increment. Verification should proceed via careful use, and a check on the scale's performance/specification. And, for an accurate assessment of a quantity's absolute error, there may be further error contributions that need to be identified, assessed, and incorporated. Clearly, achieving a result close to the true value is a significant challenge from a single measurement.

Second, and on the contrary, repeated measurements of unchanging quantities, combined with statistical methods of analysis, may offer improvement. This is particularly so if the quantity of repeated measurements exceeds about 20††:

Then a common approach is to treat the quantity's value as the average, and its absolute error as the standard deviation. And the confidence in these treatments would improve with increasing number of similar measurements.

Alternatively, plotting a histogram of the repeated measurements offers the notable benefit of highlighting their distribution. Owing

Analogue means possessing a smoothly varying change in space or time.

†Two examples:
►If using a rule with 1 mm graduations, it may be reasonable to interpolate readings to the nearest 0.5 mm, and thus claim a reading error of 0.5 mm.
►But, if using an analogue vernier-gauge with 0.05 mm increments, the human factor of poor eyesight may restrict reading to the nearest 0.1 mm, leaving this as the best claim of reading error.

Digital means possessing abrupt changes between two or more different states.

††But confidence in these statistical methods will reduce:
►If there are significantly fewer measurements.
►If the quality of the individual measurements is low – it is much better to take a few careful measurements than a large number of indifferent ones.

to its Gaussian (bell-shaped) symmetry, the normal distribution is the easiest to analyse, where the centre is taken as the quantity's value, and the half-width at half of the maximum height may be taken as its absolute error.

1.12 Error in calculation, and danger of rounding

Combining physical quantities using a formula requires care because of how their errors (Section 1.10) need to be combined. Ongoing discussions will cover only two of the simplest types of formula†:

►*Addition or subtraction of two quantities with the same units:* In cases where the quantities have uncorrelated errors the resultant absolute error is treated statistically as the square root of the sum of the squares of the individual absolute errors††.

As an example of an uncorrelated case, a length may be determined via a rule with 1 mm graduations and the formula $|x_{end} - x_{start}|$, where x_{end} and x_{start} are its end and start coordinates: If x_{end} and x_{start} are read with interpolation to the nearest 0.5 mm and have no other significant error, then both would be attributed with an absolute error of 0.5 mm. And the resultant absolute error in the length would be $[(0.5 \text{ mm})^2 + (0.5 \text{ mm})^2)]^{1/2} = 0.7$ mm†††.

►*Multiplication or division of two quantities:* In cases where the quantities have uncorrelated errors the resultant relative error is treated statistically as the square root of the sum of the squares of the individual relative errors††††.

As an example, the value of π may be checked from the circumference and diameter of a precisely circular body, with confident respective measurements of (2171 ± 3) mm and (690 ± 1) mm being taken:

The numbers of significant figures for the measurements are four for the circumference but only three for the diameter: Supposing just

†Notes:
►Such formulae can be derived from calculus based methods.
►For more on the derivation and types of formula see, for example, Taylor (2022).

††Note that uncorrelated cases feature a low likelihood that each concerned quantity has maximum deviation from its true value at the same time. However, correlated cases can exhibit strong reinforcement, and then the sum of the individual absolute errors may be a better estimate of the resultant absolute error.

††† with rounding (Section 1.9) of the final result to one significant figure (as is appropriate in many cases).

††††Notes:
►But in correlated cases, like in †† above, the sum of the individual relative errors may be a better estimate of the resultant relative error.
►Since relative error has no units, there is no unit based impediment to its combination.
►The rule also applies in terms of % relative errors.

three are chosen for calculating the value of π, then π = 2171/690 = 3.15. And each calculation of relative error, to one figure, is shown in Table 1.10.

circumference	3/|2171| = 0.001
diameter	1/|690| = 0.001
π	$[(0.001)^2 + (0.001)^2]^{1/2}$ = 0.001

Table 1.10: Associated relative errors

Also calculated to one figure, the absolute error in π follows as $3.15 \times 0.001 = 0.003$.

But the final result, at $\pi = 3.15 \pm 0.003$, is immediately seen as wrong, and its underlying acts of rounding (Section 1.9) are to be understood as needing correction:

► *Correct handling of error:* Despite there being confidence in the measurement data, the indicated range for π clearly does not include its true value. But suppose all intermediate calculations of error are conducted to two figures. Then the resultant relative error in π is doubled to a much more plausible 0.002. Indeed, the underestimate caused by rounding each stage to one figure was a mistake. But how can it be known *a priori* to use two figures for the intermediate calculations of error†?

► *Correct handling of value:* The calculated value 3.15 has one less decimal place than that of the 0.003 absolute error. This inconsistency indicates that three figures are insufficient for the intermediate calculations. Indeed, repeating the process with four figures leads to $\pi = 3.146 \pm 0.006$, which is not only notationally consistent, but is also correct to four significant figures. But how can it be known *a priori* to use four figures for the intermediate calculations of value††?

1.13 Data acquisition, presentation, and analysis

As per this Chapter's discussed good practice, a summary of worthy actions when acquiring,

†On the general handling of error:
►Identify the input error with the least number, say n, of significant figures, conduct all intermediate calculations with $n + 1$ figures, and only round the absolute-error's final result back to n figures. (Note that often $n = 1$, as in the given example. But, in well-controlled experiments, where it is possible to justify $n = 2$, the intermediate calculations would need three figures.)
►Then, and except in cases of complex multi-stepped calculation, there should be a good result free of rounding error.
►But good practice is always to check the veracity of the last point. Do this by repeating the intermediate calculations with yet one more figure until *mutatis mutandi* there is no further change in the absolute-error's final result.

††On the general handling of value:
►Identify the input value with the least number, say m, of significant figures, conduct all intermediate calculations with $m + 1$ figures, and only round the value's final result if necessary for consistency with the calculated error.
►But, like with the calculation of error, always check for the absence of rounding error in the value's final result.

recording, and manipulating data is given in Table 1.11:

> ►Noting of experimental apparatus, method, pertinent environmental conditions, *etc.*
> ►Following Section 1.11: Eliminating of systematic error, minimising of random error, reading/recording of values with all the figures that any instrument provides for clerical accuracy, and identifying/recording of associated errors.
> ►Converting of data into SI (base) units and scientific notation (Section 1.7).
> ►Manipulating of data – e.g. by averaging – as appropriate.
> ►Following Section 1.12, attaining correct final data via the appropriate handling of error and rounding at each stage.

Table 1.11: Data-handling actions prior to presentation

In terms of subsequent presentation, graphs represent an excellent form of assimilation due to their visualisation of trends and patterns between two or more variables. Furthermore, although a variety of graphical forms is available, many examples involve the ***Cartesian graphing*** of two variables – an ***exemplification*** of which is provided by Figure 1.4, opposite, where:

►One variable $T^2/(4\pi^2)$ – with T being a period of time – is considered as the input and is referenced against the horizontal axis. And the other variable L – a length – is considered as the output and is referenced against the vertical axis.

►It is common to refer to the input variable as independent, and the output one as dependent.

►Annotation includes an appropriately descriptive title, axis labelling, and some analysis (notably the derivation of a value for g – the magnitude of the Earth's near-surface gravitational acceleration).

In ***Cartesian graphing:***

►The data set of each variable is referenced against its own Cartesian axis (Section 1.2) whose scale is carefully crafted to include all the associated data, the origin (if required), and as much of the screen/paper as possible subject to those at 1:1 (where one big box is equivalent to one unit of the variable) being the easiest to plot and read.

►Each scale includes numbers, the variable's name, and possibly also a universal multiplier, units, symbol, and formula. (Note that the symbols x, y, and z should not be applied, unless they really are the chosen variable symbols.)

►Points are plotted between the referenced data sets, with particular attention paid to accurate location and clear highlighting such as via a cross-based symbol.

Such an ***exemplification*** is:

►Based on a pendulum's so-called law of length – for more information see Section 3.7's example of simple harmonic motion.

►Notably presented entirely by computer.

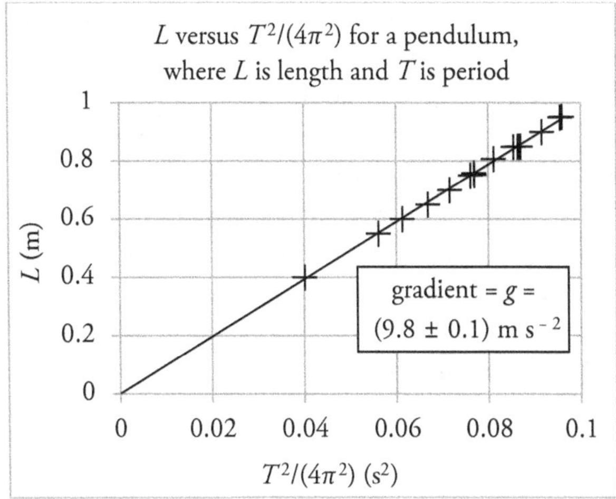

Figure 1.4: An example of 2D Cartesian graphing

Generally, once a graph is constructed it should be examined for any relationship between the variables. For example, can that relationship be approximated using some form of mathematical function†?

Further questions then arise, such as should the function go through the origin, and should any badly aligned points be excluded. Such actions require justification. A final functional fit, including all graphical presentation and analysis, is best done by computer††.

However, here is an explanation of the steps as if manual, where it is assumed that, in a Cartesian graph, there is an independent variable x, a dependent variable y, and that its functional fit is deemed to be a straight line:

►After completing the graph, manually fit a best straight line to the plotted points†††.

►Then evaluate constants m and c for the fitted line's equation $y = mx + c$:

►Constant m is the calculus gradient dy/dx. To determine it with the greatest accuracy, choose two locations on the fitted straight line that are furthest apart (i.e. its two ends), and take the difference in y divided by the corresponding difference in x. The result is positive if y increases

†Remember the example of Figure 1.4 in which the fitted function is shown as a straight line going through the origin.

††Computers employ automated function-fitting routines for the easiest and most accurate quantification of trends and their errors.

†††Notes on manually fitted best straight lines:
►Avoid the common mistake of making the line intersect the first and last points since two arbitrarily chosen points will generally not lie on the best fit.
►Use a mixture of theory and empiricism to decide whether the line should go through the origin.
►Apply the best straight line by visually minimising the average closeness of the line to the plotted points.
►Beware of residual systematic error. This can be evident if, for example, an expected intersection with the origin results in the line being excessively distant from the majority of the points.

with x, negative otherwise, and has units that are in ratio of y to x†.

►Constant c is read as the value of y where the fitted straight line intercepts the y-axis. If, for example, the intercept is at the origin, then $c = 0$. And, as each term (y, mx, and c) of the line's equation must have the same units, the units of c are the same as those of y†.

1.14 Questionnaire

†But note that, regardless of the quality of the input data and of the manual fit, and even with the dubious premise that the scale's marked locations are exact, any manually derived values (such as of m and c) have limited accuracy due to each axis comprising at most, say, 100 small boxes. Thus, even with interpolation to the nearest ½ small box, the 200 available scale locations offer manual plotting and reading accuracies of at best 3 significant figures and probably markedly less.

1Q1   Which option comparing scalar and vector quantities is always true?
a   A scalar has one component; a vector may have multiple components
b   Both have a unit
c   Both have spatial direction
d   Scalars are positive; vector-magnitudes are positive

1Q2   Select a vector quantity:
a   Energy
b   Force
c   Mass
d   Time

1Q3   Which option is not an SI base unit?
a   Amp
b   Celcius
c   Metre
d   Mole

1Q4   Which of the following quantities has its SI base units defined with a prefix?
a   Length
b   Mass
c   Temperature
d   Time

1Q5   Which of the following times is expressed in SI base units?
a   1 second
b   1 hour
c   1 day
d   1 year

1Q6   From left to right, select a prefix sequence that continually increases in size:
a   kilo, Mega, micro
b   Mega, kilo, micro
c   micro, kilo, Mega
d   micro, Mega, kilo

1Q7   The number 10^{-2} equates to which prefix?
a   centi
b   deci
c   milli
d   nano

Page 20 answers: 19c   20d   21c   22c   23a

Page 17 answers: 1a   2b   3d   4b   5a   6c   7a

1Q8 The derived SI units of force are kg m s^{-2}, and pressure is defined as force divided by area. What, then, are the derived SI units of pressure?

a   kg m^{-2} s^{-2}
b   kg m^{-1} s^{-2}
c   kg m^{2} s^{-2}
d   kg m^{3} s^{-2}

1Q9 Select a correct statement:

a   A litre is 100 cm^3
b   Density is mass divided by area
c   Frequency, and energy divided by power have the same units
d   Time is charge divided by electric current

1Q10 In the same order, what do the following three derived SI units represent?
Newton. Joule. Watt.

a   Energy. Power. Force.
b   Force. Energy. Power.
c   Power. Energy. Force.
d   Power. Force. Energy.

1Q11 Given that wavelength is calculated as speed divided by frequency, what are the derived SI units of wavelength?

a   m s^{-2}
b   m s^{-1}
c   m
d   m s

1Q12 The representations 9.1×10^{-31} kg and 2×10^{30} kg approximate respectively the mass of the electron and the mass of the Sun. Answered in the same order, which body's representation has more decimal places, and which has more significant figures?

a   Electron, electron
b   Electron, Sun
c   Sun, electron
d   Sun, Sun

1Q13 How many significant figures has the representation 0.0380 m?
a   2
b   3
c   4
d   5

1Q14 How many decimal places has the representation 0.0380 m?
a   2
b   3
c   4
d   5

1Q15 What is 5.297 m quoted to three significant figures?
a   5.290 m
b   5.29 m
c   5.300 m
d   5.30 m

1Q16 Which option correctly quotes 5267 m to three significant figures?
a   5.260 km
b   5.270 × 10³ m
c   5.26 km
d   5.27 × 10³ m

1Q17 A distance quoted as 15000 μm is actually known to only two significant figures.
         Select the best representation of that distance:
a   0.15 m
b   0.15 dm
c   15 cm
d   15 mm

1Q18 Which option is the best representation for the speed of a body that covers
         2.5 m in 0.2×10^1 s?
a 1.25 m s^{-1}
b 1.2 m s^{-1}
c 1.3 m s^{-1}
d 1 m s^{-1}

Page 18 answers: 8b   9d   10b   11c   12b
Page 19 answers: 13b   14c   15d   16d   17d   18d

1Q19 Select the best representation of absolute error for a summation calculation based on uncorrelated absolute errors of 0.1 m and 0.3 m:

a   0.1 m
b   0.2 m
c   0.3 m
d   0.4 m

1Q20 Select the best representation of absolute error for a difference calculation based on fully correlated absolute errors of 0.1 m and 0.3 m:

a   0.1 m
b   0.2 m
c   0.3 m
d   0.4 m

1Q21 Select the best representation of relative error for a product calculation based on uncorrelated relative errors of 0.1 and 0.2:

a   0.02
b   0.1
c   0.2
d   0.3

1Q22 Select the best representation of percent relative error for a division calculation based on uncorrelated percent relative errors of (1.0×10^1)% and (2.0×10^1)%:

a (1.0×10^1)%
b (2.0×10^1)%
c (2.2×10^1)%
d (2.0×10^2)%

1Q23 The product of three values, with individually one, two, and three significant figures, is most likely to have:

a   1 significant figure
b   2 significant figures
c   3 significant figures
d   6 significant figures

Chapter 2   Kinematics and Mass

2.1   Particles

Whilst a body may be characterised by size, shape, structure and rigidity, discussion starts with the concept of a **particle** – the idealised representation of a body as a single point. A collection of bodies is now treated as a system of particles wherein each particle represents one body. Furthermore, such a system is generally considered as relative to an arbitrarily defined coordinate system called a **frame** of reference.

2.2   Kinematic states

Kinematics is the treatment of the geometry of motion relative to some frame of reference (Section 2.1), and whose generic states are elucidated in Table 2.1.

As relative to the frame of reference	State of:		
	position	velocity	acceleration
stationary	constant	0	0
uniform velocity	changing	constant	0
uniform acceleration	changing	changing	constant
non-uniform acceleration	changing	changing	changing

Table 2.1: Generic kinematic states

As per Sections 1.1 and 1.2, and with immediate discussion covering both Cartesian and rotational geometries, such kinematic quantities all have a magnitude and unit; they also include both vectors and scalars, but where the vector forms notably also have direction relative to the frame of reference.

The **particle** is a classical concept beneficial to the study of bodies. But there are concerns in its application. For example:

► The matter associated with real bodies has an extended and possibly time-dependent distribution.

► The zero volume of a point implies infinite density.

► It is applicable to cases of both linear and curved translatory motion, but not spin because the spin of a point has no classical meaning.

► While small bodies may be worthy candidates, too small is a problem. Specifically, as will be seen in Section 5.3.1, entities inside atoms (Section 1.4) are treated as having a quantum based uncertainty in position – a starkly non-classical picture.

Notes on **frames:**

► Whilst the frame of reference is an essential theme in physics, there is nothing fundamental about a particular frame, and an observer is free to define the coordinate system of their choice. For conceptual ease, that observer may co-locate the coordinate origin with themselves, but there is no compunction to do so. That observer could equally define the coordinate system as translated or even moving relative to themselves. And, indeed, the topic of coordinate transformation is a further important theme in physics.

► While this text largely concerns Cartesian (Section 1.2) frames of reference, there is onward coverage throughout, but with key foundation in Sections 3.1 and 3.2.

2.3   Kinematic vectors

Assuming 3D for generality, considerations now involve various examples of vectorial kinematic quantities (Section 2.2) treated according to Cartesian geometry†:

Position: This is the vector **r** that extends from the Cartesian origin to the point of interest, has SI units of metres, and — following Section 1.2 — has the Cartesian representation $\mathbf{r} = x\mathbf{i} + y\mathbf{j} + z\mathbf{k}$, where x, y, and z are its Cartesian components, and **i**, **j**, and **k** are associated mutually perpendicular positive unit vectors††.

Instantaneous velocity: This is the vector **v** defined as the derivative $d\mathbf{r}/dt$, and is thus the gradient of the position-versus-time curve at any instant of time. Its derived SI units are m s^{-1}.

Instantaneous acceleration: This is the vector **a** defined as the derivative $d\mathbf{v}/dt$, and is thus the gradient of the velocity-versus-time curve at any instant of time. Its derived SI units are m s^{-2}. Also, $\mathbf{a} = d(d\mathbf{r}/dt)/dt = d^2\mathbf{r}/dt^2$, since $\mathbf{v} = d\mathbf{r}/dt$.

Average velocity and average acceleration: These quantities are defined in Table 2.2.

Quantity, symbol	Definition	Result
average velocity, $\bar{\mathbf{v}}$	change in position divided by change in time	$= \Delta\mathbf{r}/\Delta t$ $= (\mathbf{r}_2 - \mathbf{r}_1)/(t_2 - t_1)$
average acceleration, $\bar{\mathbf{a}}$	change in velocity divided by change in time	$= \Delta\mathbf{v}/\Delta t$ $= (\mathbf{v}_2 - \mathbf{v}_1)/(t_2 - t_1)$

Table 2.2: Average velocity and average acceleration between states 1 and 2

Associated notes:

►With notably no regard for any of the motional detail in between, Table 2.2's average quantities have concern only for parametric changes between two arbitrary states, designated here as 1 and 2†††.

►For practical purposes Δt is taken to be positive.

†Notes:
►As per Section 1.2, such geometry is notably where (1) one Cartesian axis is required per dimension, (2) in higher dimensions each such axis is mutually perpendicular to all others, and (3) the simplest, most optimally aligned such set may offer ease of calculation.
►General vectorial needs comprise addition, subtraction, trigonometric resolution along a given direction, and Pythogorean calculation of magnitude.
►For more on vectors, and much other introductory mathematics see, for example, Gould and Hurst (2009).

††Notes:
►The x, y, and z symbolism, whilst arbitrary, is chosen to indicate unique axial association with **i**, **j**, and **k**.
►Values of x, y, and z may be negative as well as positive.
►Pythagorean calculation of the position magnitude $|\mathbf{r}|$ is $|\mathbf{r}| = (x^2 + y^2 + z^2)^{1/2}$.
►In 1D, with confinement to the x-axis, **r** becomes $\mathbf{r} = x\mathbf{i}$ since $y = z = 0$. Then, the vector's direction is **i** if x is positive and $-$ **i** if x is negative. And the vector's magnitude is $|\mathbf{r}| = |x|$.

†††For example, consider the so-called displacement $\Delta\mathbf{r} = \mathbf{r}_2 - \mathbf{r}_1$ of a particle that is confined to the x-axis, and for which $\Delta\mathbf{r} = \Delta x\mathbf{i} = -2\mathbf{i}$ m. Then its position state 2 is simply 2 m from its position state 1 in the direction of $-$ **i**.

Expansion as Cartesian components: All kinematic vectors can be expanded as Cartesian components. That of 3D position is already known as $\mathbf{r} = x\mathbf{i} + y\mathbf{j} + z\mathbf{k}$, whilst Table 2.3 also includes various others:

Quantity	Definition / symbolism	Cartesian expansion
position	$\mathbf{r}$	$= x\mathbf{i} + y\mathbf{j} + z\mathbf{k}$
displacement	change of position, $\Delta\mathbf{r}$	$= \Delta x\mathbf{i} + \Delta y\mathbf{j} + \Delta z\mathbf{k}$
instantaneous velocity	$d\mathbf{r}/dt$ $= \mathbf{v}$	$= (dx/dt)\mathbf{i} + (dy/dt)\mathbf{j} + (dz/dt)\mathbf{k}$ $= v_x\mathbf{i} + v_y\mathbf{j} + v_z\mathbf{k}$
change of velocity	$\Delta\mathbf{v}$	$= \Delta v_x\mathbf{i} + \Delta v_y\mathbf{j} + \Delta v_z\mathbf{k}$
instantaneous acceleration	$d\mathbf{v}/dt$ $= d^2\mathbf{r}/dt^2$ $= \mathbf{a}$	$= (dv_x/dt)\mathbf{i} + (dv_y/dt)\mathbf{j} + (dv_z/dt)\mathbf{k}$ $= (d^2x/dt^2)\mathbf{i} + (d^2y/dt^2)\mathbf{j} + (d^2z/dt^2)\mathbf{k}$ $= a_x\mathbf{i} + a_y\mathbf{j} + a_z\mathbf{k}$

Table 2.3: Examples of 3D Cartesian kinematic vectors

Constant acceleration: Constant acceleration is an important aspect of physics due to being the consequence of a constant force†.

    Associated kinematic analysis initially involves establishing five equations concerning $\mathbf{a} = \mathbf{a}_c$ such that $\mathbf{a}_c$ is constant in time. The derivation of two of these equations is in Table 2.4.

†The concept of force is discussed in Chapter 3.

Step	Result	Equation #
separating the differential $d\mathbf{v}/dt = \mathbf{a}_c$	$d\mathbf{v} = \mathbf{a}_c dt$	-
integrating subject to constant $\mathbf{a}_c$	$\mathbf{v} = \mathbf{v}_0 + \mathbf{a}_c t$, where $\mathbf{v}_0$ is constant initial velocity	1
separating the differential in $d\mathbf{r}/dt = \mathbf{v}$ (remember that $\mathbf{v}$ depends on time, and thus its functional replacement is required before integration):	$d\mathbf{r} = \mathbf{v}dt$	-
substituting $\mathbf{v} = \mathbf{v}_0 + \mathbf{a}_c t$	$d\mathbf{r} = \mathbf{v}_0 dt + \mathbf{a}_c t dt$	-
integrating subject to constant $\mathbf{v}_0$, $\mathbf{a}_c$	$\mathbf{r} - \mathbf{r}_0 = \Delta\mathbf{r} = \mathbf{v}_0 t + (\tfrac{1}{2})\mathbf{a}_c t^2$, where $\mathbf{r}_0$ is constant initial position	2

Table 2.4: Two equations of constant acceleration in 3D

The other three equations provide no new information, and are simply a manipulation of the first two. Whilst generating these is left as an exercise, note that keeping $\mathbf{r} - \mathbf{r}_0$ as the single variable $\mathbf{\Delta r}$ leaves five variables $\mathbf{v}$, $\mathbf{v}_0$, $\mathbf{a}_c$, t, and $\mathbf{\Delta r}$. And eliminating $\mathbf{v}_0$, $\mathbf{a}_c$, or t between the first two equations will lead respectively to one of the other three. Since each of the five equations has a different set of four quantities, a careful choice of equation will lead more quickly to the required solution†.

But, for the given two equations, $\mathbf{v} = \mathbf{v}_0 + \mathbf{a}_c t$ and $\mathbf{\Delta r} = \mathbf{v}_0 t + (\tfrac{1}{2})\mathbf{a}_c t^2$, the associated 3D Cartesian components of $\mathbf{v}$ and $\mathbf{\Delta r}$ may be written as in Tables 2.5 and 2.6:

†General problem-solving tactics:
► Draw a diagram with the known/unknown quantities.
► Write down or derive the five kinematic equations.
► Choose the equation from the set of five for which the only unknown quantity is that required by the problem.
► In each required direction, calculate the component of the unknown quantity, taking into account the applicable SI units.
► Check that the results of the calculations are reasonable.

Direction	Component
i	$v_x = v_{0x} + a_{cx} t$
j	$v_y = v_{0y} + a_{cy} t$
k	$v_z = v_{0z} + a_{cz} t$

Table 2.5: 3D Cartesian components of velocity $\mathbf{v}$ under constant acceleration

Direction	Component
i	$\Delta x = v_{0x} t + (\tfrac{1}{2}) a_{cx} t^2$
j	$\Delta y = v_{0y} t + (\tfrac{1}{2}) a_{cy} t^2$
k	$\Delta z = v_{0z} t + (\tfrac{1}{2}) a_{cz} t^2$

Table 2.6: 3D Cartesian components of displacement $\mathbf{\Delta r}$ under constant acceleration

2.4   Kinematic scalars

The magnitude (Section 1.1) of any kinematic vector (Section 2.3) provides a positive associated scalar quantity (Section 1.2). And, ranging over distance, speed, and acceleration, key examples of such positive kinematic scalars are given in Table 2.7.

Quantity	Description	Formula
$\lvert \mathbf{\Delta r} \rvert$	distance, d	$d = \lvert \mathbf{\Delta r} \rvert = \lvert \mathbf{r}_2 - \mathbf{r}_1 \rvert$
$\lvert \mathbf{v} \rvert$	instantaneous speed	$\lvert \mathbf{v} \rvert = \lvert d\mathbf{r}/dt \rvert$
$\lvert \bar{\mathbf{v}} \rvert$	average speed	$\lvert \bar{\mathbf{v}} \rvert = \lvert \mathbf{\Delta r}/\Delta t \rvert = d/\Delta t$
$\lvert \mathbf{a} \rvert$	magnitude of instantaneous acceleration	$\lvert \mathbf{a} \rvert = \lvert d\mathbf{v}/dt \rvert = \lvert d^2\mathbf{r}/dt^2 \rvert$
$\lvert \bar{\mathbf{a}} \rvert$	magnitude of average acceleration	$\lvert \bar{\mathbf{a}} \rvert = \lvert \mathbf{\Delta v}/\Delta t \rvert$

Table 2.7: Examples of positive kinematic scalars

In practice, however, be aware of the concerns, opposite:

▸The quantity Δt is taken to be positive.

▸Regardless of path, if $\Delta \mathbf{r} = 0$, then both d and $|\bar{\mathbf{v}}|$ are zero.

▸Furthermore, since $d = |\Delta \mathbf{r}|$ concerns only the position states 1 and 2 it regards the intervening path to be straight. But a travelled path may be significantly longer if there are changes in direction. If the average speed is required along a length of convoluted path, then $|\bar{\mathbf{v}}|$ is calculated as $|\bar{\mathbf{v}}| = L/\Delta t$, where L is the total length of that convoluted path, and Δt is the total time taken.

▸Negative acceleration, contrary to common language, does not always result in reduced speed. Inspection of Section 2.3's equation, $v_x = v_{0x} + a_{cx}t$, shows that $|v_x|$ will increase if v_{0x} is negative as well as a_{cx}.

2.5   Rotation

Contrary to the use of Cartesian vector methods (Section 2.3), the geometry of rotational motion is often more conveniently described in terms of radial distance and rotational angle relative to some coordinate origin†.

Radial distance r is always positive. But rotational angle can be positive or negative, and hence encodes the sense of the rotation – either anticlockwise or clockwise respectively – without using unit vectors. So, whilst such a rotational sense is couched in scalar symbolism, this text affords it the language of vectors. Furthermore, rotational angle has derived SI units of radians, symbol rad††.

With related quantities treated in the radian unit of angle (unless otherwise stated), and with motion restricted to a rotation of θ in an x-y plane at constant r from the origin, ongoing analysis concerns an arbitrary point P, as schematically shown overleaf in Figure 2.1†††.

†Such radial distance and rotational angle are scalar quantities, specific values of which may be referred to as polar coordinates.

††Something of an oddity, it will be seen that the radian has an equivalence to 1 and is effectively not a unit at all. Nonetheless, both mainstream physics and this text use it for two key reasons. First, associated formulae are expressed according to the radian measure of angle, and thus require angular quantities to be expressed in radian units. Second, the relation 2π radians = 1 revolution = 360 degrees identifies the level of scaling relative to other units of angle. It may, on occasion, be reasonable to omit the rad symbol, but doing so always implies that the radian unit of angle is being used.

†††Notes on such motion:
▸It is circular.
▸θ is an angular variable that concerns rotation about an out-of-the-page axis z.
▸In general, however, treatments are 3D where two angular variables are needed, associated with mutually perpendicular axes of rotation.

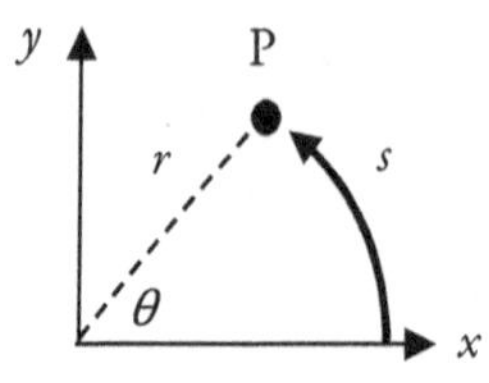

Figure 2.1: 2D angular position θ of a point P

†Notes on the $s = r\theta$ arc displacement:
►It can be positive or negative because θ can be positive or negative.
►Its magnitude, $|s| = r|\theta|$, represents the arc length.
►For a circle's $2\pi r$ circumference it can be written that
$|s| = |s_{circle}| = r|\theta_{circle}| = 2\pi r$,
where r is constant, confirming the assertion that $\theta_{circle} = 2\pi$ radians.
►Re-writing it as $\theta = s/r$ highlights θ as having no units, and thus confirms the assertion that the radian equals 1.

††There is no conflict in the unit relation m rad s^{-1} = m s^{-1} due to the radian equalling 1.

†††Notes:
►The equation $a_{centripetal} = v^2_{tangential}/r$ can be justified via a simple geometric argument based on similar triangles, and has derived SI units of m s^{-2}.
►Since $v_{tangential} = r\omega$, it follows that $a_{centripetal} = (r\omega)^2/r = r\omega^2$, where the derived SI units are still m s^{-2} due to the radian equalling 1.
►With the constancy of r, ω, and $v_{tangential}$, uniform circular motion also has constant $a_{centripetal}$.

Angular position: Point P has an angular position defined as the angle θ of subtension from the positive x-axis. This definition allows for positive values of angular position meaning anticlockwise rotations, and negative values meaning the opposite. Angular position θ has derived SI units of radians.

Arc displacement: Point P has an arc displacement s that is defined as $s = r\theta$, where s and r have SI units of metres, and θ has derived SI units of radians†.

Instantaneous angular velocity: Point P has instantaneous angular velocity ω that is defined as the derivative $\omega = d\theta/dt$. Such ω can be positive or negative, and has derived SI units of rad s^{-1}. Uniform circular motion has constant $d\theta/dt$ and ω.

Instantaneous tangential velocity: Point P has instantaneous tangential velocity $v_{tangential}$ defined as the derivative ds/dt at constant radius r, which is $ds/dt = d(r\theta)/dt = r d\theta/dt$. Accordingly, $v_{tangential} = r d\theta/dt = r\omega$, which can be positive or negative, and has derived SI units of m rad s^{-1} or simply m s^{-1}††.

With the constancy of r and ω, uniform circular motion also has constant $v_{tangential}$.

Centripetal acceleration: Since ω and $v_{tangential}$ are both constant in uniform circular motion, Table 2.1 would suggest there to be no acceleration. However, in the perpendicular radial direction there must always be an inward acceleration due to the Cartesian velocity vector for point P continuously turning towards the geometric centre of the rotation. This so-called centripetal acceleration is of magnitude $a_{centripetal}$ calculated as $a_{centripetal} = v^2_{tangential}/r$†††.

Period: The period is the time $\Delta t = T$ for one revolution by point P. For uniform circular motion, where r and $|v_{tangential}|$ are constant, T is meaningfully described as the constant quantity, $T = |s_{circle}|/|v_{tangential}| = 2\pi r/|v_{tangential}|$.

2.6   Rolling

Rolling is a combination of rotation and translation. Consider a uniform rigid circular body of radius R that is smoothly rolling over a surface so that, at the instantaneous point of contact with the surface, there is no slipping or bouncing. The rolling action is now analysed as to how the rotation and translation contribute to the forward motions relative to the surface of various points in the body perpendicular to that surface:

Rotational contributions: The rotation contributes to the body's forward motion through its tangential velocity, $v_{tangential}$, which is known from Section 2.5 to be given by $v_{tangential} = r\omega$. Such $v_{tangential}$ varies from 0 at the centre of the body ($r = 0$) to $R\omega$ at its rim ($r = R$). The sense relative to the surface is opposite, top and bottom, with that at the top being positive. The rotational contributions thus vary from $+|R\omega|$ at the top, to 0 at the centre, and $-|R\omega|$ at the bottom.

Translational contributions: Owing to the smooth rolling motion, the rotation fully drives the body's translation in the forward direction as per the following description: The point of the body that is instantaneously in contact with the surface has zero motion relative to that surface; it thus must experience a translational contribution of $+|R\omega|$ to offset the $-|R\omega|$ rotational contribution that applies there. But, owing to the body's rigidity, all of its other points must also experience the said $+|R\omega|$ translational contribution.

Forward motions: Owing to the smooth motion and the rigidity of the body, the forward motions are described as the sum of the rotational and translational contributions, and thus whose overall rates vary from $+|2R\omega|$ at the top of the body, to $+|R\omega|$ at the centre, and 0 at the bottom.

The **rest position** is where an oscillating body would settle if coming to rest.

Note that **period** as time is the default. However, for repetitive geometric patterns, ongoing discussions may refer to spatial period, which is a length.

For such a complete **cycle:**
► The start is arbitrary.
► Here is one description expressed in terms of oscillatory position: just passing through rest to maximum positive, then through rest to maximum negative, and just passing through rest again.

†Consider, for example, a pendulum's oscillating bob: With Figure 2.2 showing the state of maximum coordinate $x = x_m$, such a bob would also have $x = -x_m$ as the minimum coordinate, and $x = 0$ as the coordinate of the rest position (Section 2.7). Furthermore, if $x_m \ll L$, where L is the length of the constraining string, the naturally circular motion may be taken as confined to the x-axis, and the oscillation may thus be taken as SHM.

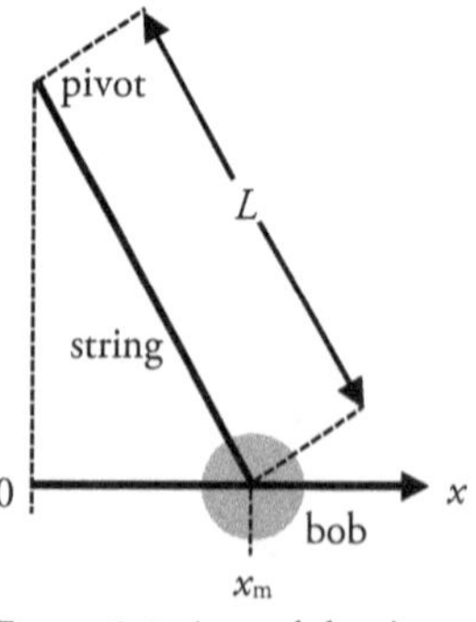

Figure 2.2: A pendulum's positive extremity of motion

2.7   Harmonic motion

Motion that repeats at regular time intervals is called harmonic. Examples include rotation and oscillation. While an oscillating body also has a mean or so-called **rest position**, two key descriptive parameters are **period** and frequency:

The period is the amount of time $\Delta t = T$ for one complete **cycle** of the repetitive motion, and has SI units of seconds. For harmonic motion the period T is constant.

Frequency f is defined as the inverse of the period – i.e. $f = T^{-1}$ – and has derived SI units of s^{-1} or Hz (hertz). For harmonic motion the frequency f is constant.

2.8   Simple harmonic motion, and the pendulum

Harmonic motion (Section 2.7), whose position is confined to a single axis and follows a sinusoidal function of time t, is called simple harmonic motion (SHM):

Simple harmonic position: Choosing the confinement to be to the x-axis, the position vector $\mathbf{r}(t)$ becomes $\mathbf{r}(t) = x(t)\mathbf{i}$. But the component $x(t)$ has a sign that in 1D fully encodes the direction of the motion†.

This text will thus take $x(t)$ as fully representing the simple harmonic position, loosely describing it in vector language. Discussions will further choose $x(t)$ to be the cosine function $x(t) = x_m \cos(at + \varphi)$ where the various terms are explained as follows:

First consider the parameter a: For $x(t)$ to advance through one cycle, the cosine argument $at + \varphi$ must advance by 2π radians as time t advances by one period T. Accordingly, $(at + \varphi) + 2\pi = a(t + T) + \varphi$, where the rad symbol is dropped because of its equivalence to 1 (Section 2.5). Thus $a = 2\pi/T = 2\pi f$, which is both positive and constant for SHM.

With f considered to be constant and the simple harmonic position $x(t)$ now becoming $x(t) = x_\mathrm{m}\cos(2\pi ft + \varphi)$, a full description of the parameters and terms is given in Table 2.8.

Term	Name	Meaning	Notes
$x_\mathrm{m}\cos(2\pi ft + \varphi)$	position	$x(t)$	►SI units of m
x_m	amplitude	$\lvert x(t)_\mathrm{maximum}\rvert$	►positive ►ideally constant ►SI units of m
$2\pi ft + \varphi$	phase	argument of cosine	►derived SI units of rad
f	frequency	concerns the rate of oscillation	►positive ►constant ►derived SI units of s^{-1}
t	time	-	►SI units of s
φ	phase angle	additional phase term	►derived SI units of rad

Table 2.8: Description of simple harmonic position

Simple harmonic velocity: This is defined in Table 2.9.

Simple harmonic velocity, $v(t) = \mathrm{d}x(t)/\mathrm{d}t$		
$= \mathrm{d}\{x_\mathrm{m}\cos(2\pi ft + \varphi)\}/\mathrm{d}t$	$= -2\pi fx_\mathrm{m}\sin(2\pi ft + \varphi)$	$= 2\pi fx_\mathrm{m}\cos(2\pi ft + \varphi - \pi/2)$

Table 2.9: Definition of simple harmonic velocity

A comparison with the simple harmonic position is given in Table 2.10.

Quantity	Equation	Relative amplitude	Relative phase
Simple harmonic position	$x(t) = x_\mathrm{m}\cos(2\pi ft + \varphi)$		
Simple harmonic velocity	$v(t) = 2\pi fx_\mathrm{m}\cos(2\pi ft + \varphi - \pi/2)$	$\times\, 2\pi f$	$-\pi/2$

Table 2.10: Velocity compared with position for SHM

The velocity thus tracks the position, but with $\times\, 2\pi f$ more amplitude, and a $-\pi/2$ shift of phase. Note that this phase-shift, being negative, is considered to be a lag†.

†This lag is equivalent to the time t of $x(t)$ being shifted by $-1/(4f)$, or $-T/4$, since then the phase of $x(t)$ would be equivalent to that of $v(t)$.

Simple harmonic acceleration: This is defined in Table 2.11.

Simple harmonic acceleration, $a(t) = \mathrm{d}v(t)/\mathrm{d}t = \mathrm{d}^2x(t)/\mathrm{d}t^2$	
$= \mathrm{d}^2\{x_\mathrm{m}\cos(2\pi ft + \varphi)\}/\mathrm{d}t^2$	$= -(2\pi f)^2 x_\mathrm{m}\cos(2\pi ft + \varphi)$

Table 2.11: Definition of simple harmonic acceleration

A comparison with the simple harmonic position is given, overleaf, in Table 2.12.

Quantity	Equation	Relative amplitude	Relative sign
Simple harmonic position	$x(t) = x_m\cos(2\pi ft + \varphi)$		
Simple harmonic acceleration	$a(t) = -(2\pi f)^2 x_m\cos(2\pi ft + \varphi)$	$\times (2\pi f)^2$	$-$

Table 2.12: Acceleration compared with position for SHM

†This mutual antiphase means that there is always a π shift of phase, or a $T/2$ shift of time, between the acceleration and position of SHM.

††Notes:
►Mass may also be conceptualised in terms of how difficult it is to move. Indeed, Newton's second law (see Section 3.3) suggests a fundamental method of quantifying mass by forcing it to undergo an acceleration.
►In a pendulum (Section 2.8), the bob is the main contributor to the oscillating mass. However, the constraining string also has mass that adds to the oscillating system. The proportionate contribution may be small enough to be ignored but, rigorously, the applicable pendulum's length would need to be considered as changed from L due to the system's different centre of mass (see Section 2.10).

†††For rigid bodies and when the applicable gravity (see Section 3.7) is taken to be constant, note that empirical determination may exploit equivalence to the concept of centre of gravity. Then, the centre of mass is the point where the application of a support just results in balance without falling.

The acceleration thus tracks the position, but with $\times (2\pi f)^2$ more amplitude, and opposing sign. The resultant mutual antiphase of acceleration and position is a hallmark of SHM†.

2.9 Mass and other constraints to motion

Constraints to the motion of a body may be external or internal. Discussed external constraints comprise the quality of a surface for a rolling body (Section 2.6) and the influence of a string on a pendulum's bob (Section 2.8). However, numerous others may be applicable.

Internal constraints certainly include the mass of the body. Differing from other notable characteristics – such as size, density, and weight (see Section 3.7) – mass is a fundamentally positive attribute whose total consideration – or net value – is the algebraically summed amount of constituent matter, expressed in the SI base unit of kg††.

Nonetheless, see Sections 5.6 and 5.7 for deeper insight on the origins of the mass of ordinary matter.

2.10 Centre of mass

Considered to contain a body's entire mass (Section 2.9), that body's so-called centre of mass is the point where it behaves like a particle. Such a point clearly may change in cases of overall motion or loss of rigidity†††.

Extending straightforwardly to a system of particles, such centre of mass is represented by the position vector $\mathbf{r}_{com}$ relative to some frame of reference (Section 2.1), and is defined in Table 2.13:

Equation	Where:
$\mathbf{r}_{com} = \dfrac{1}{M}\displaystyle\sum_{i=1}^{n} m_i \mathbf{r}_i$	►M is the total mass of the system ►m_i are the masses of the constituent particles ►$\mathbf{r}_i$ are the positions of the constituent particles ►n is the total number of constituent particles

Table 2.13: Definition of centre of mass

With a frame of reference comprising 3D Cartesian axes (Section 1.2) arbitrarily aligned to the system of interest, the components of $\mathbf{r}_{com}$ are as given in Table 2.14:

x-component	y-component	z-component
$x_{com} = \dfrac{1}{M}\displaystyle\sum_{i=1}^{n} m_i x_i$	$y_{com} = \dfrac{1}{M}\displaystyle\sum_{i=1}^{n} m_i y_i$	$z_{com} = \dfrac{1}{M}\displaystyle\sum_{i=1}^{n} m_i z_i$

Table 2.14: 3D Cartesian components of centre of mass

In general centre-of-mass problems:
►First consider whether each constituent body may be treated as an independent particle positioned at its own centre of mass.
►Choose wisely the dimensionality and alignment of the associated set of Cartesian axes – for example, if the origin is located on a constituent body's centre of mass, and the Cartesian axes are aligned along lines of symmetry within the system, working should be simplified†.

2.11   Questionnaire

†In general, calculations become particularly simple in cases of uniform mass distribution and shape. For example, for uniform annuli, disks, and spheres, $\mathbf{r}_{com}$ is simply the position of the geometric centre.

2Q1   For the three kinematic quantities – position, speed, and acceleration – how many do physicists treat as vectors?

a   0
b   1
c   2
d   3

2Q2   How many of the three features – magnitude, direction, and unit – are associated with kinematic vector quantities?

a   0
b   1
c   2
d   3

2Q3   In 1D, a particle starts at $x = 2$ m, and moves at a constant rate of -1 m s^{-1}. What is x after 2 s?

a -2 m
b   0 m
c   2 m
d   4 m

2Q4   After 4 s and considered relative to a 1D frame of reference, two particles, with initial co-location and respective constant rates of motion of $+0.5$ m s^{-1} and $+1$ m s^{-1}, become separated by:

a   1 m
b   2 m
c   3 m
d   4 m

2Q5   A particle moves between the Cartesian coordinates (1.0 m, 1.0 m) and (4.0 m, 5.0 m). What is the magnitude of its displacement?

a   3.5 m
b   5.0 m
c   5.5 m
d   7.0 m

Page 34 answers: 11a   12b   13b   14d   15b
Page 35 answers: 16a   17a   18b   19d   20b

2Q6   In 5.0 s, a particle undergoes 1D movement from the origin to a coordinate
       of 10×10^1 m. What is the particle's average speed?
a 2.0 m s^{-1}
b 20 m s^{-1}
c 25 m s^{-1}
d 40 m s^{-1}

2Q7   What is the average speed of a particle travelling 1 cm in 10 ms?
a 1×10^{-1} m s^{-1}
b 1×10^{0} m s^{-1}
c 1×10^{1} m s^{-1}
d 1×10^{2} m s^{-1}

2Q8   If a particle has changing velocity, which of the following statements about its
       acceleration must be true?
a   It is zero
b   It is non-zero
c   It is constant
d   It is changing

2Q9   If a particle has zero acceleration, which of the following statements about its
       velocity must be false?
a   It is zero
b   Its magnitude is greater than zero
c   It is constant
d   It is changing

2Q10   With motion along a positive axis, a particle's coordinate first increases
       to a maximum, and then starts to decrease. At the maximum coordinate, the
       particle's velocity is:
a   Positive
b   Negative
c   Zero
d   Maximum

Page 32 answers: 1c   2d   3b   4b   5b
Page 33 answers: 6b   7b   8b   9d   10c

2Q11 For cases of constant acceleration a_c, a later velocity equals an earlier velocity plus a_c times time. If a particle moves at an initial rate of 5.0 m s^{-1} directed vertically upwards, and that gravitational acceleration is assumed to be of constant magnitude 10 m s^{-2} and directed vertically downwards, how long does it take for the particle's height to become maximum?

a   0.50 s
b   1.0 s
c   1.5 s
d   2.0 s

2Q12 Suppose $x = t - t^2$, where x and t are variable unit-less scalars, and that speed v is calculated as $v = |dx/dt|$. What, then, is the exact value of t at which v is zero?

a   0
b   ½
c   1
d   2

2Q13 With x representing position, and t representing time, which of the following quantities represents instantaneous acceleration?

a dx/dt
b d^2x/dt^2
c dt/dx
d d^2t/dx^2

2Q14 One revolution is exactly equivalent to:
a   1 radian
b   2 radians
c π radians
d 2π radians

2Q15 Answer the following three questions in the same order: Must there always be zero acceleration for motion that has zero tangential velocity? Must there be a change of velocity when following a non-straight path? Must motions that are solely circular and constant have a constant magnitude of acceleration?

a   No. No. No.
b   No. Yes. Yes.
c   Yes. Yes. Yes.
d   Yes. Yes. No.

2Q16 If a uniform wheel of fixed radius R smoothly rolls with uniform angular
velocity $|\omega|$ along a surface, then that wheel's centre of mass moves along that
surface at a rate of:

a $R|\omega|$
b $R^2|\omega|$
c $R|\omega|^2$
d $R^2|\omega|^2$

2Q17 Regarding the equation $x(t) = x_\mathrm{m}\cos(2\pi ft + \varphi)$ for the position of simple
harmonic motion, answer, in the same order, the two questions:
What is x_m? What is $2\pi ft + \varphi$?:

a   Amplitude. Phase.
b   Amplitude. Phase angle.
c   Spatial period. Phase.
d   Spatial period. Phase angle.

2Q18 Answered in the same order, are the text's presented treatments strictly vectorial
in respect of: Cartesian motion? Rotation?

a   No. No.
b   Yes. No.
c   No. Yes.
d   Yes. Yes.

2Q19 With the hint that 'in phase' and 'out of phase' are specific expressions with
meanings to be looked up, which of the following statements about simple
harmonic position is correct?

a   It is in phase with simple harmonic velocity
b   It is out of phase with simple harmonic velocity
c   It is in phase with simple harmonic acceleration
d   It is out of phase with simple harmonic acceleration

2Q20 A linear system of particles is confined to the x-axis. The particles are at
coordinates $x = 0$ m, $x = 3$ m, and $x = 5$ m. And the particles have respective
masses of 8 kg, 4 kg, and 4 kg. Where is the system's centre of mass?

a $x = 1$ m
b $x = 2$ m
c $x = 3$ m
d $x = 4$ m

Chapter 3 Newtonian Force; Momentum and Energy

Newtonian physics:
►Is published in Newton's historic Philosophiae Naturalis Principia Mathematica (1687).
►Concerns the three laws discussed next, and the law of universal gravitation (see Section 5.1.2).
►Is fundamentally based on the concept of ***force***, whose manifestations range from contact (such as in friction) to remote (such as in electromagnetism).
►Carries the untestable notion of absolute space, but actually appeals to the apparently fixed starry backdrop as a practical frame of reference (Section 2.1) – a kinematic (Section 2.2) device later to be called an ***inertial frame*** and be recognised as just one of an infinite class of equivalent such frames.
►May be acceptably accurate in weakly non-inertial frames, such as the astronomically rotating surface of the Earth.
►Can, regardless, fail catastrophically in ***extreme scenarios:***

Extreme scenarios where Newtonian physics can fail comprise the very big, the very fast, and the very small – notably extreme gravitation, motion close to the speed of light, and the interior of chemistry's atoms (Section 1.4). These scenarios benefit from radically different treatments, such as in:
►Einstein's relativistic physics (see Section 5.1.5).
►The quantisation of particles and fields (see Sections 5.2-5.7, 6.8, and 6.9).

3.1 Newtonian physics

What causes bodies to move? Under the premise that all bodies at some time in their history are stationary, to be brought into motion they must first be accelerated. In fact, the concept of acceleration is widespread and universal.

As embodied within the scheme of ***Newtonian physics***:
►Observed accelerations originate from the concept of ***force*** whose treatment allows a comprehensive understanding of the cause of Chapter 2's various kinematic motions.

3.2 Newton's first law

The concepts behind Newton's first law and the ***inertial frame*** are inextricably linked. The law may be presented in various ways, but consider this: If an observer of a particle (Section 2.1), upon which the vector-sum $\mathbf{F}_{net}$ of all external forces is zero, sees that particle either to remain at rest or continue to move with constant speed in a straight line, then that observer is confirmed to reside within an inertial frame of reference. In this context:
►Newton's first law – that there is seen to be zero, or constancy of, speed in a straight line when $\mathbf{F}_{net} = 0$ – can be taken as the definition of an inertial frame.

►When $\mathbf{F}_{net} = 0$, the concerned particle cannot undergo a change of speed or direction, and thus cannot accelerate relative to the inertial frame.

►The forces applicable to $\mathbf{F}_{net}$ must be external to the particle†.

►$\mathbf{F}_{net}$ is evaluated from rules of vector addition.

3.3   Newton's second law, and particle-like bodies

If Newton's first law (Section 3.2) confirms observations to be from an inertial frame of reference, and there is non-zero $\mathbf{F}_{net}$ acting on some particle then, according to Newton's second law, the particle will have a 'change in motion' proportional to the 'impressed force'††.

A workable version – dubbed here the Newtonian second law – follows the **notes** as $\mathbf{F}_{net} = \Delta(m\mathbf{v})/\Delta t = \mathrm{d}(m\mathbf{v})/\mathrm{d}t = m\mathbf{a}$, where the third equality assumes constancy of mass, $\mathbf{a}$ is the particle's acceleration, and all vectors (1) are mutually directed and (2) act at the particle's instantaneous position†††.

Moreover, due to mutual perpendicular disposition, the expansion of $\mathbf{a}$ as Cartesian components has the benefit of each such component only being caused by the sum of the force components along its own axis, and not by the force components along any other axis. Table 3.1 shows the constant-mass case.

x-component	y-component	z-component
$F_{net,x} = ma_x$	$F_{net,y} = ma_y$	$F_{net,z} = ma_z$

Table 3.1: Cartesian rendition of the Newtonian second law for a particle of constant mass m

Once the components of acceleration are calculated (e.g. $a_x = F_{net,x}/m$ for constant m, etc), kinematics (Chapter 2) may be used to evaluate the particle's evolution of position – i.e. whether it follows a straight or some curved path††††.

When extending the concept from the particle to a body, the simplest case involves rigidity, constant total mass M, and a net force

†Notes on the related concept of internal forces:

►They are inapplicable within particles due to the structureless nature of a geometric point.

►They are widely applicable within extended entities – i.e. bodies.

††**Notes:**

►Rather than with acceleration (Section 2.3), Newton applied his second law with arcane geometry. However, Maxwell (1888), at least, provided modern workability by defining:

►The 'change in motion' as $\Delta(m\mathbf{v})$, where m is the particle's mass, and $\mathbf{v}$ is its velocity.

►The 'impressed force' as $F_{net}\Delta t$, where Δt is the duration of $\mathbf{F}_{net}$.

►There to be equality of the above quantities so that $F_{net}\Delta t = \Delta(m\mathbf{v})$.

†††Notes:

►The differential form covers cases of changing mass and velocity.

►$\mathbf{F}_{net} = ma$ is the familiar albeit constant-mass form.

►If $\mathbf{F}_{net}$ and m are constant, the acceleration $\mathbf{a}$ is also constant, as frequently encountered in physics.

►But, if $\mathbf{F}_{net} = 0$ and acceleration is still observed, then the reference frame is not inertial and, for acceptable accuracy of application, so-called fictitious forces need to be incorporated as a modern rendition of Newtonian physics – see, for example, Taylor (2004).

††††But remember that there is no classical spin of a geometric point.

$\mathbf{F}_{net}$ that acts at the body's centre $\mathbf{r}_{com}$ of mass (Section 2.10). Such a particle-like body behaves as if M is all located at $\mathbf{r}_{com}$, does not rotate, and accelerates everywhere according to that of its centre of mass $\mathbf{a}_{com}$ following the constant-mass Newtonian second law $\mathbf{F}_{net} = M\mathbf{a}_{com}$. And the Cartesian components of such $\mathbf{a}_{com}$ are as given in Table 3.2†.

x-component	y-component	z-component
$F_{net,x} = Ma_{com,x}$	$F_{net,y} = Ma_{com,y}$	$F_{net,z} = Ma_{com,z}$

Table 3.2: Cartesian rendition of the Newtonian second law for a particle-like body of constant mass M

3.4   Newton's third law

Newton's third law is that when one body exerts a force on a second, that second body exerts an equal and opposite force on the first. And it is often stated as there being, to every action, an equal and opposite reaction††.

Associated so-called third-law force-pairs arise in various ways, such as from contact or action at a distance. But their key broader consequence is mutual cancellation. Notably:

►They make no contribution to any external $\mathbf{F}_{net}$ applicable to a system.

►When arising within a system, they make no contribution to the motion of that system's centre of mass (Sections 2.10 and 3.3).

3.5   Importance of the inertial frame

Following Sections 3.1-3.4, Newtonian forces are seen to impart profound understanding to motional cause and effect, whilst the latterly named underlying premise – the inertial frame (Section 3.1) – gives clear reference to their application. And, for each such application, there is implicit equivalence of all inertial frames. Moreover, while over the next two centuries there would be a general sweeping aside of the quaint Newtonian notion of absolute space, the laws remain valid†††.

†But cases of non-rigidity and $\mathbf{F}_{net}$ being off-centre are likely far more complex: Here, the same $\mathbf{a}_{com}$ applies but, dependent on the ensuing detailed interaction of internal forces, as does a combination of bodily distortion and rotation.

††Notes on Newton's third law:
►For interaction-associated forces, it is always possible to identify counterparts that are equal and opposite. For example, the law may be applied to a system comprising the Earth and the Moon with these two bodies taken to interact via equal and opposite forces of gravity (see Section 3.7).
►It is conceptually easiest to apply the third law to observations from inertial frames, as Newton intended.
►However, for any fictitious forces (Section 3.1) that are used to explain observations from non-inertial frames, there is notably no third-law counterpart since such non-Newtonian forces are not associated with physical interaction.

†††And even the inertial frame represents no fundamental impediment since non-inertial motions may be accommodated via the invocation of fictitious forces (Section 3.1) and, later, via the use of Einstein's general theory of relativity (see Section 5.1.5).

3.6   Free-body diagrams

Even where there is the simplicity of, for example, bodily rigidity and centre-of-mass action (Section 3.3), applications of Newton's laws (Sections 3.2-3.4) may not be intuitive†.

But understanding often follows from so-called free-body diagrams – pictorial treatments that break each scenario down into its constituent bodies – or particles thereof – and separately consider the forces acting thereon††:

With a nod to Cartesian (Section 1.2) gravitational scenarios, Figure 3.1 gives two 1D examples where the labelled y-axis – acting as the frame of reference (Section 2.1) – is intuitively chosen to increase vertically downwards. Such a key direction importantly relates to any vector components to be determined, such as of vectorially resolved force, net force, and net acceleration:

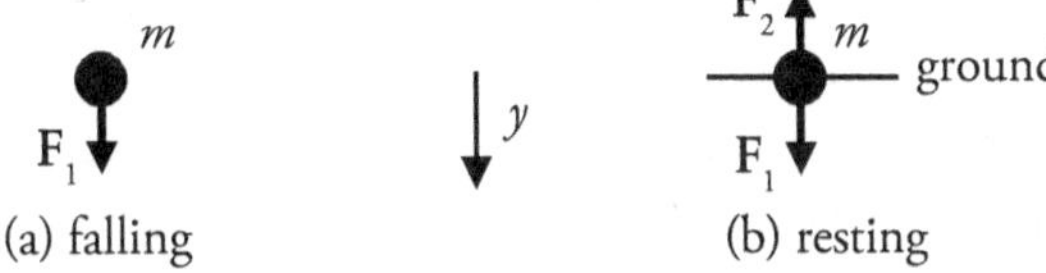

(a) falling   (b) resting

Figure 3.1: With all parameters taken as constant, two 1D free-body diagrams (a) falling, and (b) resting

For Figure 3.1(a), the constant-mass Newtonian second law, applied in the downwards direction, gives $F_{net,y} = F_{1,y} = ma_{net,y}$.

But, for Figure 3.1(b), an opposing equal magnitude force $\mathbf{F}_2$ is introduced as a third-law force-pair (Section 3.4) to ensure continued resting of the body, and then the Newtonian analysis gives $F_{net,y} = F_{1,y} - F_{2,y} = ma_{net,y} = 0$.

More typical, however, are 3D Cartesian scenarios; these would need three mutually perpendicular axes of resolution (say x, y, and z) to calculate the associated three components of acceleration (say $a_{net,x}$, $a_{net,y}$, and $a_{net,z}$)†††.

†As generally in physics' problems, start by:
►Studying the scenario until its essence is understood.
►Identifying the key bodies of interest.
►Noting the context, and all relevant physical concepts, principles and laws.

††In creating each free-body diagram:
►Represent each body, for which acceleration is to be determined, as a dot.
►For every external force associated with each dot, apply a vector arrow starting with its tail – but remember inapplicability of the internal forces (Section 3.4).
►And, with respect to each chosen Cartesian axis, apply an overall arrow to indicate the chosen direction of assessing vector components. Consistent adherence to such directions ensures that calculated quantities are determined with the correct magnitudes and signs.

†††Note that, regardless of the chosen axial directions, careful trigonometric resolution of each force along each axis will still yield components of acceleration with the correct signs. In Figure 3.1(a), for example, the component of acceleration would have worked out with opposite sign had the reference y-axis been chosen to increase vertically upwards, meaning that the applicable acceleration is still associated with the expected downward direction.

†But remember – from Section 3.3 – that the easiest applications involve particle-like (rigid) bodies, and centre-of-mass acting forces.

††Note that general treatments should also consider the effect of height:
►Over astronomical incoming distances towards the Earth, F_g, W, and a_g all increase significantly, and with gathering rapidity upon approach.
►At the Earth's surface, F_g, W, and a_g take their largest practical values. Nonetheless, typical nearby applications can take them as constant, assuming there are negligible variations in height.
►Near the Earth's surface, $|a_g|$ is often represented by the symbol g so that $|F_g| = |W| = m|a_g| = mg$.
►But g can vary by about 0.5% across the Earth's surface due mainly to variations in altitude. Thus, taking g to only two significant figures, as $g = 9.8$ m s^{-2}, is realistic in the absence of local geographic knowledge.

3.7   Examples of Newtonian forces

As observed from an inertial frame of reference, (Section 3.2), here are some examples of forces analysed via the Newtonian second law†:

Gravity and weight: The force F_g of gravity acting on a body is also referred to as the body's weight W. Thus, $W = F_g$, indicating equivalence of magnitude and direction between the two quantities. If F_g is also the net force F_{net} acting at the body's centre of mass, and the body is particle-like with constant mass m, then the Newtonian second law indicates the acceleration a_g of the body to follow $F_{net} = F_g = W = ma_g$.

In the context of the Earth, F_g and W act vertically downwards towards its centre of mass (Section 2.10). Then, for a free-body diagram (Section 3.6), such a downwards direction may be used for the F_g, W, and a_g vector arrows, as well as performing vector resolutions. But only the downwards axis is relevant and, calling it y, thus gives $F_{g,y} = W_y = ma_{g,y}$ as a full description of the scenario for some particle-like body of constant mass m††.

Force for Section 2.5's centripetal acceleration: The Newtonian second law indicates that a particle-like body of constant mass m, subject to $a_{centripetal} = v^2_{tangential}/r = r\omega^2$ of centripetal acceleration (where $v_{tangential}$, r, and ω are respectively its tangential velocity, rotational radius, and angular velocity) requires $F_{centripetal} = ma_{centripetal} = mv^2_{tangential}/r = mr\omega^2$ of centripetal force.

Force for Section 2.8's simple harmonic acceleration: The Newtonian second law indicates that a particle-like body of constant mass m, subject to $a(t) = -(2\pi f)^2 x(t)$ of simple harmonic acceleration (where f and x are its frequency and position, and t is the time) requires $F_x(t) = -m(2\pi f)^2 x(t)$ of simple harmonic force.

But f and the associated period T can be further quantified as material constants: Consider a spring aligned with the x-axis, with one end fixed, and a particle-like object of constant mass m attached to the other end. Such a mass m responds to an x-component $F_x(t)$ of restoring force within the spring given by the law of Hooke (1678) as $F_x(t) = -ke_x(t)$, where k is a positive constant quantifying the spring's stiffness (with derived SI units of $N\,m^{-1}$), and $e_x(t)$ is its extension. Furthermore, with $e_x(t) = 0$ representing rest, such $e_x(t)$ is also identified as the object's simple harmonic position $x(t)$, where $\quad F_x(t) = -ke_x(t) = -kx(t) = -m(2\pi f)^2 x(t)$ is the required simple harmonic force.

Accordingly, $f = (2\pi)^{-1}(k/m)^{\frac{1}{2}}$ (with the period T being its inverse). And, thus, a high frequency f (and associated short period T) go with a large stiffness k and small mass m†,††.

Normal force: A body resting on a horizontal surface remains stationary because the gravitational force $\mathbf{F}_g$ is exactly balanced by a reactive normal force $\mathbf{F}_n$ acting upwards from that surface. Such a pair of balanced forces, $\mathbf{F}_n = -\mathbf{F}_g$, is an example of Newton's third law (Section 3.4). Normal forces always act perpendicularly to the local plane of contact.

So, what happens if the local plane of contact is not horizontal? In this case, only part of $\mathbf{F}_g$ is balanced by $\mathbf{F}_n$. The remainder of $\mathbf{F}_g$ acts downwards along the plane, and must be exactly balanced by the force of friction acting upwards along the plane if the body is to remain stationary:

Static and kinetic friction: Fundamentally based on the existence of normal force, there are considered to be two different types of friction – namely static and kinetic – which both act to oppose motion along the local plane of contact between two surfaces, but generally differ in magnitude:

†And, of course, the converse is also true.

††But every oscillating system has some equivalent to the stiffness-to-mass ratio k/m:

For example, in the case of a pendulum (Sections 2.8 and 2.9), $k/m = g/L$, where g is the magnitude of the Earth's near-surface gravitational acceleration, and L is the pendulum's length. The equation may be re-written as the so-called law of length, $L = gT^2(2\pi)^{-2}$, notably providing a convenient route to determining g:

Comparing the law of length's parameters with those of a Cartesian straight line $y = mx + c$ (Section 1.13) identifies L with y, g with m, $T^2(2\pi)^{-2}$ with x, and 0 with c. Thus plotting L on the vertical axis against the quantity $T^2(2\pi)^{-2}$ on the horizontal axis, and fitting a best straight line going through the origin, gives a gradient equal to g. The data for the plot are easily obtained by measuring L and T for pendulums of various lengths.

†Such $\mathbf{F}_{sf}$ is essential to much surface based motion. For example, it crucially allows non-slipping contact between one's lagging foot and horizontal ground, combined with a changing vertical centre of gravity, to produce thrust for harmonically ratcheting forward motion. Regardless of its complexity, however, the enacting of such walking cannot exist if $\mathbf{F}_{sf}$ is zero.

Indeed, a body of constant mass supported by a frictionless horizontal surface, can bring itself neither into motion nor into a change of motion – i.e. it cannot accelerate.

But, upon such **slippage**, there must be work done (see Section 3.12) by $\mathbf{F}_{net}$ which notably wastes precious energy as heat (see Section 4.1) and may cause premature mechanical wear-out and failure.

††If this motion is just sufficient to remain constant it may be called friction compensated.

Predating the work of Newton, **momentum** was initially formulated by Descartes, but inappropriately expressed in terms of speed. Later, Huygens (1669) expressed momentum in terms of velocity, and showed that such vectorial momentum may be subject to conservation.

†††Where there are multiple bodies, each is first treated as a particle at its own centre of mass.

►In the case of static contact, the applicable friction is the static friction $\mathbf{F}_{sf}$. Such $\mathbf{F}_{sf}$ opposes any net force $\mathbf{F}_{net}$ existing along the local plane of contact†.

►Up to some limit, $|\mathbf{F}_{sf}|$ always equals $|\mathbf{F}_{net}|$. Here, there is mutual cancellation of $|\mathbf{F}_{net}|$ and $|\mathbf{F}_{sf}|$, and the surfaces remain in static contact.

►$|\mathbf{F}_{sf}|$ increases with $|\mathbf{F}_{net}|$, and takes a maximum possible magnitude $|\mathbf{F}_{sf}|_{max}$ that is proportional to the force $\mathbf{F}_n$ normal to the local plane of contact. Thus $|\mathbf{F}_{sf}|_{max} = \mu|\mathbf{F}_n|$, where μ is a unit-less constant dependent on the nature of the contact.

►But, at the instant that $|\mathbf{F}_{net}|$ exceeds $|\mathbf{F}_{sf}|_{max}$, mutual cancellation no longer applies, static contact is broken, and there is **slippage** between the surfaces. The so-called kinetic friction $\mathbf{F}_{kf}$, that then applies, has a magnitude that is usually less than $|\mathbf{F}_{sf}|_{max}$:

Thus, interestingly, a body experiencing a normal force from an inclined surface can maintain both stationary and sliding forms of initial motion through the specific value of the applicable type of friction. For example, there may be sufficient $|\mathbf{F}_{sf}|$ to hold the body stationary. But, if nudged into motion, and $|\mathbf{F}_{kf}| < |\mathbf{F}_{sf}|$, the body may continue to move††.

3.8   Momentum and its conservation

With derived SI units of kg m s^{-1}, and relative to some frame of reference (Section 2.1), a particle has a **momentum** vector $\mathbf{p}$ in the same direction as its velocity $\mathbf{v}$ defined as $\mathbf{p} = m\mathbf{v}$, where m is its mass. For a body, the total momentum $\mathbf{P}$ is the vector-sum of its constituent particulate momenta, and, being in the same direction as the velocity $\mathbf{v}_{com}$ of its centre of mass $\mathbf{r}_{com}$ (Section 2.10), may be written as $\mathbf{P} = M\mathbf{v}_{com}$, where M is the total particulate mass†††.

Furthermore, regardless of complexity, whether a system can be considered as having conserved momentum depends on its degree of **isolation** from the environment:

Noted first is that such a system must be closed by not permitting entry or exit of matter. The system's total mass M is then constant, and the time differential of $\mathbf{P}$ may be written as $d\mathbf{P}/dt = Md\mathbf{v}_{com}/dt = M\mathbf{a}_{com}$, where $\mathbf{a}_{com}$ is the acceleration of the system's centre of mass.

Noted second is that there must also be zero net external force, $\mathbf{F}_{net} = 0$. But, viewed from an inertial frame of reference (Section 3.2), Section 3.3 indicates that the constant-mass Newtonian second law applies as $\mathbf{F}_{net} = M\mathbf{a}_{com}$. Thus $d\mathbf{P}/dt = Md\mathbf{v}_{com}/dt = M\mathbf{a}_{com} = 0$.

Since $\mathbf{P}$ cannot then change with time, the relation $\Delta\mathbf{P} = 0$ must hold, where the Δ symbol represents the change between arbitrary later and earlier states in time†.

Furthermore, any direction where $\Delta\mathbf{P} = 0$ applies is said to conserve momentum, and then the calculation of $\Delta\mathbf{P} = 0$ is particularly useful in determining some consequences of events, such as collisions, without knowing their detail, such as how much damage is done.

Here is a summary of some characteristics of isolated systems relative to an inertial frame of reference:
- The quantities $d\mathbf{P}/dt$, $d\mathbf{v}_{com}/dt$, $\mathbf{a}_{com}$, and the external $\mathbf{F}_{net}$ are all zero.
- The ensuing temporal constancy of both $\mathbf{P}$ and $\mathbf{v}_{com}$ is held to be true regardless of the system's internal dynamics, or even extent. It is thus inconsequential whether the system's constituents are moving about and undergoing collisions, or even whether they constitute the entire universe.

For **isolation** to apply to any given system, two broad conditions must be met:
- First, it must not exchange matter with its environment. Such a system is fairly easy to achieve.
- Second, it must not exchange energy with its environment. This notably must involve zero net external force, $\mathbf{F}_{net} = 0$, so that there is no environmental exchange of work energy (see Section 3.12). But all other energy transfer mechanisms, such as via heat (see Section 4.1), must also be negligible.

†Notes on the application of $\Delta\mathbf{P} = 0$:
- Ensure that the concerned system is closed.
- And, with observations being from an inertial frame of reference, ensure that $\mathbf{F}_{net}$ is zero in up to three (preferably perpendicular) directions – such directions then have conserved momentum.
- For these directions, evaluate the total momentum $\mathbf{P}$ for two interesting states in time.
- Calculate $\Delta\mathbf{P}$ and equate to zero, noting that up to three (preferably independent) equations may ensue depending on the dimensionality of the system.
- Solve for what is required.
- But note the corollary that any direction where $\mathbf{F}_{net}$ is not zero – so that $\Delta\mathbf{P}$ is also non-zero – will not have conserved momentum.

Energy: Whether as, say, the world-regenerative ever-living fire of Heraclitus (*c.*505BC), the formalism of Young (1807), or the so-called *Lagrangian* of the standard model of particle physics (see e.g. Dodd and Gripaios (2020)), energy is arguably physics' most applicable of concepts.

Such a *Lagrangian* is a culminating formalism of energy that awaits conception of quantum gravity to complete its fundamental description.

†For further discussions of such forms see, for example, Section 3.11 for K and U, and Section 4.1 for Q.

††But such E varies across different frames of reference (see Section 3.10), and thus needs careful interpretation due to lack of absolute validity.

†††First clearly enunciated by Clausius (1865), this is referred to as the first law of thermodynamics.

††††Potentially providing simpler solutions than the vectorial Newtonian physics (Sections 3.1-3.7) and momentum (Section 3.8), the scalar $\Delta E = 0$ process notably involves:
►Choosing the frame of reference (Section 2.1).
►Identifying a system whose total energy E is constant, and thus whose ΔE is always zero (such as in isolated systems).
►Selecting two interesting states in time.
►Evaluating all associated contributions to $\Delta E = 0$.

►If **P** and $\mathbf{v}_{\text{com}}$ are found to be zero at some instant of time, they are deemed also to be zero at all other past and future times.

►And, if $\mathbf{v}_{\text{com}}$ is always zero, then (1) the centre of mass $\mathbf{r}_{\text{com}}$ cannot vary with time even if extreme internal events such as explosions are taking place, and (2) placing of the origin of the frame of reference at $\mathbf{r}_{\text{com}}$, such that $\mathbf{r}_{\text{com}} = 0$, is likely to provide the benefit of simplified calculations.

3.9   The nature, conservation, and equilibrium of energy

Providing a broad means to understanding the evolution of systems, *energy* – like numerous other physical concepts – is non-trivial and difficult to define.

Here are some initial observations:
►It is a scalar quantity.
►It has derived SI units of $\text{kg m}^2\,\text{s}^{-2}$, alternatively known as the joule, symbol J.
►It comes in numerous recognisable forms, e.g. kinetic K, potential U, heat Q, *etc*†.
►Its total instantaneous amount E within any given system is the sum of all its instantaneous forms. Thus $E = K + U + Q + \ldots$ ††.
►It may be converted from one form to another.
►It is taken to be conserved since no process of *in/ex nihilo* conversion has ever been discovered. In fact, the conservation of energy is taken as a universal axiom†††.
►For any isolated system (Section 3.8), and given frame of reference, the total value of E must be the same at all instants of time assuming that all its instantaneous forms are identified and accounted. Since such E is then considered as constant, the first law of thermodynamics may be applied as $\Delta E = \Delta K + \Delta U + \Delta Q + \ldots = 0$, where the Δ symbol refers to the change between arbitrary later and earlier states in time††††.

►When $\Delta E = 0$, the constituent Δ terms tend towards a state of **equilibrium**.

►If also $\Delta Q + \ldots$ terms are negligible, then $\Delta E = \Delta K + \Delta U = 0$, and there can be conversions of energy only between K and U. Furthermore, while mechanical energy is defined as $K + U$, the relation $\Delta E = \Delta K + \Delta U = 0$, or equivalently $\Delta K = - \Delta U$, defines its conservation.

►If also $\Delta U = 0$, then $\Delta E = \Delta K = 0$ and there can be conversions of energy only between multiple K terms. This is when there is a so-called elastic redistribution of kinetic energy, such that $\Delta E = \Delta K = \Sigma \Delta K_i = 0$ for a system of i colliding bodies.

3.10 Approach to analysing energy

Connection to the inertial frame (Section 3.2) and the Newtonian second law (Section 3.3): Relative to an inertial frame of reference, the Newtonian second law is $\mathbf{F}_{net} = m\,d\mathbf{v}/dt$ for a particle-like body of constant mass m moving with velocity $\mathbf{v}$†.

But applying the position differential dot product .$d\mathbf{r}$ to both sides gives a relation in units of energy (Section 3.9) such that $\mathbf{F}_{net}.d\mathbf{r} = m\,(d\mathbf{v}/dt).d\mathbf{r}$. And, replacing $d\mathbf{r}$ on the right-hand side with $\mathbf{v}dt$, and integrating, gives $\int\mathbf{F}_{net}.d\mathbf{r} = m\int\mathbf{v}.d\mathbf{v}$.

Recipe for ongoing discussion: In the interests of clarity, discussions will proceed, with continued reference to Section 3.9, by:

►Considering, in Cartesian geometry (Section 1.2), changes of energy relative to an inertial frame reference††.

►Putting under careful consideration any relation purporting to be of absolute energy due to its inconsistency across frames†††.

►Considering only those changes that are reversible – i.e. where full conversions are possible from one group of energy-forms to another, and vice versa††††.

Such **equilibrium** may be dynamic if there is temporally sustained uniformly-repetitive change between constituent energies, but typically becomes static in time where each Δ term tends to zero.

†As per Section 3.3, remember that the Newtonian second law may be applied to both particles and bodies. And, for the latter, application is most easy when (1) internal forces hold rigidity of structure, and (2) $\mathbf{F}_{net}$ acts at the centre of mass so that there is negligible rotational effect.

††Remember generally that, regardless of the frame of reference, the sum of the changes of the constituent energies is always assessed to be zero for isolated systems. Thus, in conservation problems, any change to a constituent energy is a key consideration.

†††Consider, for example, possible inter-frame variations of v and y in the following:
►$\tfrac{1}{2}mv^2$ as a possible measure of 1D kinetic energy K associated with mass m and speed v.
►mgy as a possible measure of 1D near-Earth's-surface gravitational potential energy U associated mass m, magnitude of gravitational acceleration g, and vertical coordinate y.

††††This notably requires $\Delta Q = 0$ such that there is:
►Zero conversion of energy into heat Q.
►Zero change of so-called entropy (See Section 7.5).

►Assessing, for a system of constant mass, both mechanical energy $K + U$ (Section 3.9) and the relation $\int \mathbf{F}_{net}.\mathbf{dr} = m\int \mathbf{v}.\mathbf{dv}$ to describe the conversion/conservation of energy within, and the effect of work done without†:

3.11 Conversion/conservation of energy within systems

As per the recipe of Section 3.10 and an inertial frame of reference, consider $\int \mathbf{F}_{net,int}.\mathbf{dr} = m\int \mathbf{v}.\mathbf{dv}$ to describe an isolated system (Section 3.8) of mechanical energy (Section 3.9) that has an internal net force $\mathbf{F}_{net,int}$ acting on a constituent particle-like body of constant mass m moving at velocity $\mathbf{v}$. This is where the following analyses may apply:

Change of kinetic energy: Such ΔK is taken to be defined by the energy term $m\int \mathbf{v}.\mathbf{dv}$, so that $\Delta K = m\int \mathbf{v}.\mathbf{dv}$. Cartesian (Section 1.2) evaluation then gives:

►$\Delta K = \tfrac{1}{2}m[v_x^2 + v_y^2 + v_z^2]_{state1}^{state2}$ in 3D cases.

►$\Delta K = \tfrac{1}{2}m[v^2]_{state1}^{state2}$ in 1D cases††.

Now the key question arises what is the origin and fate of such ΔK? Generally, the natural tendency is for ΔK to convert, via friction (Section 3.7), into heat (see Section 4.1). But the isolative and mechanical constraints of the defined system restrict ΔK's origin and fate to a change of the system's potential energy:

Change of potential energy: This is taken to be defined by the negated energy term $-\int \mathbf{F}_{net,int}.\mathbf{dr}$ so that $\Delta U = -\int \mathbf{F}_{net,int}.\mathbf{dr}$. Such ΔU thus depends on both the internal net force $\mathbf{F}_{net,int}$ and the ensuing change $\mathbf{dr}$ of position. In particular, the definition's negative sign reflects the general natural tendency towards loss of potential energy. Consider, specifically, a system comprising a particle falling towards the Earth. The $\mathbf{F}_{net,int}$ acting on the particle is then that due to the Earth's field of gravitation. But, as the

†Note, further, that ongoing discussions generally assume particle-like behaviour to avoid the complications of rotations and changes of shape.

††For 1D cases, absolute K is indicated as $K = \tfrac{1}{2}mv^2$, clearly increasing with speed v.

particle falls, the vectors $\mathbf{F}_{net,int}$ and $\mathbf{dr}$ are in the same downwards direction. This makes the quantity $\int\mathbf{F}_{net,int}.\mathbf{dr}$ positive, meaning that the action of $\mathbf{F}_{net,int}$ expends a positive amount of energy. Such positive energy may appear in various forms (here, restricted to increased K), but must come from a commensurately reduced U. And the associated negative change, or loss, is accommodated via ΔU's negated definition.

Change of mechanical energy: Furthermore, with $\int\mathbf{F}_{net,int}.\mathbf{dr} = m\int\mathbf{v}.\mathbf{dv} = -\Delta U = \Delta K$ as a complete description of the scenario (with its attendant lack of ΔQ and all other Δ energy terms), the full reversibility between ΔU and ΔK, indicated by the relation $\Delta E = \Delta K + \Delta U = 0$ (Section 3.9), is guaranteed via $\mathbf{F}_{net,int}$ acting in a so-called conservative way in which $\int\mathbf{F}_{net,int}.\mathbf{dr}$ evaluated along any path depends only on the path's start and end positions, is independent of the path's shape, and notably evaluates to zero if the path returns to its start.

Cases of ongoing discussion: Specifically involving **collinear** $\mathbf{F}_{net,int}$ and $\mathbf{dr}$, three cases follow, ranging over gravitation, spring-based action, and the conservation of mechanical energy (Section 3.10)†:

Case 1 – the change in potential energy due to gravitation by the Earth nearby its surface: Here are some circumstances under which the associated $\Delta U = -\int\mathbf{F}_{net,int}.\mathbf{dr}$ may be evaluated:
- Given the expectation of U increasing with height, the inertial frame of reference is arbitrarily chosen to be represented by a y-axis increasing vertically upwards.
- $\mathbf{F}_{net,int}$ is the gravitational force $\mathbf{F}_g$.
- The system is 1D such that $\mathbf{F}_g$ is described by the y-component $F_{g,y}$.
- $F_{g,y}$ is considered to be constant over small vertical movements dy near the Earth's surface.

Collinear and non-collinear vectors:
- Two vectors $\mathbf{F}$ and $\mathbf{dr}$ are collinear if they are of the same or opposite direction; otherwise they are non-collinear.
- Assuming $\mathbf{F}$ to be a constant force, $\mathbf{dr}$ to be a change in position, and some mathematical knowledge, $\int\mathbf{F}.\mathbf{dr} = |\mathbf{F}||\mathbf{r}|\cos\theta = |\mathbf{F}|d\cos\theta$, where d is the distance over which $\mathbf{F}$ acts, θ is the angle in radians (Section 2.5) between $\mathbf{F}$ and $\mathbf{dr}$, and here is the meaning and consequence of three particular values of θ:
(a) 0 ($\cos\theta = 1$): $\mathbf{F}$ and $\mathbf{dr}$ are in the same direction, and the expended energy is positive and maximum.
(b) $\pi/2$ ($\cos\theta = 0$): $\mathbf{F}$ and $\mathbf{dr}$ are mutually perpendicular, and the expended energy is zero.
(c) π ($\cos\theta = -1$): $\mathbf{F}$ and $\mathbf{dr}$ are in opposite directions, and the expended energy is negative and maximum.

†In general internal analyses, key questions include:
- Is the reference frame defined, and is it sufficiently inertial? (Beware of the rotating Earth's surface.)
- Is the system fully defined?
- Is the system isolated so that $\Delta E = 0$?
- Are all relevant internal Δ energy terms identified, including ΔQ?
- Have all interesting internal forces been identified, including those of third-law force-pairs (Section 3.4), and are they conservative?
- Does the angle between each relevant $\mathbf{F}_{net,int}$ and $\mathbf{dr}$ differ from collinearity?

►At the Earth's surface, however, that constant $F_{g,y}$ has a magnitude that Section 3.7 gives as mg, where m is the mass of some gravitationally affected body – taken here as particle-like and constant – and g is the magnitude of the nearby gravitational acceleration. It is thus necessary to assign $F_{g,y} = -\,mg$ since $\mathbf{F}_g$ resolves negatively with respect to the upwards direction.

►And, then, ΔU becomes as given in Table 3.3.

$\Delta U = -\int\mathbf{F}_{\text{net,int}}\cdot d\mathbf{r} = -\int F_{g,y}\,dy = -F_{g,y}\int dy = -(-mg)\int dy = mg\,[y]_{\text{state1}}^{\text{state2}} = mg\Delta y$ for particle-like constant mass m, and vertically-upwards increasing y.
Notes: ►Such ΔU increases with Δy, applies only near the Earth's surface, and can be presented in the absolute form $U = mgy$ where the $y = 0$ origin benefits from a sensible designation such as the start of the motion.   ►But Δy and changes in y must be small enough to ensure sufficient constancy of gravitational force.   ►Calculations are independent of path, and gravitation is generally taken as conservative.

Table 3.3: Change in potential energy due to the Earth's near-surface gravitation

Case 2 – the change in potential energy due to the action of a spring: A spring, considered to be a 1D body, has a restoring force-component F_x given by Section 3.7 as $F_x = -\,kx$, where k is the spring's stiffness – here taken as constant – x is the free-end's component of position such that $x = 0$ defines its rest position, and the spring's other end is fixed. And, accordingly, ΔU becomes as given in Table 3.4.

$\Delta U = -\int\mathbf{F}_{\text{net,int}}\cdot d\mathbf{r} = -\int F_x\,dx = -\int(-kx)\,dx = k\int x\,dx = \tfrac{1}{2}k\,[x^2]_{\text{state1}}^{\text{state2}}$ with the $x = 0$ origin defining the rest position of the moving end of the spring.
Notes: ►Such ΔU can be presented in the absolute form $U = \tfrac{1}{2}kx^2$.   ►Calculations are independent of path, and the action of springs is generally taken as conservative.

Table 3.4: Change in potential energy of a spring

Case 3 – scenarios of conserved mechanical energy: Involving both isolation (Section 3.8) and the energy conservation relation $\Delta E = \Delta K + \Delta U = 0$ (Section 3.9), here are two scenarios of conserved mechanical energy:

►For an isolated gravitational system, a particle-like body of constant mass m and speed v undergoes small movements Δy referenced against a y-axis increasing vertically upwards from the surface of the Earth. This is where Table 3.5 applies.

$\Delta E = \Delta K + \Delta U = \tfrac{1}{2}m[v^2]_{\text{state1}}^{\text{state2}} + mg[y]_{\text{state1}}^{\text{state2}} = 0.$
As a check on signs, it should be noted that when the particle is moving, say, downwards:
►$[v^2]_{\text{state1}}^{\text{state2}}$ is positive, giving positive ΔK.
►$[y]_{\text{state1}}^{\text{state2}}$ is negative, giving negative ΔU.

Table 3.5: Conserved mechanical energy in the case of gravitation

►For an isolated simple harmonic (Section 2.8) system of constant k and m (stiffness and mass), conserved mechanical energy $\Delta E = \Delta K + \Delta U = 0$ may be verified over all values of time t via the information summarised in Table 3.6†.

†Notes:
►Verification is left as an exercise.
►Ideally, such a simple harmonic system remains in a state of dynamic equilibrium (Section 3.9).

Quantity	Formula	Notes
position	$x(t) = x_{\text{m}}\cos(2\pi ft + \varphi)$	►x_{m} is the simple harmonic amplitude. ►f is the simple harmonic frequency, which follows Section 3.7 as $(2\pi)^{-1}(k/m)^{\frac{1}{2}}$. ►$\varphi$ is the simple harmonic phase angle.
kinetic energy	$K(t) = \tfrac{1}{2}mv^2(t)$	►absolute, 1D (SHM is 1D).
potential energy	$U(t) = \tfrac{1}{2}kx^2(t)$	►absolute, via analogy with Case 2 (spring-based action is also 1D).

Table 3.6: Information underlying conserved mechanical energy in the case of simple harmonic motion

3.12 Changes of total system energy; effect of external work done

If a system is no longer isolated (Section 3.8), external forces can act on it doing **work**. If $\mathbf{F}_{\text{net,ext}}$ is the net external force, then the work W done on the system – following Section 3.10 – is given by $W = \int \mathbf{F}_{\text{net,ext}} \cdot d\mathbf{r}$. Note that, when the two vectors $\mathbf{F}_{\text{net,ext}}$ and $d\mathbf{r}$ are in the same direction, W is positive; thus positive work is done, and the system's energy E increases. And when the two vectors are in opposite directions, the opposite applies and E decreases††.

Such **work** is synonymous with energy.

††But note that the source of $\mathbf{F}_{\text{net,ext}}$ must lose an equivalent amount of energy when W is positive, and gain the same when W is negative.

The work done W causes a change ΔE in the system's energy such that $W = \Delta E$. Generally, such W becomes arbitrarily distributed amongst the system's Δ energy terms. But, in the case of changed mechanical energy (Section 3.9), $W = \int\mathbf{F}_{net,ext}.\mathbf{dr} = \Delta K + \Delta U = \Delta E$, as elaborated in Table 3.7 following Section 3.11's definitions:

$$W = \int\mathbf{F}_{net,ext}.\mathbf{dr} = \Delta K + \Delta U = m\int\mathbf{v}.\mathbf{dv} - \int\mathbf{F}_{net,int}.\mathbf{dr} = \Delta E$$

Table 3.7: Work done on a mechanical system of particle-like constant mass

But $\Delta U = 0$ and $\Delta K = 0$ are even simpler cases:

Work done and kinetic energy: The condition $\Delta U = 0$ means that none of W feeds into potential energy. This requires $\mathbf{F}_{net,ext}$ to be perpendicular to any applicable internal net force $\mathbf{F}_{net,int}$, so that there is no induced aligned motion, and that W fully feeds into ΔK associated with perpendicular motion.

In such $\Delta U = 0$ cases, the work W follows $W = \int\mathbf{F}_{net,ext}.\mathbf{dr} = \Delta K = \Delta E$ known as the ***work-energy theorem***. Thus positive W leads to increased kinetic/system energy, with increased speed perpendicular to any applicable internal net force. And ***negative*** W leads to the opposite.

Work done and potential energy: The condition $\Delta K = 0$ means that none of W feeds into kinetic energy. This is possible only if, by being equal and opposite, $\mathbf{F}_{net,ext}$ balances any applicable internal net force $\mathbf{F}_{net,int}$ and thus can just move a particle-like body to a position of changed potential energy, but with negligible ΔK.

In such $\Delta K = 0$ cases, the work W follows $W = \int\mathbf{F}_{net,ext}.\mathbf{dr} = \Delta U = - \int\mathbf{F}_{net,int}.\mathbf{dr} = \Delta E$. And, as a ***gravitational*** example, such W becomes $W = \int\mathbf{F}_{net,ext}.\mathbf{dr} = \Delta U = mg\Delta y = \Delta E$, so that positive W leads to increased potential/system energy, with increased height arising from positive Δy. And ***negative*** W leads to the opposite.

Work-energy theorem:
►Note that this specifically covers scenarios where $W = \Delta K = \Delta E$ applies.
►Furthermore, for systems of particle-like constant masses, such W also equals $m\int\mathbf{v}.\mathbf{dv}$.

Notes on *negative* work:
►When negative work is done, the source of $\mathbf{F}_{net,ext}$ actually gains the lost system energy.
►Such physical description perhaps conflicts with the seemingly effortful slowing of a moving body or gradual lowering of a gravitationally affected one.

Such a *gravitational* example follows Section 3.11, where m is a particle-like constant mass, g is the magnitude of the Earth's near-surface gravitational acceleration, and y is an axis increasing vertically upwards.

3.13 Power

Power is the temporal rate at which energy is converted to another form, and is a scalar quantity with derived SI units of $J\,s^{-1}$, usually written as W (the watt). Instantaneous power P is defined as $P = dE/dt$, whilst average power $P_{average}$ is defined as $P_{average} = \Delta E/\Delta t$.

3.14 Questionnaire

3Q1   A force of 1 N equals:
a 1 kg m s^{-2}
b 1 kg m s^{-1}
c $1 \text{ kg}^{-1} \text{ m}^{-1} \text{ s}$
d $1 \text{ kg}^{-1} \text{ m}^{-1} \text{ s}^{-2}$

3Q2   Supposing that there are balanced Newtonian external forces, which of the
       following statements regarding an affected particle must be false?
a   It has zero velocity
b   It has constant non-zero velocity
c   It has zero acceleration
d   It has constant non-zero acceleration

3Q3   The practice of observing from an inertial frame is most consistent with ensuring:
a   System closure
b   Applicability of Newton's laws
c   Constancy of centre of mass
d   Mutually perpendicular coordinate axes

3Q4   Arising from a variety of contributory forces, a Newtonian net force $\mathbf{F}_{net}$ acts on a
       body of mass m, and consists of components F_x, F_y, and F_z associated with
       mutually perpendicular coordinate axes respectively x, y, and z. Which of the
       following statements about F_x is false?
a   It equals the algebraic sum of the x-components of the contributory forces
b   It equals $\mathbf{F}_{net} - F_y - F_z$
c   It is given by ma_x where a_x is the x-component of the associated acceleration
d   It equals $(|\mathbf{F}_{net}|^2 - F_y^2 - F_z^2)^{\frac{1}{2}}$

3Q5   In analysing a body's motion, which of the following statements is false?
a   An arbitrarily aligned set of Cartesian axes may be used
b   Internal forces may mutually cancel
c   Net external action may be consistent with translation
d   Net centre-of-mass action may be consistent with rotation

3Q6   Considering simple harmonic motion and its restoring force being proportional
       to extension, which of the following statements is false?
a   Relative to the position, the velocity is shifted in phase by $-\pi/2$
b   Relative to the position, the acceleration is shifted in phase by π
c   The constant of proportionality to extension has derived SI units of N m^{-1}
d   The restoring force and extension take the same sign

Page 54 answers: 13b   14b   15b   16a   17b
Page 55 answers: 18b   19a   20c

3Q7   Regarding the Newtonian analysis of a moving particle, upon which there is no net force, which of the following is a non-zero constant?
a   Position
b   Displacement
c   Velocity
d   Acceleration

3Q8   Relative to the Earth's centre of gravity, there is a stationary particle on a stationary horizontal surface. Which option, then, most accurately lists significant vertically-acting Newtonian forces applicable to the particle:
a   Gravity
b   Normal
c   Gravity, and normal
d   Friction, gravity, and normal

3Q9   For a body of mass m near the Earth's surface, assume (i) that y is an axis increasing vertically upwards, (ii) that the applicable net force $\mathbf{F}_{net}$ acts vertically downwards due to the gravitation of the Earth, and (iii) that g is the magnitude $|\mathbf{a}|$ of its acceleration $\mathbf{a}$. Which of the following statements, then, is false?
a $|\mathbf{F}_{net}|$ equals $|F_y|$
b g is approximately 9.8 m s^{-2}
c $a_y = g$
d $|\mathbf{F}_{net}|$ equals mg

3Q10   For which option is the subsequent example not consistent with the quoted quantity:
a   Constant velocity: Obeying of Newton's first law
b   Constant velocity: Motion resulting from non-zero net force
c   Constant acceleration: Free-fall under gravity near the Earth's surface
d   Constant magnitude of acceleration: Uniform circular motion

3Q11   A particle of mass 4.0 kg undergoing uniform circular motion at a radius of 2.0 m and tangential velocity 0.50 m s^{-1} must be subject to a centripetal force given by:
a   0.25 N
b   0.50 N
c   1.0 N
d   2.0 N

3Q12   Regarding a system's centre of mass, which of the following statements is false?
a   It behaves as if it contains all the system's mass
b   Its velocity equals the system's total momentum divided by the system's total mass
c   Its velocity will change if there is an explosion internal to the system
d   It accelerates as the system's net external force divided by the system's total mass

Page 52 answers: 1a   2d   3b   4b   5d   6d
Page 53 answers: 7c   8c   9c   10b   11b   12c

3Q13 Which of the following is most likely to enjoy substantial temporal parametric
       change:
a   Gravitational acceleration near the surface of the Earth
b   The modelling of multiple states of an evolving system
c   Kinetic energy in a conserved gravitational system at constant height
d   The position of an oscillating pendulum seen only at rest

3Q14 Momentum has derived SI units of:
a $kg\ m^{-1}\ s^{-1}$
b $kg\ m\ s^{-1}$
c $kg\ m^{-1}\ s^{-2}$
d $kg\ m\ s^{-2}$

3Q15 Suppose, relative to some point on the Earth's surface, a particle experiences a
       Newtonian net horizontal force **F** that acts through a small distance d. Then,
       which of the following statements must be false?
a   The work done is $|F|d$
b   The body's change in gravitational potential energy is $|F|d$
c   The body's change in kinetic energy is $|F|d$
d   The body's vertical momentum is conserved

3Q16 A simple harmonic oscillator has a spring constant of $10\ N\ m^{-1}$ and an
       amplitude of 0.40 m. What is its total energy?
a   0.80 J
b   1.6 J
c   2.0 J
d   4.0 J

3Q17 In practice, the most likely purpose of carefully aligning a set of coordinate axes
       to a system is to achieve:
a   Compatibility with closure
b   Easy resolving of vectors
c   Maximised gravitational potential
d   Correct analysis of conserved energy

3Q18 According to an inertial observer, which of following statements about an
      isolated system must be true:
      1) Its momentum does not change.
      2) Its total energy does not change.
      3) Its centre of mass does not change.
a   None
b   Only 1) and 2)
c   Only 2) and 3)
d   All

3Q19 An elastic collision is particularly concerned with conserving which of the
      following types of energy?
a   Kinetic
b   Potential
c   Mechanical
d   Work

3Q20 How much work is done by a conservative constant force of 2.0 N that acts at an
      angle of $\pi/3$ rad through a distance of 4.0 m?
a   1.0 J
b   2.0 J
c   4.0 J
d   8.0 J

Chapter 4   Energetic Propagation

The study of physical systems frequently requires an understanding of large-scale particulate and in-vacuo mechanisms of transporting energy. Relating respectively to the idealised concepts of the **bulk medium** and **free space**, new mechanisms of treatment are thus needed to cover scenarios where the number of constituent particles ranges from innumerable down to zero†.

Overall, a compendium of physics follows ranging over thermodynamics, flows, and waves – wherein it is notable that particulate media are necessary for all mechanical transport mechanisms, and that free space can also support the propagation of light.

4.1   Thermodynamics

The treatment of thermodynamics describes the energy of systems in terms of the topics of temperature and heat:

4.1.1   Temperature, heat, and thermal equilibrium

Although temperature is **classically** conceived as proportional to average atomic kinetic energy (Sections 1.4 and 3.11), it is also thermodynamically concordant with the so-called **zeroth** law, such that it may be taken as

---

Bulk medium: This is considered to be a particulate (Section 2.1) medium of infinite extent. Real physical systems are bounded; they can, however, be good approximations to bulk media sufficiently far inside their boundaries.

Free space: This is an idealised concept for the complete absence of matter – i.e. a perfect vacuum. However, it does approximate to reality, for example, within artificial vacuum chambers and in outer space. There are circumstances under which even the Earth's atmosphere can be considered a free-space environment.

†Remember that outside these regimes, Section 3.14 has already covered the treatment by which the energy of a system can change by means of work done by an external force.

The **classical** consideration of thermodynamic temperature and heat concerns the average motion of atoms relative to all others, and thus does not require a separate frame of reference (Section 2.1).

The **zeroth** law of thermodynamics was postulated by Fowler and Guggenheim (1939) as: 'If two assemblies are each in thermal equilibrium with a third assembly, they are in thermal equilibrium with each other.'

the physical property that links thermally equilibrated systems. Temperature may thus be uniquely measured via a scale that is marked and used under conditions of thermal equilibrium. Consider, for example, a thermometer's scale:

If the scale is marked with a temperature value when in thermal equilibrium with a known medium, and that the same mark is reached with a second equilibrated medium, then that mark also indicates the second medium's temperature. The process may be repeated with another known medium, providing the scale with two possible measures of temperature†.

But the scale can now be extended via interpolation and extrapolation to create a practical thermometer with a uniformly incrementing scale offering many possible measures of temperature.

The SI system (Section 1.3) adopts the absolute scale of temperature whose SI base unit is the **kelvin** (K). Some examples of kelvin temperatures are given in Table 4.1.

†Commonly used calibrating media comprise water at its repeatable physical points of freezing and boiling.

Kelvin: This SI unit must always be used in calculations. Note that if a temperature T_C is expressed in Celsius (C) units, its conversion to T_K on the kelvin scale is via the relation $T_K = T_C + 273.15$ K.
Note that such an additive relation is possible only because the C unit is equivalent to the K unit.

Value	Description	Notes
0 K (exact)	absolute zero (by definition)	lowest possible temperature, consistent with atoms having minimum kinetic energy††
273.15 K	onset of freezing of water	at atmospheric pressure
373.15 K	onset of boiling of water	at atmospheric pressure

Table 4.1: Examples of kelvin temperatures

Whilst being in thermal equilibrium is essential, thermometry also requires a practical process of attaining such thermal equilibrium. Clausius (1865), however, indicated that, if two nearby systems are at different temperatures, energy will naturally transfer from the hotter one to the colder one until such time as the two systems come to the same temperature. Such transferred energy is called heat, and has derived SI units of joules†††.

There are three main applicable transfer mechanisms, namely thermal conduction, radiated heat, and convection:

††But note that the classical limit of zero energy at 0 K is not possible due to quantum physics indicating there to exist non-zero ground-states.

†††Notes:
►If the total heat transferred to a system is positive, then the system's internal energy will increase, and vice versa.
►Once two systems have reached the same temperature, and hence are in thermal equilibrium, there is no further net transfer of heat.

4.1.2 Thermal conduction

Consider temperature T to change by $\mathrm{d}T$ between the faces of a slab of material of cross-sectional area A, and thickness $\mathrm{d}x$. As long as $\mathrm{d}T$ is non-zero, heat Q will transfer between the faces at a rate given by Fourier (1822) as $\mathrm{d}Q/\mathrm{d}t = -kA\mathrm{d}T/\mathrm{d}x$, where t is the time, and k is the thermal conductivity of the slab†.

There are two main processes of thermal conduction. One involves vibrational energy being randomly passed in a slow statistical way, from one atom to the next, deeper into the medium. The other involves the extended motion of energetic mobile electrons, and is particularly significant in metals because their values of thermal conductivity k can be orders of magnitude greater than in other materials.

4.1.3 Radiated heat

All bodies radiate heat over a range of electromagnetic wavelengths dependent on their temperature. Approximately following the physics of so-called blackbodies, such radiated heat has a peaked spectral profile where the greater the temperature of the body, the shorter the wavelength at the peak of emission††.

4.1.4 Convection

The transfer of heat via the motion of matter is called convection. The process requires mobile states of matter – specifically liquids and gasses. Suppose heat-induced expansion causes a local volume to contain less matter, and hence be less affected by gravity. Being more buoyant, the associated matter rises, progressively gives up its heat to the cooler environment, contracts, and falls. Convective cyclical motion of both matter and heat thus occurs in the associated region†††.

4.2 Flow

A flow is the movement of a medium that results from a force (Section 3.1) acting tangentially to its surface. Media that flow are called fluids.

---

†Known as Fourier's law, the quantity, $\mathrm{d}Q/\mathrm{d}t$, has derived SI units of J s^{-1} or W, while k is a material constant having derived SI units of W m^{-1} K^{-1}.

††For further discussions on electromagnetic waves and blackbody physics see respective Sections 4.3.7 and 6.8.

†††Convective heat underpins many processes such as:
► The weather.
► The circulation of water in lakes that is essential to support animal and plant life.
► Space heating via artificial forced-hot-air systems.

4.2.1   Introduction to fluids

Fluids comprise gasses and liquids, but with a key difference. Gasses are highly compressible, while liquids are not. In helping to understand the physics of such fluids, here are some introductory topics:

Buoyancy and Archimedes; apparent weight and floating: If a body enters a fluid, some of that fluid – say of mass m_f – must flow elsewhere. Near the Earth's surface, the weight (Section 3.7) of the departed fluid has a magnitude of $m_f g$, where g is the magnitude of the acceleration there due to gravity. Such $m_f g$ was previously supported by the fluid beneath it, but now that same support acts upwards on the body. The ensuing buoyancy is known as **Archimedes' principle**, with $m_f g$ being said to be the magnitude of the associated buoyant force.

Furthermore, with m being the body's mass, and mg being the magnitude of the body's weight, a so-called apparent weight of magnitude $mg - m_f g$ applies to the body. And, if $m_f g = mg$, the apparent weight is zero and the body may float††.

Flow lines, and lift: The concept of lines of flow is essential in advanced treatments, and is not just a matter of whether the flow is following smooth lines, or not. Of critical importance is when the flow is first straight and then becomes curved (or vice versa) since then the flowing matter has undergone a centripetal acceleration (Section 2.5), and thus must have been subject to a centripetal force (Section 3.7). In applying this idea to an aerofoil, for example, whenever a flow of air curves around the top surface, it must have experienced a centripetal force towards the ground, and the aerofoil must, by Newton's third law (Section 3.4), have experienced an equivalent force towards the sky. This effect is the origin of lift†††.

Archimedes' principle: Although difficulties in application may arise when other forces are present – such as surface tension – Archimedes (*c.*250BC) provides an ancient principle that retains its relevance today.

††Notes:
►Of course, zero upwards external force is needed to hold a floating body (as well as any of the pre-existing fluid that its introduction displaced).
►Whilst weight is traditionally measured in air, it should be remembered that even the relative rarity of air has some buoyancy. The errors may be small but, strictly, such measurements are of air-referenced apparent weight.

†††Why there can be curving of the air-flow around an aerofoil's surface, however, is a complex matter of surface friction (Section 3.7).

Density: Density ρ is a positive scalar quantity defined as the amount of mass m (Section 2.9) divided by the associated amount of volume V. Hence $\rho = m/V$. In **bulk media**, the concept of density is often more convenient than that of mass alone. This is particularly so in the case of uniform bulk media wherein ρ is considered constant throughout the volume V†.

Pressure: Pressure p is a positive scalar quantity defined as $p = |\mathbf{F}|/A$, where $\mathbf{F}$ is considered as the force applied normally (Section 3.7) to, or by, some area A of surface. With such p implicitly considered to be uniform over all of A, its concept may be more readily applied than that of vectorial force.

Furthermore, the pressure at a given position varies with the amount fluid above that position. Indeed, as a mountaineer ascends, the amount of air above decreases and the pressure falls but, as a diver descends, the amount of water above increases and the pressure rises. Overall, a positive change Δp of pressure requires a negative change Δy of an observer's height, with the y-axis defined to be increasing vertically upwards††.

4.2.2   Analysis of ideal fluids

Following Section 4.2.1, and unless an exception is given, the ongoing discussion of fluids assumes them to be incompressible, have no viscosity, and exhibit steady flow when in motion. Such fluids are referred to as ideal†††:

Change of pressure with height in an ideal fluid: Regardless of the complexity of the connective path within a continuous body of ideal fluid, there is no change in pressure when there is no change of height (i.e. $\Delta p = 0$ when $\Delta y = 0$). Otherwise, the positive change Δp of pressure, that Section 4.2.1 indicates to require a negative change Δy of height, may be written in cases of ideal fluids near the Earth's surface as $\Delta p = -\rho g \Delta y$, where ρ is the density of the fluid, g is the magnitude of the Earth's

---

Bulk medium – an idealised particulate (Section 2.1) medium of infinite extent.

†The assumption of constancy of density is:
►Good for uniform incompressible media, such as liquids and solids.
►Generally not applicable to compressible media such as gasses.

††Notes on pressure:
►The concept is readily applied to liquids and solids where the volume V and density ρ are both considered to be constant. But both V and ρ are likely to change significantly in gasses.
►The quantity Δp, represented as, say, $p - p_0$, is referred to as a differential pressure. Numerous types of pressure gauge measure the difference between a fluid pressure p and an internal reference pressure p_0.

†††Notes on ideality in fluids:
►Liquids and solids are usually taken to be incompressible. Gasses, however, are highly compressible.
►Viscosity relates to media that are resistive to flow, such as treacle or tar.
►Flow that is not smooth is called turbulent.
►Accordingly, compressible, viscous, and turbulent fluids are generally excluded as not ideal. But, even water, which is usually a well-behaved ideal fluid, can have turbulent flow. Clearly, great care is necessary in applying the concept of the ideal fluid because of the many exceptions.

near-surface gravitational acceleration, the y-axis is defined to be increasing vertically upwards, and the following further notes apply†:

►The density ρ must be independent of Δy to fulfil the ideal requirement of incompressibility. This is usually fine for liquids and solids. But, for gasses, ρ can change strongly with Δy due to Δp inducing a change in volume. Thus, for gasses, Δy must be small for ρ justifiably to be taken as constant.

►The quantity g, too, must be independent of Δy for ideality. This is fine for many practical purposes because its variation around the Earth's surface is fairly weak.

►The associated relation $p - p_0 = \Delta p = -\rho g \Delta y$, following Section 4.2.1, is an expression of ideal differential pressure near the Earth's surface.

►And the ensuing relation $p = p_0 - \rho g \Delta y$ is an expression of ideal absolute pressure near the Earth's surface.

Equation of continuity for an ideal fluid: Consider the scenario of water being fed into a uniform pipe at a given volume V_{in} per unit time Δt. The input rate is thus $V_{in}/\Delta t$. And, with the assumptions that no water is compressed, expanded, lost, created, or stored within the pipe, the output rate $V_{out}/\Delta t$ must be the same – i.e. $V_{out}/\Delta t = V_{in}/\Delta t$.

But suppose that the pipe is not uniform and that the output and input cross-sectional areas are A_{out} and A_{in}. Then V_{out} must be contained within a length Δx_{out} of pipe given by $V_{out} = A_{out}\Delta x_{out}$. And, with the input volume V_{in} treated in a similar way, $A_{out}\Delta x_{out}/\Delta t = A_{in}\Delta x_{in}/\Delta t$.

But $\Delta x/\Delta t$ defines the speed v of the flow, and consequently $A_{out}v_{out} = A_{in}v_{in}$, which is known as the equation of continuity for ideal fluids. According to such continuity, if there is a decrease in the cross-sectional area of a pipe, the internal flow speed for an ideal fluid must increase††.

†To confirm the relation $\Delta p = -\rho g \Delta y$:
►Consider that the pressure p over some horizontal area A within the fluid is due to the weight $\mathbf{W}$ of the overburdening fluid.
►Combine Section 3.7's $|\mathbf{F}| = |\mathbf{W}| = mg$ with Section 4.2.1's $p = |\mathbf{F}|/A$ and $\rho = m/V$ to give $p = \rho Vg/A$ where m, ρ and V are respectively the mass, density and volume of the overburdening fluid.
►Recognise V/A as the thickness $t - y$ of the overburden, where t is the fluid's total vertical thickness and y is the vertical location of the start of the overburden referenced, say, from the bottom of the fluid.
►And, due to $p = \rho g(t - y)$, finally write $\Delta p = -\rho g \Delta y$.

††Such as might have been experienced when partially closing off a garden hose.

Pascal's principle in an ideal fluid: Pascal (1653) enunciated the principle that a change in pressure applied to an enclosed ideal fluid is transmitted undiminished to every portion of the fluid and into the walls of its containment vessel. A well-known example is the **hydraulic lever** (or jack), which is essentially a fluid-filled tube:

If the fluid within the jack is ideal, it is known from Pascal's principle that a change of pressure at the input gives the same change of pressure at the output. Furthermore, if the input and output are at the same height, the absolute pressures will be the same, and thus, $p_{out} = p_{in}$. Following Section 4.2.1, this becomes $p_{out} = p_{in} = |\mathbf{F}_{out}|/A_{out} = |\mathbf{F}_{in}|/A_{in}$. And, rearranging as $|\mathbf{F}_{out}|/|\mathbf{F}_{in}| = A_{out}/A_{in}$ shows that making A_{out} bigger than A_{in} results in amplification of the force – as required for a jack†.

Bernoulli's equation in an ideal fluid: Bernoulli (1738) applied the principle of conservation of energy (Section 3.11) to an ideal fluid flowing along a line of arbitrary shape. The result is an equation, expressible in variety of forms, one of which is $p + \frac{1}{2}\rho v^2 + \rho gy = \text{constant}$, where v is the speed of flow, and y is the height. Inspection of this equation indicates that, if the line of flow stays at constant height y, then an increase in speed v means a reduction in pressure p††.

4.3 Waves

Waves are an essential constituent of many physical systems configured for the large-scale transmission of energy (Section 3.9) and information (see Section 6.11).

Ongoing discussion first concentrates on characteristics common to all waves, and later progresses to the two main – and fundamentally different – categories known as mechanical waves and light†††.

Hydraulic lever: This device has the key characteristic that it can amplify a force, so that a mere human can raise a body (such as a car) many times their mass.

†What is the penalty for such bravado? Since, for an ideal fluid, the output and input volumes must balance, $A_{out}\Delta y_{out} = A_{in}\Delta y_{in}$, giving $\Delta y_{out} = (A_{in}/A_{out})\Delta y_{in}$. And since A_{out} is needed to be bigger than A_{in}, the height Δy_{out} through which the body can be jacked is significantly less than the distance Δy_{in} through which the applied force $\mathbf{F}_{in}$ acts.

Nonetheless, due to combined increased output force but reduced output distance, it is easy to verify that the energy (Section 3.12) got out of an ideal jack equals the energy put in.

††Notably constrained by the horizontally straight (constant y) line of flow, this specific example of Bernoulli-induced reduction of pressure is an often misconceived basis for the explanation of lift which, as covered in Section 4.2.1, requires a curved line of flow.

†††In wider contexts, physicists consider other categories, such as the gravitational waves of space-time, and the probabilistic waves of quantum physics.

4.3.1   What and where is a wave?

Existing as a continuously translating local oscillation, a **wave** is a form of energetic propagation. Furthermore:

►In an unbounded medium, the energy flows in one direction as a travelling wave. But, in a bounded medium, the energy can reflect back and forth between the boundaries to create a so-called standing wave.

►Relative to the axis of the energy flow, wave oscillations that are (1) collinear are called longitudinal, (2) perpendicular define an axis of so-called polarisation and are called **transverse**, and (3) circulatory are called torsional.

►Longitudinal waves exist in 1D. Transverse waves exist in 2D. Torsional waves exist in 3D. And a real physical medium may support a combination of longitudinal, transverse, and torsional waves, and a multitude of propagation directions.

►Waves are generated via energetic oscillatory sources whose frequency and strength feed into harmonic oscillation of the local elements of a medium. And propagation ensues via continuous oscillatory transfer from one local element to the next.

►Forward local elements of the medium are treated as at their rest positions (Section 2.7) until the wave's leading edge arrives, just as they are treated as returning to rest as the lagging edge has passed.

►Thus, the propagatory **hallmark** of a wave is specifically not that of local elements, but rather the extended and directed transfer of oscillatory energy from one local element to the next.

►Additionally, continuing local persistence through typically multiple cycles (Section 2.7) propagates a **coherent** extended oscillatory wave-portion known as a wavetrain†.

Such a **wave** oscillation notably involves harmonic (Section 2.7) local elemental disturbance:

►That is subject to a continuously acting process of excitation and restoration.

►Whose manifestation is strikingly different for each category of wave – specifically, for example, it is particulate for mechanical waves (see Section 4.3.6), and electromagnetic for light waves (see Section 4.3.7's discussion on 'electromagnetic propagation and speed').

Transverse waves are thus said to be polarised.

Whilst energy is the propagatory **hallmark** of a wave, the local elements are still temporarily transmitted up to the amplitude of their oscillations. But this amplitude is generally small compared to the wave's propagation distance and, regardless, returns to zero upon passing of the oscillatory energy.

†Key notes:

►The duration (or length) of a wavetrain is known as coherence time (or length).

►The **coherence** of a wavetrain is due to its phase (Section 2.8) undergoing uniform monotonic change.

►But arbitrarily different starting phases are likely to apply to successive wavetrains from a given local oscillator, as well as those from independent local oscillators.

†Such a wave may be exemplified as the vertical undulations of the sea's surface progressively travelling towards the shore, and appreciated in two different ways:
► Either by taking a fixed location, and observing the local water level rise and fall repeatedly over time.
► Or by taking a snapshot in time, and appreciating the wave crests and troughs extending over space.

Non-*classical*, i.e. relativistic (see Section 5.1.5), renditions of Doppler's treatment apply:
► When the source and receiver speeds are large.
► In all cases where the wave is of light.

This *axis* defines the propagation direction of the wave, and along which the medium's rest positions (Section 2.7) are ideally taken as uniformly distributed, and temporally fixed – i.e. stationary.

††Note that scenarios where f_r is negative or infinite need careful interpretation:
► The negative f_r associated with a receding v_r exceeding v cannot be received.
► An infinite f_r results when an approaching v_s equals v. Then, new waves may reach a receiving point at the same time as older ones to give a high total energy known as a shock wave.
► A negative f_r also results from an approaching v_s exceeding v. Here new waves may be received before older ones indicating an apparent reversal of time.

4.3.2 Features and equation of a wave

To explore wave-behaviour further, consider a sinusoidal transverse travelling wave†:

Frequency, and the Doppler effect: The wave is generated, with an assumed stationary source, at the frequency f of the source, and has a transverse temporal variation $y(t)$, at a fixed point x in space, like the portion shown in Figure 4.1.

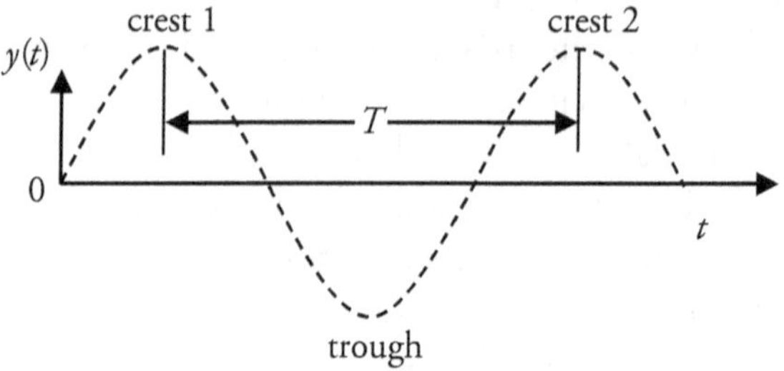

Figure 4.1: Portion of a sine wave in time, t

The time $\Delta t = T$ between adjacent similar wave features – taken here to be crests – is the temporal period of the wave. Ideally, T and $f = 1/T$ (Section 2.7) are constant. But f changes for all waves if sourced and received under relative motion. And f of intense light can double upon certain crystal interactions. On the former:

With the wave sourced at frequency f_s and propagated at speed v, Doppler (1842) gave an arbitrary point's **classically** received frequency f_r as $f_r = f_s(v \pm v_r)/(v \pm v_s)$, where:
► Each v is a speed that applies along, and relative to, a given source-receiver *axis*, such that v_s concerns the source, and v_r concerns the receiver.
► The sign of each $\pm$ symbol is chosen to make f_r greater for approaching motions, and smaller for receding ones††:
► If $v_r = 0$, then $f_r = f_s v/(v \pm v_s)$, and, for the quintessential emergency siren, $f_r = f_s v/(v - v_s)$ if approaching and $f_r = f_s v/(v + v_s)$ if receding.
► In calculating f_r for a complex system, each part with changing values or signs requires its own application of Doppler's formula with carefully instigated linkage to its predecessor.

Wavelength: The wave has a transverse spatial variation $y(x)$, at a fixed time t, like the portion shown schematically in Figure 4.2.

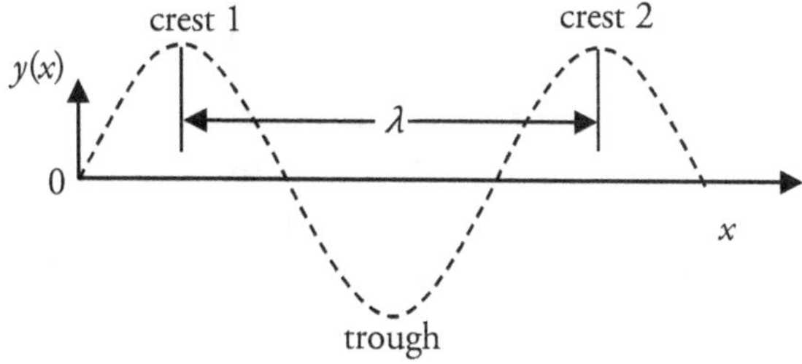

Figure 4.2: Portion of a sine wave in space, x

The distance $\Delta x = \lambda$ between wave crests is the spatial period of the wave, known as wavelength.
Speed: A spatial period of one wavelength $\Delta x = \lambda$ corresponds to one temporal period $\Delta t = T$. And, with λ and T ideally being constant, the wave's speed $v = \Delta x / \Delta t$ (Section 2.4) is ideally $v = \lambda / T$†.
Amplitude, phase, and equation: Figures 4.1 and 4.2 are different views of the same uniform wave, represented respectively as t and x dependent sinusoidal transverse functions. But the two functions are usefully combined together as $y(x,t)$, whose simplest sinusoidal form is $y(x,t) = y_m \sin(ax \pm bt + \varphi)$ and where y_m, a, and b are parameters needing to be identified††:

The quantity y_m is the maximum value of $|y(x,t)|$, and occurs when the sine term equals 1. Such y_m is accordingly the transverse distance from the x and t axes to any crest or trough, and is referred to as amplitude.

For the quantity a, it is to be noted that the waveform in Figure 4.2 repeats in x after λ, so that $y(x,0) = y(x + \lambda, 0)$. Accordingly, $ax + \varphi = a(x + \lambda) + \varphi + 2\pi$, and thus $a\lambda = 2\pi$.

But the waveform in Figure 4.1 repeats in time after T, so that $y(0,t) = y(0,t + T)$. Accordingly, $\pm bt + \varphi = \pm b(t + T) + \varphi + 2\pi$, and thus $\pm bT = 2\pi$.

By using the established three positive relations, $v = \lambda / T$, $a\lambda = 2\pi$, and $bT = 2\pi$, the

†And hence ideally $v = f\lambda$ since $f = 1/T$.

††With similarities to the terminology of simple harmonic motion (Section 2.8), here is some initial commentary on $y(x,t) = y_m \sin(ax \pm bt + \varphi)$:
➤ y_m is a positive quantity to be identified.
➤ $\sin(ax \pm bt + \varphi)$ is an oscillatory term.
➤ $ax \pm bt + \varphi$ is an amount of so-called phase.
➤ a and b are positive constants to be identified.
➤ $\pm$ is selected in sign according to the direction of propagation. If negative, increasing time means that x has to increase for the phase to remain the same, and hence indicates the propagation to be in the increasing-x direction. The positive sign, conversely, indicates the opposite.
➤ φ is the phase at $x = t = 0$, and called phase angle. In regarding a single wave, there is freedom to set $y(x,t) = 0$ at the $x = y = 0$ origin by arbitrarily choosing $\varphi = 0$. However, where two or more waves are present, the consideration of relative phase may become necessary.

equation of the transverse travelling wave can now be written as in Table 4.2.

$$y(x,t) = y_{\mathrm{m}}\sin\left[\frac{2\pi}{\lambda}(x \pm vt) + \varphi\right]$$

Table 4.2: Equation for transverse travelling waves

4.3.3 Wave strength, and propagative loss

A measure of the energy of a single wave is the sum of the its potential and kinetic energies (Section 3.11) integrated over one wavelength. And a measure of the power of a single wave is the aforementioned energy divided by the wave's temporal period. Such measures of energy and power are notably both dependent on the square of the amplitude (Section 4.3.2) of the wave.

With ensembles of waves, however, not only is there are a considerable **variation** of power across practical sources, but a fundamentally more useful description is via the concept of intensity I, defined as $I = P/A$, where P is an amount of power that passes through an amount A of area.

Nonetheless, whatever values pertain to the original directions of propagation, P and I will both be subject to continual reduction due to various effects that include divergence, reflection, refraction, absorption, scattering and diffraction:

Effect of divergence: The propagating intensity will substantially decrease in cases of strong divergence relative to the original propagation directions:

Suppose a localised power P_{s} diverges uniformly, and without loss, in all directions. Then P_{s} will spread uniformly over a spherical area of $4\pi r^2$ at distance r, which is associated with an intensity I of $I = P_{\mathrm{s}}(4\pi)^{-1}r^{-2}$, and a detected power P_{d} of $P_{\mathrm{d}} = A_{\mathrm{d}}I = A_{\mathrm{d}}P_{\mathrm{s}}(4\pi)^{-1}r^{-2}$ for a detector of active area A_{d}†.

Effects of reflection and refraction: Between two dissimilar media is an interface where wave energy can be lost from the original propagation

In appreciation of such **variation** consider just a few watts of visible light from an incandescent bulb and the awesome destruction associated with tsunamis and seismic activity.

†Notes:
► The derived relations for I and P_{d} thus both have an r^{-2} dependence.
► Any quantity with likewise dependence is said to follow an inverse-square law.
► Inverse-square laws are frequently encountered in physics.
► For further discussion in the specific contexts of light and astronomy, see Section 7.2.1.

directions via the effects of reflection and refraction, with the former returning energy into the first medium, and the latter transmitting energy at a different angle into the second medium†.

Effects of absorption and scattering: Energy may be lost from the original propagation directions via irreversible interaction with its host medium. For example, it may be progressively absorbed and converted into heat (Section 4.1), or it may suffer progressive random scattering potentially into any direction†.

Effect of diffraction: Diffraction is a fundamental propagative effect that involves the unavoidable spreading of wave energy away from the original propagation directions, and into numerous different forward directions††:

4.3.4 Wavefronts, Huygens, and diffraction

In the specific case of uniform media, an ensemble of waves may be considered to propagate as a uniformly translating locus where:

►The phase (Section 4.3.2) of all constituent waves is constant.

►The extended locus of constant of phase is said to define a wavefront and to exhibit spatial coherence (Section 4.3.1).

►At each point on a wavefront, the outward perpendicular direction is that of the local propagation.

►The uniformity of the medium means that there is a uniformity of separation between adjacent wavefronts.

►Taking that separation, for example, to be one wavelength makes all wavefronts representable as a common wave feature – often chosen to be crests. And, then, in the specific cases of plane and circular wavefronts, uniform propagation may be illustrated as in Figures 4.3 and 4.4 – the former like the distinctive linear illumination from some types of laser, and the latter like ripples diverging from a local impact on water.

†See Section 4.3.7 for detailed discussions in the specific context of light.

††Furthermore, the onward discussion of Section 4.3.5 notably indicates that diffracted waves may also mutually superpose to cause a structured redistribution of energy – that could equally be a loss or a gain relative to the original propagation directions – according to the effect known as interference.

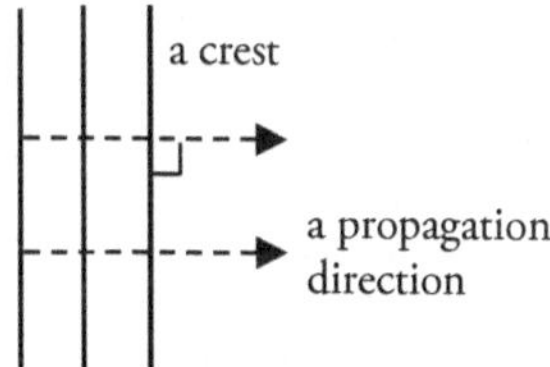

Figure 4.3: Uniformly propagating crests of a plane wavefront

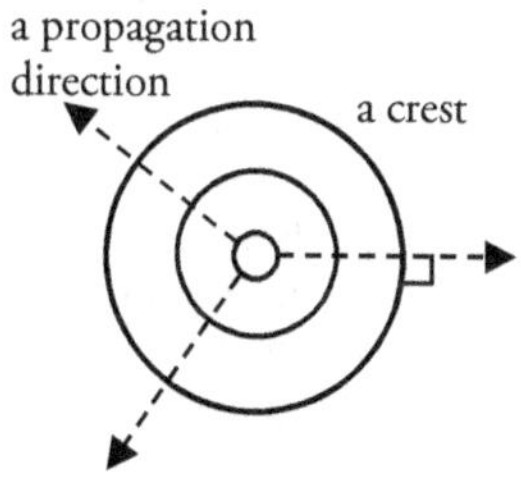

Figure 4.4: Uniformly propagating crests of a circular wavefront

†This principle may be enunciated as follows:
►Consider each point on a wavefront, or Huygens' envelope, as the source of a spherical wavelet that, dependent on the medium's local properties, diverges at its own propagation speed v to its own radius r.
►Choose some small amount Δt of time: Calculate r_1 for wavelet 1 as $r_1 = v_1\Delta t$. Repeat for wavelet 2, and others, as needed. And plot all forward-directed wavelets.
►Take the new locus of constant phase to be the wavelets' forward-directed surface tangent, or envelope:
And, notably, Anderson (2021) justified the *ad hoc* ignoring of (1) reverse propagation, and (2) wavelet-portions outside the original wavefront – as per, for instance, the labelling of Figure 4.5.

††Note that, being dependent on the chosen Δt, the envelope's phase may differ from that of the original wavefront.

†††Simple discussions follow, but note here that:
►An interferometric net wave can significantly differ from its superposing waves.
►Interference can result in a strongly contrasting disturbance of bright and dark regions in space referred to as fringes.
►Diffractive superposition is strongest from media with a wavelength-sized structure, and where such micro-structure has spatially uniform, extreme repetition.

Huygens' principle: For widened applications, that contrast with the ideality of Figures 4.3 and 4.4, Huygens (1690) extended the concept of the wavefront by promulgating its constancy of phase to evolve geometrically as an envelope of locally diverging wavelets†.

As illustrated in Figures 4.5 and 4.6, the wavefront's forward evolution after a small time Δt depends on each wavelet's local speed v, and its consequent radius $r = v\Delta t$ of divergence††:

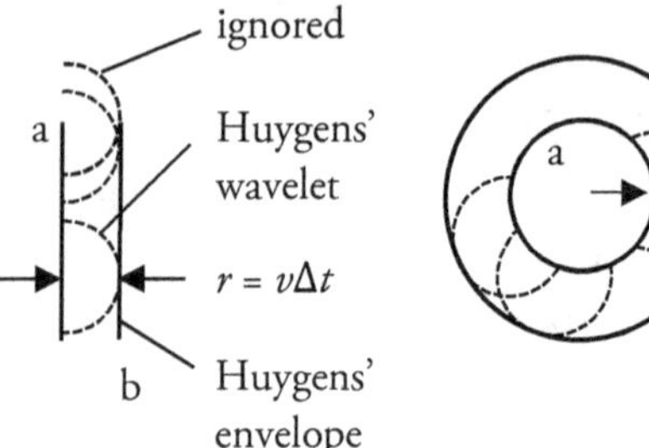

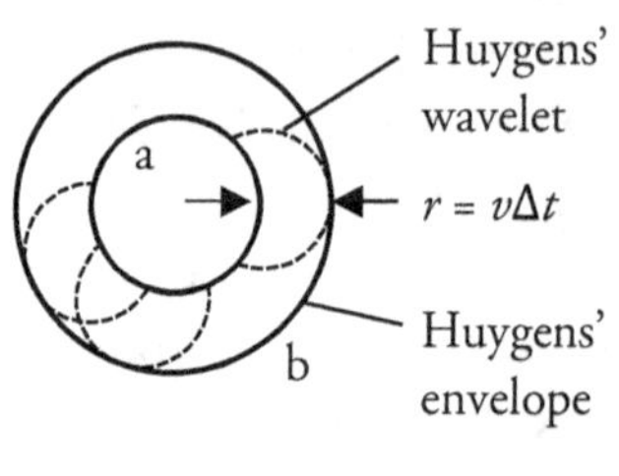

Figure 4.5: Plane wavefront (a), and Huygens' envelope of constant phase (b)

Figure 4.6: Circular wavefront (a), and Huygens' envelope of constant phase (b)

With propagation treated geometrically as the local divergence of wavelets, Huygens' principle provides a powerful means of tracing the evolution of a wave that:
►Is highly applicable in many geometric cases, such as in reflection and refraction.
►Is conveniently implemented by computer.
►In the case of non-planar propagation, has innate, but relatively coarse, geometric characterisation of spreading.

Beyond Huygens: But understanding of the fine detail of the diffractive spreading of waves (Section 4.3.3) would also require an analysis of phase based interactions between the wavelets. And an associated treatment would need to address both the mechanism of combination and the associated local functional detail of the ensuing net wave, referred to respectively as superposition and interference†††:

4.3.5   Superposition and interference

In **treating** waves beyond Huygens' principle (Section 4.3.4), first consider the two extreme inter-relationships of phase shown in Figure 4.7:

The specific **treating** of light sees further discussion in Section 4.3.7.

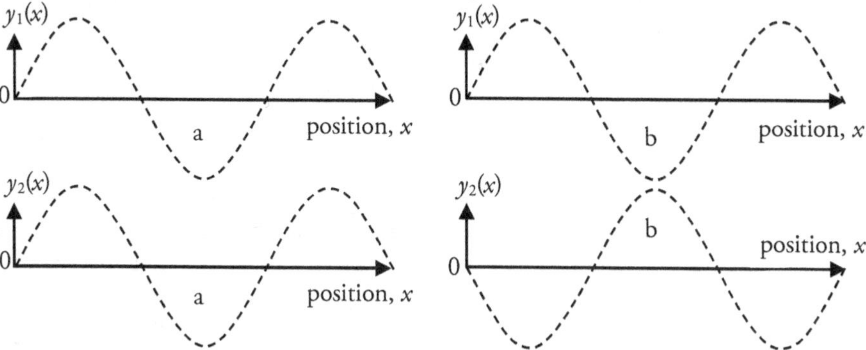

Figure 4.7: In-phase (a) and out-of-phase (b) relationships

Thus in-phase waves feature mutual alignment of common associated features (such as crests), while out-of-phase waves feature alignment of the crests of one with the troughs of the other. Arbitrary pairs of waves, however, may have some intermediate inter-relationship of phase.

But, when two such arbitrary waves propagate along the same axis, Bernoulli (1755) postulated them to combine (or superpose) as their algebraic sum. Thus two individual waves, $y_1(x,t)$ and $y_2(x,t)$, superpose as the net wave $y_{net}(x,t) = y_1(x,t) + y_2(x,t)$†.

Furthermore, an introductory summary of three key cases is given in Table 4.3 where:
► The inter-relationship of phase between $y_1(x,t)$ and $y_2(x,t)$ varies from in phase to out of phase, and also according to counter-propagation, and a difference of frequency.
► Standard trigonometric identities are invoked to elucidate the local functional detail – i.e. the so-called interference – exhibited by the net wave $y_{net}(x,t)$.
► Substantial difference between $y_{net}(x,t)$ and the superposing waves is verified as largely due to the latter's specific inter-relationship of phase.

†Note that general analyses would need to address:
► Interference as an extended effect that must be analysed system-wide to determine the instantaneous distribution of total energy – e.g. does some energy appear along a specific arm of an interferometer, become reflected, or become intercepted on a screen, *etc*?
► The duration of each wavetrain (Section 4.3.1) due to its limiting of the time over which mutually correlated phase – and hence interference – can exist.
► Arbitrary numbers of waves – note that if increased, for example, there is likely to be less coherence and weaker interference.
► Dynamic effects – e.g. is energy building up within a multiply reflecting laser cavity, or is feedback within a system changing the energy emitted by its source?
► The number of wave cycles (or equivalent response time) over which any detector integrates.

Case	Superposing waves	Relative form of $y_2(x,t)$	Theme of ongoing discussion of interference
1	$y_1(x,t) = y_\mathrm{m}\sin\left[\frac{2\pi}{\lambda}(x - vt)\right]$ $y_2(x,t) = y_\mathrm{m}\sin\left[\frac{2\pi}{\lambda}(x - vt) + \varphi\right]$	$+\varphi$ of phase	constructive, destructive, and intermediate
2	$y_1(x,t) = y_\mathrm{m}\sin\left[\frac{2\pi}{\lambda}(x - vt)\right]$ $y_2(x,t) = y_\mathrm{m}\sin\left[\frac{2\pi}{\lambda}(x + vt)\right]$	counter-propagation due to the $+ vt$ term (e.g. due to reflection)	standing waves, nodes and antinodes
3	$y_1(x,t) = y_\mathrm{m}\sin\left(\frac{2\pi x}{\lambda_1} - 2\pi f_1 t\right)$ $y_2(x,t) = y_\mathrm{m}\sin\left(\frac{2\pi x}{\lambda_2} - 2\pi f_2 t\right)$	different frequency ►Note 1: v is replaced by $f\lambda$ ►Note 2: subscripts are introduced to λ since different wavelengths will generally be associated with different frequencies.	beating

Table 4.3: The three cases of superposition under consideration

Case 1 (Table 4.3, $+ \varphi$ of phase): Subjecting $y_1(x,t) + y_2(x,t)$ to trigonometric analysis leads to the $y_\mathrm{net}(x,t)$ interference as given in Table 4.4.

$y_1(x,t)$	$y_\mathrm{m}\sin\left[\frac{2\pi}{\lambda}(x - vt)\right]$
$y_2(x,t)$	$y_\mathrm{m}\sin\left[\frac{2\pi}{\lambda}(x - vt) + \varphi\right]$
$y_\mathrm{net}(x,t)$	$2y_\mathrm{m}\cos(\varphi/2)\sin\left[\frac{2\pi}{\lambda}(x - vt) + \varphi/2\right]$
amplitude of $y_\mathrm{net}(x,t)$	$2y_\mathrm{m}\lvert\cos(\varphi/2)\rvert$

Table 4.4: Interference due to $+ \varphi$ of phase

►Consider $\varphi = 0$: Here, $y_2(x,t)$ is in phase with $y_1(x,t)$, and the net wave has twice the amplitude of each superposing wave. Called constructive interference, and arbitrarily taking $t = 0$, the result is shown in Figure 4.8.

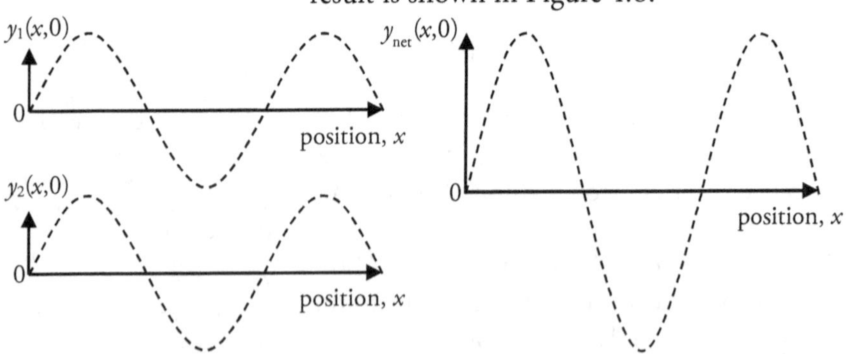

Figure 4.8: The phenomenon of locally constructive interference

►Consider $\varphi = \pi$: Here, $y_2(x,t)$ is out of phase with $y_1(x,t)$, and the net wave is zero everywhere. Called destructive interference, and arbitrarily taking $t = 0$, the result is shown in Figure 4.9†.

†Note that increasing x by $\lambda/2$ increases $2\pi x/\lambda$ by π. Thus $\varphi = \pi$ is equivalent to the waveform shifting by $\lambda/2$ along the x-axis.

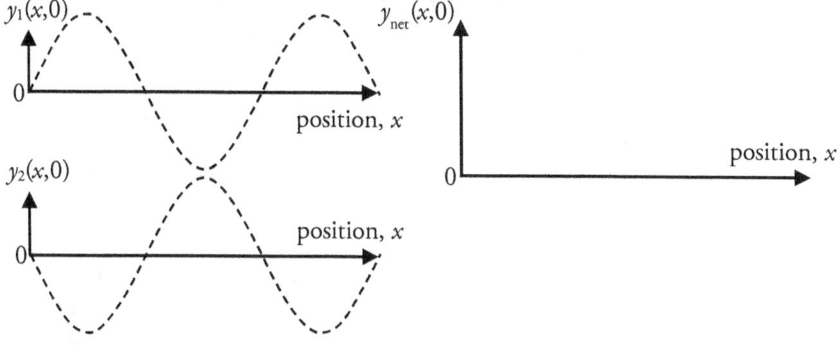

Figure 4.9: The phenomenon of locally destructive interference

►Consider $0 < \varphi < \pi$: Such a condition covers intermediate interferometric states between constructive and destructive.

Overall, in Case 1, there are two severe conceptual concerns. The local constructive interference has apparently caused a doubling of total energy, and the local destructive interference has apparently caused a complete loss of energy††.

††Remember that, according to Section 4.3.3, the energy of a wave is proportional to the square of its amplitude.

But energy conservation (Section 3.9) cannot be violated; the explanation being that the given local description is incomplete at the system level. In general, bringing coherent waves together will always result in nearby regions with a variety of constructive and destructive interferences†††.

†††Remember from Section 4.3.1's discussion of the wavetrain, that waves, which are coherent with one another, have a persistence of mutually correlated phase.

To be fully understood, superposition must be considered subject to the instantaneous system-wide conservation of energy. It will then be found that an increase in constructive interference in one locality is always balanced by an increase in destructive interference in another.

Case 2   (Table 4.3,   counter-propagation): Subjecting $y_1(x,t) + y_2(x,t)$ to trigonometric analysis leads to the $y_{net}(x,t)$ interference as given in Table 4.5.

$y_1(x,t)$	$y_m \sin\left[\frac{2\pi}{\lambda}(x - vt)\right]$
$y_2(x,t)$	$y_m \sin\left[\frac{2\pi}{\lambda}(x + vt)\right]$
$y_{net}(x,t)$	$2y_m \sin\left(\frac{2\pi x}{\lambda}\right)\cos\left(\frac{2\pi vt}{\lambda}\right)$
amplitude of $y_{net}(x,t)$	$2y_m \left|\sin\left(\frac{2\pi x}{\lambda}\right)\right|$

Table 4.5: Interference due to counter-propagation

Due to explicit separation of the x and t variables, $y_{net}(x,t)$ has no resemblance to either $y_1(x,t)$ or $y_1(x,t)$, and is not a travelling wave. Instead, it features an x-dependent sinusoidal amplitude, and is called a standing wave. The sinusoidal dependence, $\sin(2\pi x/\lambda)$, is analysed in Table 4.6:

$\sin\left(\frac{2\pi x}{\lambda}\right) =$	Associated values of x	Meaning
0	$x_n = n(\lambda/2)$ where $n = 0,1,2,...$	x-coordinates of zero amplitude known as nodes
1	$x_p = (p + \frac{1}{2})(\lambda/2)$ where $p = 0,1,2,...$	x-coordinates of maximum amplitude known as antinodes

Table 4.6: Nodes and antinodes due to counter-propagating waves

Case 3   (Table 4.3,   different   frequency): Subjecting $y_1(x,t) + y_2(x,t)$ to trigonometric analysis leads to the $y_{net}(x,t)$ interference as given in Table 4.7.

$y_1(x,t)$	$y_m \sin\left(\frac{2\pi x}{\lambda_1} - 2\pi f_1 t\right)$			
$y_2(x,t)$	$y_m \sin\left(\frac{2\pi x}{\lambda_2} - 2\pi f_2 t\right)$			
$y_{net}(x,t)$	$2y_m$	$\times$	$\cos\left[2\pi\left(\frac{1}{2\lambda_1} - \frac{1}{2\lambda_2}\right)x - 2\pi\left(\frac{f_1 - f_2}{2}\right)t\right]$ Note: factor representing a low-frequency transverse travelling wave	$\times$	$\sin\left[2\pi\left(\frac{1}{2\lambda_1} + \frac{1}{2\lambda_2}\right)x - 2\pi\left(\frac{f_1 + f_2}{2}\right)t\right]$ Note: factor representing a high-frequency transverse travelling wave

Table 4.7: Interference due to different frequencies

The net wave is thus the product of two transverse travelling waves where:
► One has a high frequency at $(f_1 + f_2)/2$.
► The other provides an envelope of low frequency at $|f_1 - f_2|/2$, and where zeroes of amplitude appear at twice this rate, giving a so-called beat frequency of $|f_1 - f_2|$†.

4.3.6 Mechanical waves

A mechanical wave relies on the presence of a particulate medium that can provide a force (Section 3.1) to restore particles moved away from their rest positions (Section 2.7). For each such particle, the restoring force supports oscillatory transfer to its neighbour, and the ensuing wave may exist in various states of matter. Examples range from vibrations in taut media, to sound, and ripples on water. Features pertinent to mechanical forms of wave will be examined next. But, first, it will be useful to recount applicability of the generic material of Sections 4.3.1-4.3.5:

Summary of discussed material: Often treated with sinusoidal forms of analysis, and with relative source/receiver motion-dependent frequency, an individual mechanical wave may be transverse or longitudinal, and it may be travelling or standing. As a transverse wave it is polarised. And a random ensemble of such transverse waves may be filtered down to a few polarisation states via passage through a suitable medium. Whilst the power of an individual wave depends on the square of its amplitude, the intensity of an ensemble of waves diverging from a localised source into a lossless uniform medium reduces according to an inverse-square law with distance. Furthermore, mechanical waves can also be subject to reflection, refraction, absorption, scattering, diffraction and superposition††.

Ongoing discussions provide some deeper treatment:

†An explanation of the beating: If the two waves start off in phase, the local constructive interference produces a new wave of twice the amplitude. However, over time, the waves gradually become out of phase due to the difference of frequency. When fully out of phase, local destructive interference causes cancellation. Later, the waves again become in phase and the beat cycle repeats.

The resultant beating is strongest when the superposing waves have identical amplitudes, and subjectively most pronounced when f_1 and f_2 are close together, making $|f_1 - f_2|$ much smaller than f_1 and f_2 individually.

††Contingent with this summary, it is to be remembered that, over an extended scale, a mechanical wave can only transmit oscillatory energy. The particles of the wave, other than to the extent of their temporary oscillatory amplitude, are not transmitted.

†The wave equation notably:
► Applies whether travelling or standing, as well as to sound.
► Is sometimes called linear due its $x \pm vt$ dependence, despite the underlying wave treatments being sinusoidal.

Wave equation, and propagation speed: Although propagation speed v is readily measured, it is also theoretically linked to sinusoidal $x \pm vt$ variations in space x and time t via the so-called wave equation. Derivation is given in Table 4.8 in the case of Section 4.3.2's equation for transverse travelling waves†:

Quantity	Equation
Transverse travelling wave	$y(x,t) = y_{\mathrm{m}}\sin\left[\frac{2\pi}{\lambda}(x \pm vt) + \varphi\right]$
Second-order partial derivative with respect to x	$\dfrac{\partial^2 y(x,t)}{\partial x^2} = -\left(\dfrac{2\pi}{\lambda}\right)^2 y(x,t)$
Second-order partial derivative with respect to t	$\dfrac{\partial^2 y(x,t)}{\partial t^2} = -\left(\dfrac{2\pi}{\lambda}\right)^2 v^2 y(x,t)$
The wave equation arising from the previous two rows	$\dfrac{\partial^2 y(x,t)}{\partial x^2} = \dfrac{1}{v^2}\dfrac{\partial^2 y(x,t)}{\partial t^2}$

Table 4.8: Appreciation of the wave equation

Furthermore, should a medium's characteristics be known, and be shown to comply with the wave equation, the propagation speed v theoretically follows††:

††Such characteristics include, for example, internal tension and elemental mass.

Taut media, and resonation: At the two ends of each element of, say, a taut string or surface, there is considered to be outwards-acting tangential tension. For 2D simplicity, consider a taut string:
► Then, at rest, the outwards-acting tangential tensions of each element not only must be in the same axis as the whole, but also must be in balance†††.
► But, with transverse movement from rest, there is increasingly off-axis tangential tension, whose newly arising ***transverse*** components differ significantly with shape between the two ends of each element, and (2) whose ***axial*** components, conversely, have small proportionate variation to those at rest, and are typically considered as unchanged.
► Now, representing the rest axis as x, the transverse axis as y, the magnitude of the axial tension as constant T, and considering a general element as having some arbitrary small change of

†††A taut string without transverse motion must remain at rest.

If such ***transverse*** components are imbalanced across a local element, they act to restore that element, and thus cause the propagation of a transverse wave.

Regardless of the string's shape, such ***axial*** components are thus considered always to be of constant magnitude T, and hence also always to be in balance.

shape with small values of y, Table 4.9 shows significant steps in calculating the wave's propagation speed v†.

†Tip: Draw and annotate a portion of changed shape to imbue deeper understanding.

Elemental quantification	Result	
With the portion of changed shape considered to extend from x_1 to larger x_2, given small $y(x,t)$: approximate length: approximate mass:	$x_2 - x_1 = \Delta x$ $\rho\,\Delta x$, where ρ is the mass per unit length	
At the ends of said portion: outwards tangential tensions: respective angles against the x-axis: increasing-x resolution of $\mathbf{T}_2$: increasing-x resolution of $\mathbf{T}_1$:	$\mathbf{T}_2$ and $\mathbf{T}_1$ θ_2 and θ_1 $T_2\cos\theta_2 = T$ $-T_1\cos\theta_1 = -T$	
With increasing-y resolutions of $\mathbf{T}_2$ and $\mathbf{T}_1$, application of the constant-mass Newtonian second law (Section 3.3):	$T_2\cos(\pi/2 - \theta_2) - T_1\cos(\pi/2 - \theta_1) = \rho\,\Delta x\dfrac{\partial^2 y(x,t)}{\partial t^2}$ or $T_2\sin\theta_2 - T_1\sin\theta_1 = \rho\,\Delta x\dfrac{\partial^2 y(x,t)}{\partial t^2}$	
Using the previous two rows to eliminate T_2 and T_1, noting that $\tan\theta = \partial y/\partial x$:	$\dfrac{1}{\Delta x}\left(\dfrac{\partial y(x,t)}{\partial x}\Big\|_{x_2} - \dfrac{\partial y(x,t)}{\partial x}\Big\|_{x_1}\right) = \dfrac{\rho}{T}\dfrac{\partial^2 y(x,t)}{\partial t^2}$	
Taking the limit as Δx tends to zero:	$\dfrac{\partial^2 y(x,t)}{\partial x^2} = \dfrac{\rho}{T}\dfrac{\partial^2 y(x,t)}{\partial t^2}$	
Recalling the wave equation, noting specifically that v represents the speed of propagation:	$\dfrac{\partial^2 y(x,t)}{\partial x^2} = \dfrac{1}{v^2}\dfrac{\partial^2 y(x,t)}{\partial t^2}$	
Comparing the previous two rows:	$\dfrac{\rho}{T} = \dfrac{1}{v^2}$ or $v = (T/\rho)^{\frac{1}{2}}$	Note: T cannot be zero – a slack string does not support a wave.

Table 4.9: Speed of a transverse wave of a taut string

But following Section 4.3.1:

►A taut string may also support torsional waves wherein oscillation of the local elements involves to-and-fro circulation around the axis of propagation††.

►The tautness requires the string to be rigidly clamped at both ends. Such clamping implies the possibility of reflective counter-propagation and, according to **Case 2** of Section 4.3.5, defines the nodes of a standing wave. Moreover, such standing waves resonate at particular frequencies

††Note that the propagation speed of such torsional waves would be expected to differ from the transverse ones due to there being different processes of excitation and restoration.

Case 2's forward and reverse directions of propagation would be expected to be at the same speed due to applicability of the same processes of excitation and restoration.

†For the loudspeaker, a rapid fore and aft movement of the cone initiates a pressure pulse within the air, with regions of compression caused by entering air molecules, and regions of rarefaction caused by exiting ones. A uniform succession of such pressure pulses initiates a sinusoidal longitudinal pressure wave within the air, with oscillatory longitudinal energy constantly being transferred between air molecules along the direction of propagation.

Frequencies: Name ►Notes
< 20 Hz: Infrasound ►Can be felt rather than heard.
20 Hz to 20 kHz: Audible sound ►The greater the frequency, the higher the so-called pitch. ►E.g. 256 Hz defines the pitch of so-called middle C. ►And adjacent Cs differ by a factor of two in frequency, known as an octave.
> 20 kHz: Ultrasound ►Cannot be heard. ►Is often used in sonar and imaging.

Table 4.10: Frequencies of mechanical waves

††Such an open end – for instance that of an organ pipe – acts as an antinode, whilst the other (closed) end acts as a node. The scenario contrasts with a doubly clamped string, which has a node at both ends.

described as follows: For a mutually aligned x-axis, and with λ as the propagating wavelength, taking $n = 0$ in Case 2's relation $x = n\lambda/2$ defines the location $x = 0$ of the first clamp and first node. And, while subsequent nodes follow with $n = 1,2,3,\ldots$, the relation $x = n\lambda/2$ must also be true at the location, say $x = L$, of the second clamp. Replacing x by L, and λ by v/f (Section 4.3.2) then indicates the supported resonant frequencies f_n to be given by $f_n = nv/(2L)$, where $n = 0,1,2,\ldots$, v is the speed of propagation, and L is the axial distance between the clamps.

Sound, pipes, and resonation: Existing in all states of matter – gasses, liquids and solids – waves of sound feature periodic compressions and rarefactions along the axis of propagation, and are thus quintessentially longitudinal (Section 4.3.1). Such waves may be initiated by various sources – that range from seismic activity to mechanical impact, the larynx and the loudspeaker – while onward propagation is sustained via the restoring force generated within the local compressions†.

As indicated in Table 4.10, sound is categorised over a wide range of frequencies, far beyond what is audible.

Sound also follows the wave equation, allowing calculation of propagation speed v. Such v tends to be greater in media of high density and low compressibility – notably liquids and solids – for example, about 1.5×10^3 m s^{-1} in water, but only about 0.33×10^3 m s^{-1} in air.

Furthermore, the body of air within an air-filled pipe can sustain a resonant longitudinal standing wave of sound. The standing waves arise from reflection between the ends of the pipe. But, if one end of the pipe is left open, sound energy may escape as an external travelling wave††.

Water waves: Taking above the surface to be a significantly different medium – such as air – a body of water is a complex 3D system:

Near the surface, movement is mostly transverse, and is governed by an interplay of forces: Gravitation, and to a lesser extent surface tension, provide the restorative mechanisms. And friction with superficial wind provides a means of energising the wave towards greater amplitude.

Deeper, there is progressively less transverse energy. And at sufficient depth from the surface – where there is no mechanism for transverse oscillation – only longitudinal waves can exist. But these deeper longitudinal waves may approach and interact with the surface. Indeed, since reflection is generally stronger when adjacent media have increasingly dissimilar density, the water/air interface internally reflects most incident longitudinal energy, with the remaining energy being transmitted via refraction into the air†.

However, efficient capturing of the interfacial energy is exploited in various applications. In particular, detection of reflected ultrasound is used in both sonar depth-finding and medical imaging††:

For **static** applications of sonar, if a ship emits a pulse of ultrasound vertically downwards and the reflection from a submarine returns a time t later, then the depth of the submarine is $vt/2$, where v is the speed of propagation.

In terms of medical imaging, pulses of ultrasound may be used to probe within the human body, where their reflection from parts of interest provides for **diagnostic** imagery. The technique is harmless and non-invasive, and is applied to the beating heart, the flow of blood, the foetus, organs, muscle, and soft-tissue interfaces with bone. Implementation involves placing a **piezoelectric** transducer in contact with

†The physics of this reflection and refraction is akin to that of light (see Figures 4.10 and 4.11 of Section 4.3.7).

††It is to be noted here that:
►The medical applications of ultrasound extend beyond imaging, where much higher intensities may be used for therapy and surgery – for example in the puncturing of cysts, breaking up of gallstones, and excision of brain tumours.
►For further general introduction to the associated medicine see, for example, Keevil *et al.* (2024).

Note that, for non-**static** applications, analysis involves the increased geometric complexity of relative lateral movement between the source and reflective surface.

Ultrasound for medical **diagnostic** purposes has:
►an intensity that is at the harmless level of about $10 \ \mathrm{W \ m^{-2}}$.
►a frequency that is typically in the range (1-20)MHz.

Piezoelectric transducers change shape in response to a change in applied voltage. Fast voltage changes, typically of (1-20)MHz are used to emit ultrasound of the same frequency. The reverse is also true – incident ultrasound can generate a change in shape and voltage at the same frequency.

†Forms of echo presentation:
►A 1D graphical display of echo strength on one axis versus round-trip propagation time on a perpendicular axis: The echo strength depends on the reflectivity of a body-part, but also generally weakens with propagation depth.
►An enhanced version of the above where the echo strength is encoded as the brightness of spots, with the other axis showing depth, assuming an in-body propagation speed of about 1.5×10^3 m s^{-1}.
►Rendering of detailed 2D and 3D imagery via a combination of multiple sensing elements, movement of the transduction head, and increasingly sophisticated computer based signal processing.

(Aside: The *human eye* also enjoys analogous diagnostics via so-called optical coherence tomography, which involves not only sliced imagery, but also the shifting of the echo principles into the infrared region of the electromagnetic spectrum (see Section 4.3.7). The frequency f is thus increased by many orders of magnitude, and micron-level resolutions can be achieved. Mainstream implementation is limited to a depth range of about 2 mm, sufficient for retinal examinations.)

††Derivation is left as a tricky exercise, where both applications of Doppler's equation (Section 4.3.2) need careful consideration of the applicable parameters and signs, and v is assumed to be much larger than v_{bp}.

the patient's skin — usually aided by gel to minimise reflective loss of acoustic energy — and emitting from that transducer a short-duration pulse of ultrasound. Body-parts in the line of propagation then reflect some of the ultrasound, and the same transducer can detect the returning echoes. For ease of interpretation, the echoes are presented, often in real-time, in various forms†.

Dependent primarily on the need for a high frequency f of ultrasound, spatial resolution is typically 0.5 mm axial to the beam (with associated dependence on the pulse duration), and 1.5 mm to 1 mm transverse (with associated dependence on the beam width). But note that the body's strong absorption of high-frequency ultrasound limits f typically to the range (1-10)MHz, with a notable exception being the **human eye**, whose low absorption allows 20 MHz frequencies to be used.

Doppler ultrasound: Ultrasound may be combined with beating (Case 3, Section 4.3.5) caused by a Doppler-shift of frequency (Section 4.3.2), giving a highly effective means of detecting moving body-parts. The technique is based on the frequency of detected echoes being changed by the approaching or receding motion of the body-part of interest. Full understanding notably requires the appreciation of two Doppler shifts: When a source frequency f_s is incident on the approaching/receding body-part, the associated frequency f_{bp} at that body-part follows from a first Doppler shift. But, now, f_{bp} is subject to its own Doppler shift by being reflected — as a secondary source — off the moving body part, and thence the echo may become received at frequency f_r. Finally, f_r and f_s beat together at a frequency given by $|f_s - f_r| = 2f_s v_{bp}/v$, where v_{bp} is the speed of the body-part's approach/recession, and v is the speed of the ultrasound in the intervening medium††.

The beat frequency $|f_s - f_r|$ is usually in the audible range, and can either be visualised on a monitor screen, or heard through headphones. Experienced clinicians are able to notice unusual beat frequencies of *inter alia* the motion of the foetus, the flow of blood, and the operation of heart valves.

4.3.7   Electromagnetic waves

Observed to propagate not just in particulate media, but also in environments that closely approximate **free space**, discussions will start on the familiar topic of light, although its connection to waves and its fundamental electromagnetic origin will soon be revealed. But, first, it will be useful to recount applicability of the generic material of Sections 4.3.1-4.3.5:

Summary of discussed material: Often treated with sinusoidal forms of analysis, and with relative source/receiver motion-dependent frequency, light waves may be travelling or standing. But all are transverse. Thus, being polarised, each has one of a potentially large number of possible polarisation states; and a random ensemble may be filtered down to a few such states via passage through a suitable polarising medium. Whilst the power of an individual wave depends on the square of its amplitude, the intensity of an ensemble of waves diverging from a localised source into a lossless uniform medium reduces according to an inverse-square law with distance. Furthermore, light waves can also be subject to reflection, refraction, absorption, scattering, diffraction, and superposition†.

Ongoing discussions provide some deeper treatment:

Reflection and refraction: The simplest treatment of introductory optics – such as of reflection and refraction – is purely geometric. Known as **geometric optics**, an application may involve tracing a large number of

Free space is discussed in the introduction to Chapter 4.

†Contingent with this summary, it is to be remembered that light waves serve only to transmit energy. Also, being supported in environments akin to free space, particles clearly have no fundamental relevance to their onward propagation.

In the absence of significant phase based effects, **geometric optics** may be successfully applied to systems of optical elements – such as lenses and mirrors – and generally involves:
- Defining the source.
- Specifying the disposition, shape, and composition of each optical element.
- Comparing the system's performance against intended function by tracing, preferably via a computer, a large manifold of rays tightly distributed in both height and angle from the source through to the system's output.

inter-connected straight-line segments, known as rays, to characterise the variable cross-section and direction of a beam of light passing through a system of optical elements:

An arbitrary central axis is chosen for the system. Then, relative to this axis and, for each ray, the evolution of height and angle, system-wide, is assessed using a mixture of geometry, and the local processes of reflection and refraction at each interface between adjacent media as defined by the laws given in Figures 4.10 and 4.11†.

†Notes:
►The angles according to geometric optics and the locally applied laws are not necessarily the same. There is an equality of angles only if the associated interfaces are perpendicular to the chosen central axis of the system.
►The chosen central axis is sometimes referred to as the system's optical axis.
►An arbitrary interface will generally impart some mixture of reflection and refraction.
►Ongoing discussion is presented in 2D, but extension to 3D is straightforward.

A *normal* is a perpendicular line that may be drawn at any point on an interface, and against which local angles may be defined. Such normals may – or may not – align with the system's chosen central axis.

The *plane of incidence* is defined by the input ray and its associated normal. For Figures 4.10 and 4.11, such a plane is that of the page.

Denoted by the symbol n, the *refractive index* – or optical density – of a medium is the factor by which the supported light-propagation speed v is less than the free-space speed c. Such a factor, $n = c/v$, is an example of a quantity without units.

Law of reflection – Euclid (c.300BC): A ray incident at angle θ_1 to the **normal** to an interface between medium 1 and medium 2 reflects back into medium 1, within the **plane of incidence** and also at angle θ_1, but on the opposite side of the normal:

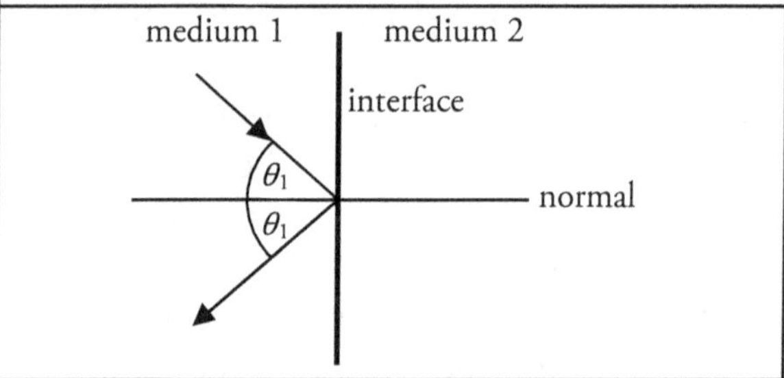

Figure 4.10: Reflection at an interface

Law of refraction – Snell (1621): A ray incident at angle θ_1 to the normal to an interface between medium 1 and medium 2 refracts into medium 2 along a direction that lies within the plane of incidence and at an angle θ_2 on the opposite sides of both the interface and normal according to the relation $\sin\theta_2/\sin\theta_1 = n_1/n_2$, where n_1 and n_2 are the respective so-called **refractive indices** of the two media:

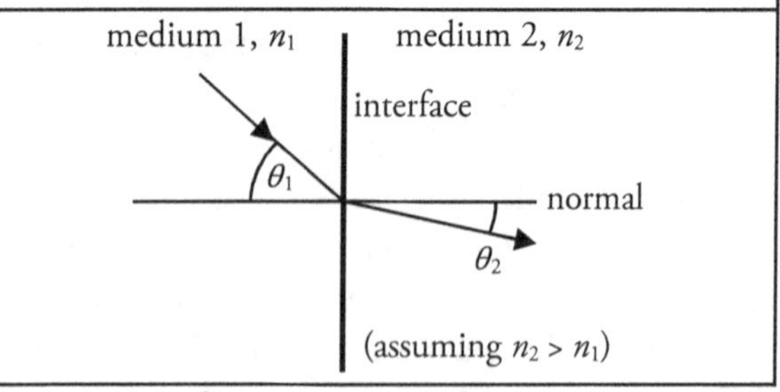

Figure 4.11: Refraction at an interface

Snell's law, $n = c/v$, and the use of $v = f\lambda$ at constant frequency f (Section 4.3.2) lead to the speed v and wavelength λ dependent relations $\sin\theta_2/\sin\theta_1 = v_2/v_1 = \lambda_2/\lambda_1 = n_1/n_2$, of which key refractive outcomes are presented in Table 4.11:

Critical angle: This concept can apply only when medium 2 is less optically dense, i.e. $n_2 < n_1$.

Conditions	Outcomes	Notes
$n_2 > n_1$	$\theta_2 < \theta_1$ $v_2 < v_1$ $\lambda_2 < \lambda_1$	The ray is refracted (sometimes called bent) towards the normal.
$n_2 = n_1$	nothing new	Medium 2 is optically equivalent to medium 1 and, with effectively no interface, there is no refraction. The ray simply continues onward at angle θ_1.
$n_2 < n_1$	$\theta_2 > \theta_1$ $v_2 > v_1$ $\lambda_2 > \lambda_1$	The ray is refracted away from the normal.
$n_2 < n_1$ and $\theta_1 = \theta_c$	$\theta_2 = \pi/2$	When θ_1 is increased to the so-called **critical angle** θ_c, the refracted ray propagates along the interface, and $1/\sin\theta_c = v_2/v_1 = \lambda_2/\lambda_1 = n_1/n_2$, where all parametric ratios are > 1.
$n_2 < n_1$ and $\theta_1 > \theta_c$	no refraction	When θ_1 is increased beyond θ_c, there is no refraction, and the incident ray is confined to medium 1 via reflection at angle θ_1 – an effect known as **total internal reflection**.

Table 4.11: Analysis of refraction

Absorption and scattering: If propagating light has a frequency that **matches** the natural frequency of the atomic **transitions** within a host medium, it can be absorbed by that medium and thus be increasingly attenuated with propagation distance. Given the ideal scenario that the propagating beam is collimated – i.e. that it is of constant cross-section – and that the medium is of uniform absorbance, Bouger (1729) offered a descriptively-couched law that the beam's remaining intensity $I(z)$ is an exponential function of propagation distance z. In accordance, $I(z)$ may be written mathematically as $I(z) = I(0)e^{-\alpha z}$, where α is defined as the fraction of the intensity absorbed per unit length. Furthermore, α is generally a function of wavelength, so that optical materials may absorb one colour but not another†.

Total internal reflection can be a means to confine light within the core of an optical fibre due to the periphery (or cladding) of the optical fibre being of lower refractive index.

When there is such a **matching** of frequency there is said to be resonation.

Atomic **transitions** involve changes of energy levels and are commonly associated with electrons.

†Such selective absorption underlies perceived colouration: For example, rubies appear red due to absorbing the blue and green, whilst transmitting or reflecting the red.

†Known as Rayleigh scattering, this is where, due to the λ^{-4} dependence:
►Short wavelengths suffer stronger scattering than longer ones.
►The often blue appearance of the day-time sky may be explained by the preferential scattering, by atmospheric gasses, of blue wavelengths towards the Earth as sunlight passes by overhead.

Charge is an attribute of certain entities usually found within atoms, notably protons and electrons.

††Such is the means by which radiant light and heat energy approaches from the Sun, and vast electromagnetic propagation distances are possible through the deep vacuum of outer space.

†††This relation is remarkable since ε_0 and μ_0 were previously known only from the physics of electricity and magnetism.
    As presently accepted:
►$c = 299\ 792\ 458$ m s^{-1} (exact by definition).
►$\varepsilon_0 = 8.854\ 187\ 8128(13) \times 10^{-12}$ kg^{-1} m^{-3} s^4 A^2.
►$\mu_0 = 1.256\ 637\ 062\ 12(19) \times 10^{-6}$ kg m s^{-2} A^{-2}.

††††Having the further wave behaviours of polarisation reflection, refraction, scattering, diffraction and superposition, Fizeau's light and Hertz's radio were both confirmed via Maxwell's theory as electromagnetic in origin and real examples of electromagnetic waves.

But, if the light suffers a random change of propagation direction after interacting with the medium, it is said to be scattered. The total light energy is ideally unchanged, but the amount remaining in the forward direction decreases. For collimated propagation within a uniform medium, the equation for the remaining forward-directed intensity is like the mathematical rendition of Bouger's law except that, according to Strutt (1871), the α-parameter is replaced by a function proportional to λ^{-4}†.

Electromagnetic propagation and speed: Maxwell (1865) made a range of remarkable contributions to physics that included:

►Predicting that the acceleration of a *charge* creates an entity known as an electromagnetic wave that can propagate in both particulate media and free space.

►Revealing that a created electromagnetic wave can sustain itself with no further need for the presence of charge or, indeed, any form of matter – and, in principle, can continue to propagate through free space without limit††.

►Predicting that all electromagnetic waves propagate with fixed speed c in free space, given by $c = (\varepsilon_0\mu_0)^{-\frac{1}{2}}$, where ε_0 and μ_0 are respectively its so-called permittivity and permeability†††.

But what is the physical reality of Maxwell's electromagnetic waves? One clue came from Fizeau (1849) who, prior to Maxwell's theory, measured the speed of light via its time of flight between a rapidly rotating toothed wheel and a distant mirror. The result was within 5% of $(\varepsilon_0\mu_0)^{-\frac{1}{2}}$. Later, Hertz (1892) reported radio signals that also propagated with speed close to $(\varepsilon_0\mu_0)^{-\frac{1}{2}}$††††.

But the electromagnetic spectrum surpasses light and radio. Electromagnetic waves range continuously from short wavelength gamma rays (hundredths of nanometres) to long wavelength radio waves (many metres) – and potentially infinitely beyond – whilst in between are ultraviolet, visible, infrared, and various other loosely defined electromagnetic bands. The electromagnetic spectrum, in its entirety, is known as **Maxwell's rainbow.**

The speed of light – i.e. of all of Maxwell's rainbow – is always less than c in a particulate medium. Indeed, following Table 4.11's notes on refractive index n, an exemplification of the speed $v = c/n$ in a medium is given in Table 4.12†:

Medium	Speed, v (m s^{-1})	Refractive index, n
free space	c (by definition)	1 (by definition)
air	2.99×10^8	1.00
water	2.25×10^8	1.33
quartz	2.05×10^8	1.46
diamond	1.24×10^8	2.42
germanium	0.730×10^8	4.10

Table 4.12: For selected media, approximate values of the speed of light, and refractive index

Maxwell's rainbow and the euphemism of 'light': Although light is traditionally considered as pertaining to visibility, ongoing discussion will use the term to refer to all of Maxwell's electromagnetic rainbow.

†Notes:
► The quantities v and n both vary weakly with wavelength and temperature.
► Some contrasts: Light can exist in free space, mechanical waves cannot. Light slows in higher optical densities, mechanical waves tend to hasten in higher material densities.

Refractive index n may usefully be incorporated into the equation (Section 4.3.2) for sinusoidal transverse travelling waves, as shown in Table 4.13.

Quantity	Equation (with $\varphi = 0$)	Notes
wave in free space	$y(x,t) = y_{\mathrm{m}}\sin\left[\frac{2\pi}{\lambda_0}(x - ct)\right]$	subscript 0 designates free space
wave in a medium	$y(x,t) = y_{\mathrm{m}}\sin\left[\frac{2\pi}{\lambda}(x - vt)\right]$	λ and v refer to the medium
speed in free space	$c = f\lambda_0$	
speed in a medium	$v = f\lambda$	f is often treated as independent of the medium
refractive index, n	$n = c/v$	
n-based representation of a wave in a medium	$y(x,t) = y_{\mathrm{m}}\sin\left[\frac{2\pi}{\lambda_0}(nx - ct)\right]$	follows from the previous four rows

Table 4.13: Light-wave equations incorporating refractive index

But Maxwell not only confirmed light waves to be transverse, but also revealed them as an energetic propagation of mutually embracing oscillations of electric and magnetic entities known as fields, which:

►Are both transverse to the direction of propagation.

►Are perpendicular to each other.

►Follow the wave equation (Section 4.3.6).

►Satisfy $c = E_m/B_m = (\varepsilon_0\mu_0)^{-\frac{1}{2}}$, where E_m and B_m are the amplitudes of the electric and magnetic field-oscillations.

►Have no relative phase (i.e. both have $\varphi = 0$).

►Are generally treated vectorially as **E** and **B**, but, in the simple scalar form of Table 4.13, are as given in Table 4.14:

Scalar representation of electric **E** field	Scalar representation of magnetic **B** field
$E(x,t) = E_m \sin\left[\frac{2\pi}{\lambda_0}(nx - ct)\right]$	$B(x,t) = B_m \sin\left[\frac{2\pi}{\lambda_0}(nx - ct)\right]$

Table 4.14: Scalar representations of the electric **E** and magnetic **B** fields of light

Polarisation, and associated media: Being transverse, every light wave is polarised, and has a state of polarisation defined as the axis of oscillation of its electric field. If such an axis is aligned with a medium's so-called polarising axis, ideally 100% transmission ensues. But, if perpendicular, there is ideally 100% absorption or reflection. In practice, there is likely to be an intermediate state of alignment, and partial transmission.

And, for such a polarisation-based optical filter, there may be further operational complexity if there is an ensemble of incident light waves. Overall, here is the possible range of outcomes for the transmitted intensity I given an incident intensity I_0:

►$I = \frac{1}{2} \times I_0$ when the incident ensemble is ***unpolarised***.

►I varying between I_0 and zero, according to the $I = I_0\cos^2\theta$ law of Malus (1808), when the incident ensemble is ***polarised*** at angle θ to the medium's polarising axis.

►I being in some combination of the above in intermediate cases – as is likely in real scenarios.

Unpolarised and ***polarised*** represent two ideal extremes of possible polarisation distributions, where:
►Unpolarised means that there is a random distribution of constituent polarisation states (as approximately emitted, for example, by filament-based bulbs).
►Polarised means that all constituent polarisation states are the same (as approximately emitted, for example, by some lasers).

Interference, and the concept of differential accumulated phase: From Table 4.14, the phase of a light wave propagating in the direction of increasing x in a medium of refractive index n is $(2\pi/\lambda_0) \times (nx - ct)$, where λ_0 is the free-space wavelength, c is the free-space propagation speed, and t is the time. With $t = 0$ as a snapshot in time, $(2\pi/\lambda_0) \times n_{medium}x_{medium}$ may thus be considered as an accumulation of phase within some arbitrary medium, and notably where x_{medium} is a propagative length that may be considered as applicable to any direction†.

The notation may be shortened to $(2\pi/\lambda_0)n_1x_1$, where the subscript 1 associates the refractive index and propagative length with a wave 1. And, with a wave 2 treated similarly, the differential accumulated phase φ between the two waves is $\varphi = (2\pi/\lambda_0) \times |n_2x_2 - n_1x_1|$††.

But, from Section 4.3.5, Case 1, when there is φ of differential phase between two otherwise identical waves, interference ensues with amplitude proportional to $|\cos(\varphi/2)|$, which equals 1 and 0 if respectively constructive and destructive. The general analysis of such interference cases is presented in Table 4.15.

†Note that the product of refractive index and the associated propagative length is called optical path length.

††The quantity $|n_2x_2 - n_1x_1|$ is notably a difference in optical path length.

Type	Condition	Analysis	Where
Constructive	$\lvert\cos(\varphi/2)\rvert = 1$	$\frac{1}{2} \times (2\pi/\lambda_0) \times \lvert n_2x_2 - n_1x_1\rvert = m \times \pi$ $\Rightarrow \lvert n_2x_2 - n_1x_1\rvert = m\lambda_0$	$m = 0,1,2,\ldots$
Destructive	$\lvert\cos(\varphi/2)\rvert = 0$	$\frac{1}{2} \times (2\pi/\lambda_0) \times \lvert n_2x_2 - n_1x_1\rvert = (p + \frac{1}{2}) \times \pi$ $\Rightarrow \lvert n_2x_2 - n_1x_1\rvert = (p + \frac{1}{2})\lambda_0$	$p = 0,1,2,\ldots$

Table 4.15: Type of interference due to φ of differential accumulated phase

And Table 4.16 presents simplification in cases of common propagative index, $n_1 = n_2 = n$.

Interference type	Analysis	Where
Constructive	$\lvert x_2 - x_1\rvert = m\lambda$	$m = 0,1,2,\ldots$
Destructive	$\lvert x_2 - x_1\rvert = (p + \frac{1}{2})\lambda$	$p = 0,1,2,\ldots$
Note 1: λ is the wavelength in the medium.		
Note 2: It is easy to verify that $\lambda_0/n = \lambda$.		

Table 4.16: Simplification of Table 4.15's analysis for a common propagative medium

Such *physics* notably indicates significant practical constraint – see, for example, Sections 7.2.2 and 7.2.4 for its impact in the field of astronomy.

†Note that diffraction is very likely in such scenarios (even for elements as simple as an edge), but the strength of any subsequent interference is dependent on the configuration.

A *diffraction grating* is a diffractive element comprising a large number of narrow slits.

Such *concepts* require the time over which the incident light is coherent (Section 4.3.1) at least to match that associated with any considered difference in optical path length – such incident light is said to be temporally coherent.

Collimated means that constituent wave propagations are as parallel as practically possible. The incident wavefronts are then planar (Section 4.3.4), and such incident light is said to be spatially coherent (Section 4.3.1).
    Furthermore, with normal incidence, such spatial coherence may be maintained across the diffractive element.

Monochromatic means that all constituent waves are of the same wavelength as closely as practically possible. The emission from some lasers is particularly monochromatic, often referred to as narrow linewidth.

Diffractive superposition: The analysis of Tables 4.15 and 4.16 offers a simple means to move beyond Huygens' wavelet description of geometric propagation (Section 4.3.4), and to explain a broad remit of **physics** where superposition (Section 4.3.5) associated with differences of diffractive phase causes significant interference. And, as introduction to onward discussion, Table 4.17 presents four associated cases where each involves a diffractive element having the common key feature of size being comparable to the propagating wavelength†.

Case	Diffractive element
1	a narrow slit
2	a small circular hole
3	a pair of narrow slits
4	*a diffraction grating*
Note that the ongoing discussion uses (1) the propagative concepts of geometric optics in the preceding subsection 'reflection and refraction', (2) the interference **concepts** of Tables 4.15 and 4.16, and (3) the following assumptions: ►Incident light is both **collimated** and at normal incidence to the diffractive element. ►Constituent collimation/interference is enabled via sufficiency of spatial/temporal coherence. ►Incident light may also be **monochromatic** depending on the application. ►The diffraction pattern is viewed at a point far from the diffractive element, and hence all the light observed there is taken to arrive at the same angle θ. ►θ is defined as the angle between the line of view to the diffractive element and the axis of the normal incidence. ►The propagating wavelength is λ in an arbitrary medium, or approximately the free space value λ_0 in air. ►The refractive index is n in an arbitrary medium, or approximately 1 in air.	

Table 4.17: Discussed cases of diffractive superposition

Diffractive superposition from a narrow slit (Table 4.17, Case 1): When collimated light is normally incident on a slit, the light passing near the centre is undiffracted and propagates onwards as a linear bright central band. Such behaviour is consistent with geometric optics, assuming propagation to be in a straight line. It is also consistent with Huygens' principle (Section 4.3.4) whereby each location across the slit is considered as a point source. But the emission from all such sources is spatially coherent due to the normally-incident collimation, and, assuming there also to be sufficiency of temporal coherence, their superpositional interference (Section 4.3.5) determines the observed profile of intensity extending from the bright centre†.

Further notes specific to Case 1 follow:

► Due to the linear geometry, the ensuing dark and bright fringes extending from the central maximum are also linear.

► For a narrow slit, there is a moderate strength of diffraction away from the central maximum leading to a relatively broad profile.

► Nonetheless, owing to the large number of coherent sets of Huygens' wavelets from locations extending across the slit, large angles of diffraction tend to be associated with more differences of phase, leading to increased likelihood of destructive interference.

► The overall result is that of a low intensity being diffracted into the first bright fringe, and the intensity of the subsequent bright fringes falling away rapidly††.

► The case involves diffraction into a common medium and thus Table 4.16 applies.

► The value $m = 0$, such that there is a zero difference $|x_2 - x_1|$ in propagative length, defines the central maximum.

► Now, for distant viewing at a given angle θ, suppose that the maximum of $|x_2 - x_1|$ is equal to one wavelength, λ. For such a **condition**, not only would the destructive interference condition $|x_2 - x_1| = \lambda/2$ apply between one edge and the centre – i.e. to a separation of $a/2$ for a slit of width a – but it would also apply to all other

---

†General notes for many cases:

► The bright centre is called the central maximum.

► For normal incidence, the central maximum is centred on the axis of incidence.

► The superpositional interference extending from the central maximum generally results in a broad profile of intensity with a succession of dark and bright regions referred to as minima and maxima.

► Such minima and maxima are also called fringes.

††Associated notes:

► The central maximum is by far the most intense.

► And only a few subsequent bright fringes are likely to be visible.

► Furthermore, such fringes appear at different angles for different wavelengths, and consequently the clearest demonstrations involve monochromatic light.

Such a **condition** is interesting because of its heuristic consistency with a limiting of the extent of the central maximum. Indeed:

► As a criterion of constructive interference, it could only apply to light from the slit's most distant points – i.e. its two edges.

► And that light from any other two arbitrarily selected points across the slit would inevitably exhibit some degree of destructive interference.

$a/2$-separated pairings progressively extending across the slit.

►Furthermore, for each such $a/2$-separated pairing, a simple geometric consideration leads to $|x_2 - x_1| = (a/2)\sin\theta$.

►Thus, for distant viewing at angle θ, the first dark fringe is described by $a\sin\theta = \lambda$.

Diffractive superposition from a small circular hole (Table 4.17, Case 2): Broadly following the behaviour of Case 1, there is now a circular geometry which leads to a disk-shaped central maximum and increasingly distant annular fringes. The circular geometry complicates the analysis. However, following Rayleigh (1879), $d/1.22$ can be considered as the approximate effective width of a hole of diameter d. Thus, for distant viewing at angle θ, the first dark fringe is described by $(d/1.22)\sin\theta = \lambda$.

Diffractive/coherent superposition from a pair of narrow slits (Table 4.17, Case 3): Effectively an extension to Case 1, such that additional diffraction from a second slit provides coherent superposition with the first, Young (1802) reported an experiment involving a pair of slits, whose combined diffractive and interferometric behaviour is a famously lucid demonstration of the wave-nature of light:

The slit separation d is assumed to be much larger than the slit width a. Accordingly, inspection of the form of Case 1's dark fringe condition indicates there to be changes in the profile of intensity that are associated with much smaller changes of θ. Indeed, the resultant profile of intensity is a combination of single-slit diffraction and superimposed rapidly spatially-varying dark and bright fringes:

In particular, Figure 4.12 shows an idealised configuration of Young's experiment, where (1) the propagative medium is uniform, (2) the depicted wavefronts are crests, (3) the intersections of their diffractive superpositions define lines along which interference is constructive, but (4) in between such lines, crests align with troughs, and interference is destructive†.

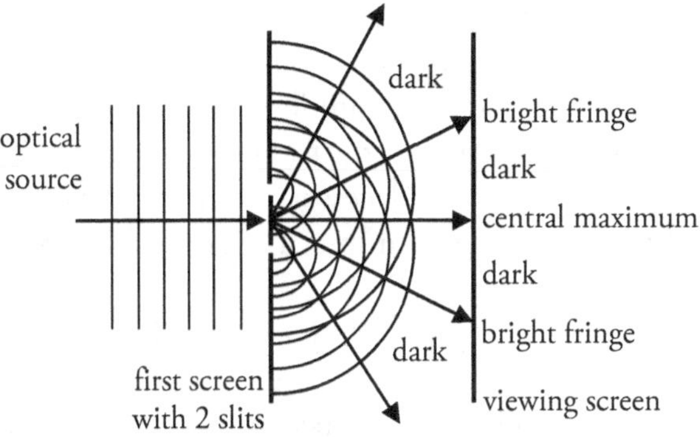

Figure 4.12: Young's double slit experiment

With propagation into a common medium, and with revelation of the entire fringe pattern via a distantly placed viewing screen, the rapidly spatially-varying dark and bright fringes may be analysed via Table 4.16 as follows:

► For the dark fringes, the condition on the difference $|x_2 - x_1|$ in propagative length is $|x_2 - x_1| = (p + \tfrac{1}{2})\lambda$, where $p = 0,1,2,\ldots$. But, for distant viewing at angle θ, a simple geometric consideration leads to $|x_2 - x_1| = d\sin\theta$, where d is the slit separation. Thus, for distant viewing at angle θ, the dark fringes follow $d\sin\theta = (p + \tfrac{1}{2})\lambda$, where $p = 0,1,2,\ldots$ ††.

► For the bright fringes, the condition on the difference $|x_2 - x_1|$ in propagative length is $|x_2 - x_1| = m\lambda$, where $m = 0,1,2,\ldots$. Thus, for distant viewing at angle θ, the bright fringes follow $d\sin\theta = m\lambda$, where $m = 0,1,2,\ldots$.

Diffractive/coherent superposition from a diffraction grating (Table 4.17, Case 4): The diffraction grating is one of the most useful devices in spectroscopy – the wavelength based study of the emission and absorption of light. Such gratings have a large number of uniformly spaced slits, called rulings, that are tightly packed at typically several thousand per mm.

†Note that, whilst the representation of Figure 4.12 ideally applies anywhere along the axes of the slits (i.e. out of the plane of the page), for the as-shown in-page depiction:
► The optical source provides a monochromatic normally-incident wavetrain.
► With each slit ideally acting as a point source, two sets of Huygens' wavelets arise that are both temporally and spatially coherent.
► The medium either side of the first screen is both common and uniform.
► Straight lines to the left are crest-based wavefronts, each separated from its neighbour by one wavelength.
► Semicircular lines to the right are also crest-based wavefronts, and each is also taken to be separated by one wavelength $\lambda = v\Delta t$ for some common speed v, and appropriately chosen common small amount of time Δt.

††And the first dark fringe is thus described by $d\sin\theta = \lambda/2$, contrasting with $a\sin\theta = \lambda$ for Case 1.

Except with the key practical difference that the input illumination is no longer monochromatic, analysis follows that of Case 3's pair of slits – indeed the same distant bright fringe conditions apply but, with each additional slit, a new set Huygens' wavelets adds to the interstitial destructive interference:

►Assuming each new slit to be separated by the same d from its predecessor, the initial effect is subtle, with a new minimum appearing between each bright fringe.

►But, with the growing number of intervening minima, the extent of their darkness grows and the bright fringes become narrower and brighter.

►When there is a very large number of slits, the intervening spaces tend towards complete darkness, and the bright fringes tend towards lines†.

►Furthermore, the fringe pattern is replicated at each wavelength within the input illumination, but seen at different angles θ of view. This is key to the practice of spectroscopy, which requires unambiguous spatial separation of closely spaced wavelengths.

►Confining operation to one order – i.e. at constant m – the differential of the bright-fringe condition becomes $d\cos\theta\,\Delta\theta = m\Delta\lambda_0$, where $m = 0,1,2,\dots$.

►The related quantity $\Delta\theta/\Delta\lambda_0 = m/(d\cos\theta)$ is called dispersion, and should be maximised for high-resolution spectroscopic applications. This implies operating in a high order m, and the use of a small slit separation d.

►Note that there is no dispersion for $m = 0$; whilst much spectroscopy is actually conducted in the first order, $m = 1$††.

Coherent superposition via the interferometer of Michelson and Morley (1887): Where the fundamental effect of diffraction (Section 4.3.4) is taken as insignificant, scenarios of coherent

†Notes:
►Then, for practical purposes, only the bright fringes remain of interest.
►In particular, a grating's total number of slits may be increased, within engineering limits, to achieve bright fringes of maximum brightness, and minimum geometric width.

††It is possible to conduct spectroscopy in higher orders, i.e. with $m \geq 2$, but then there is increasing likelihood of higher order fringes overlapping lower ones. The associated problem of interpretation may be overcome by using an optical filter to block the spectral regions of the input illumination whose fringes are party to the overlapping. But such a practice reduces the usable input spectral range.

superposition (Section 4.3.5) are dominated by the concepts of geometric optics and differential accumulated phase†:

An important simple example, where there are just two distinct optical paths, is the so-called Michelson interferometer. Notably offering the measurement of optical lengths – or changes thereof – with great accuracy, an illustration is provided in Figure 4.13:

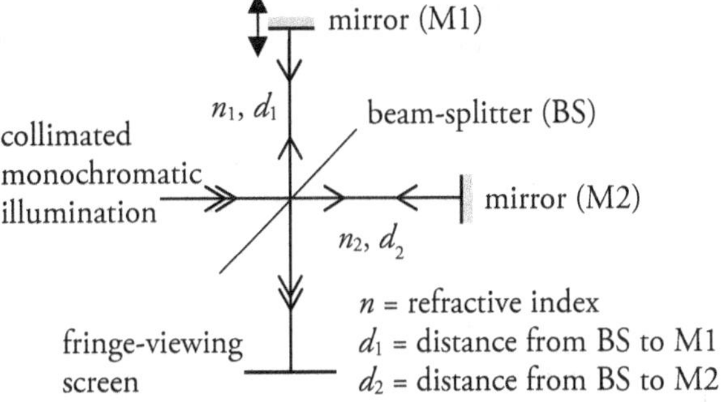

Figure 4.13: Michelson's interferometer

The beam-splitter is key since it both splits and recombines the input illumination, defining the two distinct optical paths for which the differential accumulated phase is to be assessed††.

Then, with the applicability of various **conditions**, interference will cause a succession of equal-intensity bright fringes to be seen across the output from the beam-splitter. For example, if the two paths are of refractive indices n_1 and n_2, then Table 4.16 indicates the bright fringes to follow $2|n_2 d_2 - n_1 d_1| = m\lambda_0$ and the intervening dark fringes to follow $2|n_2 d_2 - n_1 d_1| = (p + \frac{1}{2})\lambda_0$, with $m,p = 0,1,2,\dots$.

Reliant on measuring a shift of the fringe pattern upon some change of $2|n_2 d_2 - n_1 d_1|$, such interferometers are often used to determine (1) the optical path lengths of some transparent body inserted into one path, or (2) a movement of one of the mirrors.

†Please refer to these preceding subsections:
►'Reflection and refraction' for geometric optics.
►'Interference, and the concept of differential accumulated phase' – in particular Table 4.16.

††Notes:
►One optical path length is from BS to M1 back to BS, represented by $2n_1 d_1$.
►The other optical path length is from BS to M2 back to BS, represented by $2n_2 d_2$.
►Conversely, the input to BS and the output from BS represent common propagative paths, and thus ideally have no effect the differential accumulated phase.

Such **conditions** include:
►The illumination having sufficient temporal coherence – i.e. that the length of its wavetrain exceeds the interferometer's difference in optical path length.
►The collimation having sufficient spatial coherence.
►The monochromaticity providing sufficient clarity.
►Recombination by the beam-splitter retaining the collimation and spatial coherence.

4.3.8 Mechanical versus electromagnetic waves

Both types of wave:	Differences	
	Mechanical	Electromagnetic
Embody energy/information sourced as:	The oscillation of entities with mass.	The oscillation of electric and magnetic fields from oscillating entities with charge, notably electrons.
Maintain oscillation:	Via mechanical restoration and continuous transfer to deeper elements of mass within a host medium.	Internally, via continuous mutual embrace of their oscillating electric and magnetic fields.
Have a local frequency of oscillation that depends not only on that of their source, but also on any source/receiver motion relative to the host medium:	Often described by Doppler's treatment.	Requires relativistic Dopplerian treatment.
That, in free space:	Are not supported.	Are supported at speed c.
That, in a particulate medium, have a local speed of propagation calculated as the local frequency multiplied by the local wavelength:	►Which is usually very much less than c, being limited by the masses under oscillation and available restoring forces. ►But which generally increases in media of higher (material) density.	►Which is often not much less than c. ►But which decreases in media of higher optical density.
Can continue to propagate in a straight line (assuming negligible diffraction).	Requires linearly disposed presence of mass.	Does not require mass, or even the originating charge.
Can ideally propagate over large distance that is:	Limited by the size of practical media.	Limited by the size of the universe.
Can possess polarisation:	Exceptions: All longitudinal forms.	Exceptions: None.
Can, as an ensemble, be polarised via a medium:	Not often implemented.	Frequently implemented.
Can, as an ensemble, exhibit inverse-square-law based divergence.	Conditional on a uniform lossless medium.	Unconditional in free space.
Can be reflected, refracted, absorbed, scattered, diffracted and superposed.	-	-

Table 4.18: Comparison of mechanical and electromagnetic waves

4.4 Questionnaire

4Q1   Select an incorrect statement about heat:
a   Its classical absence is consistent with 0 K
b   It can arise from the movement of atoms
c   It can be associated with electrons
d   Its transfer arises from thermal equilibrium

4Q2   Which of the following statements about density is false?
a   Its definition is mass divided by volume
b   It is a scalar quantity
c   It generally varies with temperature
d   It has a pressure dependence that is roughly constant regardless of physical state

4Q3   On the lifting of a body, select a factor that is always significant in there being
       differences of effort between when partially submerged and fully submerged:
a   Viscosity
b   Buoyancy
c   Surface tension
d   None of the others

4Q4   How many of the following four attributes apply to a so-called ideal fluid?
       Not turbulent. Not moving. Not compressible. Not viscous.
a   1
b   2
c   3
d   4

4Q5   For a continuous 3D body of fluid:
a   Horizontal constancy of pressure ideally requires connectivity at constant height
b   There is constant pressure over the periphery
c   A Δp change of pressure appearing at some location ideally appears everywhere else
d   The pressure has a rate of change with height that is ideally zero

4Q6   Answer the following two questions in the same order regarding the pistons of an
       hydraulic lever:
       Which has bigger area? Which moves through bigger distance?
a   The input. The input.
b   The input. The output.
c   The output. The input.
d   The output. The output.

Page 98 answers: 30d   31b   32c   33c   34b   35c   36b
Page 99 answers: 37d   38b   39c   40d   41b   42d

4Q7   Via inspection of the two equations $A_1v_1 = A_2v_2$, and $p_1 + \frac{1}{2}\rho v_1^2 = p_2 + \frac{1}{2}\rho v_2^2$ at constant ρ, select the correct option regarding the following two statements: 1) When A increases, v decreases. 2) When v decreases, p increases.

a   Neither is true
b   Only 1) is true
c   Only 2) is true
d   Both are true

4Q8   With x representing a variable positional component, t representing time, and λ, T, φ, and C all taken as constant, the phase $(2\pi/\lambda)x - (2\pi/T)t + \varphi = C$ of a uniform wave may be differentiated to yield which of the following as a measure of speed?

a λ/T
b T/λ
c λT
d $(\lambda T)^{-1}$

4Q9   Which of the following statements about a uniform transverse travelling wave is false?

a   The distance between adjacent crests is its wavelength
b   The height between the troughs and crests is twice its amplitude
c   The inverse of the time between a crest and an adjacent trough is its frequency
d   The time between adjacent crests equals time between adjacent troughs

4Q10 Regarding the equation $y(x,t) = y_m\sin\left[\frac{2\pi}{\lambda}(x \pm vt) + \varphi\right]$ for a transverse travelling wave, which of the following statements is false?

a $2y_m$ is the wave's amplitude
b $\sin\left[\frac{2\pi}{\lambda}(x \pm vt) + \varphi\right]$ is the wave's oscillatory term
c $\frac{2\pi}{\lambda}(x \pm vt) + \varphi$ is the wave's phase term
d φ is the wave's phase angle

4Q11 If there is halving of an observer's distance to a source that is emitting waves uniformly in all directions into a lossless medium, then the intensity seen by that observer:

a   Halves
b   Remains the same
c   Doubles
d   Changes, but is not halved or doubled

4Q12 If a lossless uniformly spherically diverging propagation has an intensity of
5.0 W m^{-2} at 1.0 m, what is the intensity at 5.0 m?
a 2.5 W m^{-2}
b 1.0 W m^{-2}
c 0.50 W m^{-2}
d 0.20 W m^{-2}

4Q13 Which of the following statements regarding Huygens' principle is false?
a   All points on a wavefront serve as forward-propagating point sources
b   After a time t, a local wavefront of constant speed v has progressed a distance of t/v
c   The wavefront at any given time is a surface tangent to all secondary wavelets
d   It is without concern for phase based superposition

4Q14 Which of the following statements is false regarding the net wave resulting from
the superposition of two identical waves?
a   It is treated as being in phase with both superposing waves
b   Its phase angle is treated as the same as both superposing waves
c   It is treated as having four times the superposing energy
d   It may provide an incomplete system-level description

4Q15 If a first uniform wave is superposed by another which differs only in having $+\varphi$
of relative phase, then which of the following statements is false?
a   The net wave has $+\varphi/2$ of phase relative to the first
b   The net amplitude is twice that of the first when φ is zero
c   Destructive interference ensues when φ makes the individual waves out of phase
d   The value $\varphi = \pi$ renders the superposing wave appearing identical to the first

4Q16 Which of the following statements about sinusoidal transverse travelling waves is
false?
a   They may encompass a 90-degree variation in oscillation axis
b   They may be mechanical
c   They may be electromagnetic
d   They may possess nodes of oscillation

4Q17 Which of the following comments on standing waves is false?
a   They arise from the superposition of counter-propagating waves
b   Their amplitude is independent of time
c   They are said to resonate
d   Their existence stems from at least a partially bounded medium

4Q18 The superposition of two waves of frequencies f_1 and f_2 produces a net wave which beats at a frequency of:

a $f_1 + f_2$
b $(f_1 + f_2)/2$
c $|f_1 - f_2|$
d $|f_1 - f_2|/2$

4Q19 Which of the following media is likely to support the fastest sound waves?

a   Gas
b   Water
c   Wood
d   Rock

4Q20 A mechanical wave of wavelength 2.00 m and frequency 4.00 Hz propagates with a speed of:

a 0.125 m s^{-1}
b 0.500 m s^{-1}
c 2.00 m s^{-1}
d 8.00 m s^{-1}

4Q21 If $T = \rho v^2$ and $v = f\lambda$, where T is tension, ρ is mass per unit length, v is speed, f is frequency, and λ is wavelength, then what is λ?

a $f^{-1}(T/\rho)^{\frac{1}{2}}$
b $f(T/\rho)^{\frac{1}{2}}$
c $f^{-1}(\rho/T)^{\frac{1}{2}}$
d $f(\rho/T)^{\frac{1}{2}}$

4Q22 Which of the following statements about mechanical waves is false?

a   They are governed by Newton's laws
b   They are an aspect of a particulate medium
c   They propagate via large-scale transport of matter
d   They require some form of restoring force

4Q23 How many of the following three actions can create a compression pulse in a medium and hence initiate a longitudinal wave? Action of a loudspeaker cone on air. Mechanical impact on a solid. Seismic activity.

a   0
b   1
c   2
d   3

4Q24 Select a true statement about a longitudinal wave propagating in an unbounded
      medium:
a   It is transverse
b   It can be torsional
c   It is compressive
d   It can be standing

4Q25 With an internal propagation speed taken as 300 m s^{-1}, an air-filled tube of
      3.00 m length closed at both ends supports a lowest standing-wave frequency of:
a   50.0 Hz
b   100 Hz
c   200 Hz
d   900 Hz

4Q26 The medical uses of ultrasound encompass:
a   Diagnostics only
b   Therapy only
c   Diagnostics, and therapy only
d   Diagnostics, therapy, and surgery

4Q27 The Doppler-shifted form of ultrasound diagnostics is particularly useful for
      which of the following?
a   Muscle
b   Injuries
c   Interfaces with bone
d   Heart

4Q28 Suppose that a beat frequency is inversely proportional to speed. If the speed
      becomes half of its original value, what then happens to the beat frequency?
a   It stays the same
b   It increases by a factor of 2
c   It decreases by a factor of 2
d   It changes by a factor of 4

4Q29 An incident wave of frequency $f =$ is 1.0×10^{6} Hz and propagation speed
      $v = 1.5 \times 10^{3}$ m s^{-1} beats with its Doppler-shifted echo from a body moving at
      $v_{body} = 0.015$ m s^{-1}. What is its $2fv_{body}/v$ beat frequency?
a 2.0×10^{0} Hz
b 2.0×10^{1} Hz
c 2.0×10^{2} Hz
d 2.0×10^{3} Hz

Page 96 answers: 18c   19d   20d   21a   22c   23d
Page 97 answers: 24c   25a   26d   27d   28b   29b

4Q30 For an entity to travel at $c = 299\,392\,458$ m s^{-1}, it must:
a   Have longitudinal oscillations
b   Be within a medium of zero refractive index
c   Be a particle
d   Be within a perfect vacuum

4Q31 Which of the following statements about electromagnetic waves is false?
a   They propagate faster in media of reduced optical density
b   They tend to propagate faster in media of increased material density
c   They can propagate faster than any other physical entity
d   They can propagate in free space

4Q32 Which of the following statements on geometric optics is false?
a   It is consistent with continued propagation as a plane wavefront
b   It takes propagation to be in a straight line in a uniform medium
c   It is always consistent with diffraction
d   It has no concern for phase

4Q33 Which of the following statements about a reflected ray is false?
a   It lies in the plane defined by the incoming ray and the normal
c   It is on the same side of the normal as the incoming ray
b   Its angle with the normal has the same magnitude as that of the incoming ray
d   It is on the same side of the interface as the incoming ray

4Q34 The refraction of a wave is taken to involve:
a   A speed that does not change
b   A frequency that does not change
c   A wavelength that does not change
d   A propagation direction that does not change

4Q35 Which of the following options about Snell's law is false?
a   It implies the concept of critical angle
b   It implies the concept of total internal reflection
c   It relates an angle of reflection to an angle of incidence
d   It suggests ratiometric equivalence of two refractive indices and two speeds

4Q36 How many of the following five items could be considered as a locus of constant
        phase? A wave. A wavefront. A wavelength. A Huygens' wavelet. A ray.
a ≤ 1
b   2
c   3
d ≥ 4

4Q37 Regarding the fields of a Maxwell's wave, which statement is wrong:
a   They are transverse
b   They are electromagnetic
c   They have the same phase
d   They are mutually aligned

4Q38 Wave superposition is most strongly associated with:
a   Polarisation
b   Recombination from an interferometer's arms
c   Snell's description of the effect of an interface
d   Huygens' description of wavelets

4Q39 Select a false statement about diffraction:
a   It is strongest when light passes wavelength-sized features
b   Its central maxima can largely be described by geometric optics
c   From a grating, it typically consists of bright and dark regions of equal width
d   Detailed understanding can arise through an analysis of phase

4Q40 Select a false statement about a difference in optical path length:
a   It is dependent on refractive indices
b   It is dependent on propagation distances
c   In the case that it changes, different interference can result
d   It is $\cong |d_2 - d_1|$ for a Michelson interferometer with arms of air and lengths d_1 and d_2

4Q41 Of these three comparisons how many are correct? Light waves are longitudinal,
       but ripples are transverse. Light waves transport energy, but mechanical waves
       transport matter. Ripples can exist on the surface of water, but not deep inside.
a   0
b   1
c   2
d   3

4Q42 How many of the following three activities are possible via waves?
       Communication. Transmission of force. Transport of energy.
a   0
b   1
c   2
d   3

Chapter 5   Interactions and Unification

Name: Effect. ►Limit to dominating distance.	
Weak: Transmutations between protons and neutrons. ►About 10^{-18} m.	
Strong: Binding of atomic nuclei, and of each constituent proton and neutron. ►About 10^{-14} m, i.e. the size of a large atomic nucleus.	
Electromagnetic: Attraction and repulsion between charges (see Section 5.2.1). ►10^{b} m, limited via b to some practically small extra-atomic distance. (But, in the impossible scenario of isolation from all other charges, the dominating distance could be infinite.)	
Gravitational: Attraction between masses. ►10^{b} m to ∞.	

Table 5.1: Comparison of observed interactions

Such **binding** is at distances of about 10^{-10} m.

Inter-atomic:
►Bonding is at distances of about 10^{-10} m.
►Contact is at an approach of about 10^{-8} m, marked by a significant rise of electronic repulsion between atoms, and manifestation of bulk phenomena such as normal forces, pressure, and friction (but where Section 3.1-3.7's Newtonian based treatments are generally preferred).

†Such a universe would have zero net charge, and offer electromagnetic shielding.

Marked by practical dominating distances from within atoms (Section 1.4) to the vastness of space, Table 5.1 presents the various observed interactions:

►With the shortest and next-shortest mediations respectively, **weak** and **strong** both affect the quarks of an atom's protons and neutrons.

►**Electromagnetic** concerns atomic **binding** of electrons, **inter-atomic** bonding and contact, and also small-scale extra-atomic distances marked by the physicists' expectation that the universe has large-scale tendency to homogenise its structure, with balanced negative and positive charges†.

►Thereafter, **gravitational** – which is conversely always positive, and has no shielding – dominates through to infinity.

Furthermore, whilst the interactions are usually treated separately, ongoing revelation of their unification tantalisingly suggests the deeper physics of a single unifying theory of everything.

5.1   Gravitation

Early cosmological modelling is a supreme example of progress stalled through human belief preventing the acceptance of change – in this case lasting for two thousand years:

5.1.1   Kepler's rejection of geo- and heliocentricity

With the orthodoxy maintaining the supremacy of the Earth, Eudoxus (*c.*380BC) originated a geocentric model of the universe with the Earth at its centre. Nonetheless, in recognition of its mounting inconsistencies, Copernicus (1543) bravely published an alternative heliocentric model. Brahe (1588), conversely, remained partly wedded to tradition, proposing a hybrid model of geoheliocentricity†.

Brahe died in 1601, and Kepler used his astronomical data. As a result, Kepler disproved all previous models, and instead enunciated three significant statements on planetary kinematics (Section 2.2) about the Sun:

►Sometimes referred to as the law of orbits, Kepler (1609) stated that the planets orbit along elliptical paths with the Sun at one focus. But the shape of the ellipse varies with the planets. For example, a nearly circular path applies to the Earth, while much stronger ellipses apply to the more distant planets.

►Sometimes referred to as the law of areas, Kepler (1609) stated that a straight line that connects a planet to the Sun sweeps out equal elements dA of area in equal intervals dt of time, so that the **rate** dA/dt is constant. Accordingly, relative to the Sun, an orbiting planet moves most slowly when it is most distant, and vice versa††.

►Sometimes referred to as the law of periods, Kepler (1619) stated that the temporal period T for one orbit is related to the average orbital Sun-to-planet distance r according to the relation $T \propto r^{3/2}$†††.

†To prove his geoheliocentric model, Brahe commissioned a state-of-the-art observatory, and systematically measured the positions of the Sun's planets to one minute of arc (see Section 7.2) – a tremendous accomplishment prior to the establishment by Galileo (1610) of telescope based astronomy, and ten times better than earlier work.

Kepler's statement on constancy of the **rate** dA/dt is equivalent to the law of conservation of momentum, but in an angular sense rather than the Cartesian one underpinning Section 3.8.

††Indeed, when the planet is most distant, the assumptions of (1) the Sun being a an inertial frame of reference (Section 3.2), and (2) the Sun/planet system being isolated (Section 3.8), so that its energy is conserved (Section 3.9), mean that it would be reasonable to expect:
►The Sun/planet system to have maximum potential energy (Section 3.11).
►The planet then to have minimum kinetic energy (Section 3.11).

†††As exemplified in Section 7.3, however, practical applications may involve a modestly different definition of r, as well as careful identification of the constant of proportionality.

5.1.2   Newton's universal gravitation

Together with the implicit premise of the inertial frame of reference (Section 3.2), Newton (1687) explained Keplerian kinematics (Section 5.1.1) as originating from an attractive force that arises between any pair of bodies with mass (Section 2.9). Known as Newton's law of universal gravitation, such a force is proportional to both masses, and has an inverse-square relationship with their separation†:

Algebraically, $\mathbf{F} = -Gm_1m_2r^{-2}\hat{\mathbf{r}}$, where $\mathbf{F}$ is the force of a mass m_1 on a separate mass m_2, $G = 6.674\,30(15) \times 10^{-11}$ m^3 kg^{-1} s^{-2} is the so-called gravitational constant, $\hat{\mathbf{r}}$ is a positive unit vector specifying the direction from m_1's centre of mass (Section 2.10) to that of m_2, r is the separation between the two centres of mass, and the negative sign is included because $\mathbf{F}$ acts in opposition to $\hat{\mathbf{r}}$††.

Taking the system of m_1 and m_2 to be isolated (Section 3.8), the acceleration $\mathbf{a}_g$ of m_2, observed from, say, its **barycentre**, follows the constant-mass Newtonian second law (Section 3.3) such that $\mathbf{F} = -Gm_1m_2r^{-2}\hat{\mathbf{r}} = m_2\mathbf{a}_g$. Thus, with $|\mathbf{a}_g| = Gm_1r^{-2}$, it is notable that $|\mathbf{a}_g|$ is independent of its associated m_2 mass, but can be significant if the attracting m_1 mass is large†††.

Table 5.2 gives some examples of $|\mathbf{a}_g| = Gm_1r^{-2}$ when m_1 is the mass of the Earth (about 5.97×10^{24} kg), and r is the sum of radius r_E of the Earth (about 6.37×10^6 m) and some height.

Value of r (m)	Associated location	Acceleration (m s^{-2})
$r_E + 0$	its surface	9.8 ($= g$)
$r_E + 4.0 \times 10^4$	highest crewed balloon	9.7
$r_E + 4.0 \times 10^5$	space-shuttle orbit	8.7
$r_E + 4.0 \times 10^7$	communication satellite	0.19

Table 5.2: Approximate gravitational accelerations due to separations, r, from the Earth's centre

†Notes:
► It is key to appreciate that objects in space, largely, are immune to mundane matters such as normal force and friction, and are free to roam along complex orbital paths guided solely by the gravitation of all others.
► Newton's universal gravitation notably applies generally, contrasting with Section 3.7's special case of nearby the Earth's surface.

††With each always first treated as a particle at its instantaneous centre of mass, arbitrary numbers of bodies may be accommodated by treating the net force on each as the instantaneous vector sum of the contributions from all others.

A **barycentre** is the centre of mass of multiple bodies, and notably acts as an inertial frame of reference.

†††But the manifestation of $\mathbf{a}_g$ depends on the initial conditions. Following Section 2.5, if there is no tangential velocity, $\mathbf{a}_g$ acts to accelerate the bodies towards one another, but typically $\mathbf{a}_g$ contributes to centripetal acceleration and orbit.

Furthermore, the calculation of orbital paths is a perennial problem:
► Newton solved the case of an isolated pair of gravitating bodies, such that each harmonically (Section 2.7) orbits their **barycentre**.
► Otherwise complex integral and numerical techniques, such as introduced by Von Hoerner (1960, 1963), are required since even with only three bodies there is no general solution.

Notes following Table 5.2:

►The Earth's gravitational acceleration varies strongly with height.

►The quoting of g to two significant figures, at 9.8 m s^{-2}, is realistic in the absence of precise local knowledge†.

►Following Newton's third law (Section 3.4), and the same line of argument, the m_2 mass must also attractively accelerate m_1, but with significant caveats††.

►In rigorously treating the special case of two isolated gravitating bodies, both Newtonian accelerations align with the axis of their centres of mass and are directed towards their barycentre.

5.1.3   Potential energy

Section 5.1.2 gives the force **F** of universal gravitation as $\mathbf{F} = -Gm_1m_2r^{-2}\hat{\mathbf{r}}$ and, from Section 3.11, is both conservative, and where a change ΔU of potential energy is $\Delta U = -\int\mathbf{F}.\mathbf{dr}$. Radial integration between initial and final values of r, now yields the **general** ΔU formula $\Delta U = -Gm_1m_2r_{\text{final}}^{-1} + Gm_1m_2r_{\text{initial}}^{-1}$, which furthermore suggests $U = -Gm_1m_2r^{-1}$ as an expression of absolute potential energy. Such absolute U, although negative, sensibly provides a zero at infinite r, and decreases as r decreases†††.

5.1.4   Escape speed

Having sufficient initial kinetic energy $K_{\text{initial}} = -\frac{1}{2}m_2v_{\text{initial}}^2$ (Section 3.11), so that a body of mass m_2 can just reach infinite distance with $K_{\text{final}} = 0$, is a key requisite for that body to escape the gravitation of another of, say, mass m_1. For such a scenario, v_{final} is also zero, and v_{initial} is called the escape speed v_{escape}.

Then, with the assumption that the m_1 mass being departed is an inertial frame of reference, such v_{escape} may be calculated as follows:

►As per Section 3.11, the escaping m_2 mass has a change ΔK of kinetic energy given by $\Delta K = \frac{1}{2}m_2[v^2]_{\text{escape}}^{\text{final}} = -\frac{1}{2}m_2v_{\text{escape}}^2$.

†This is because r_E can vary by about 0.5% across the Earth's surface.

††The Earth's $\mathbf{a}_\text{g}$ will not only be small due to typical m_2 masses being very small, but it is to be remembered as correctly observed only from inertial frames of reference, and certainly not from the likely strongly accelerating frame of m_2:

In general applications of Newtonian physics, it is critical to ensure that the chosen reference frame is sufficiently inertial. In particular:

►Barycentres are ideal.

►Newton's starry backdrop is rigorous but inconvenient.

►Centres of overwhelming mass are likely good approximations.

►But centres of low mass should be excluded as likely strongly accelerating.

Such a **general** ΔU formula contrasts with the analysis of Section 3.13, which indicates $\Delta U = m_2g\Delta y$ for a mass m_2 undergoing small vertical movements Δy near the Earth's surface, and where g is the nearby magnitude of acceleration. It is left as an exercise to check equivalence of the two ΔU formulae near the Earth's surface.

†††Note that such decreases in U mean that, as would be expected, a positive amount of gravitational potential energy is released as r decreases.

†Since this ΔU is positive, the system gains gravitational potential energy upon the escape.

††But all assumptions should be identified and their impact assessed – e.g:
►That gravitation is conservative.
►That the Earth's m_1 mass is large.
►That the Earth is an inertial frame of reference whose geometric centre approximates the system's barycentre (Section 5.1.2).
►That the system of m_1 and m_2 is isolated – i.e. that there is negligible gravitational influence from any other masses.
►That the rocket's propulsion starts and stops at $r_{initial} = R$, and confers no change of mass.
►That the rocket's motion is radial (but not tangential) relative to the Earth.

Such an *absence*, and its implicit assumption of instantaneous interaction and observation, mean that Newtonian physics would progressively fail in cases of increasingly remote gravitation should there, indeed, be such a limit.

Notes on *acceleration:*
►Newtonian physics is limited to coordinate based calculations relative to inertial frames of reference.
►Its true (usually called proper) values are reference-frame invariant, directly measurable e.g. via accelerometers, and are frequently handled within advanced treatments of relativity – including those of Einstein's special theory.

►With the motion of m_2 taken as being from the $r_{initial} = R$ radius of the m_1 body to $r_{final} = \infty$, Section 5.1.3 indicates the system of m_1 and m_2 to have a ΔU change in gravitational potential energy (Section 5.1.3) given by $\Delta U = Gm_1m_2R^{-1}$†.

►And, assuming the system of m_1 and m_2 to be isolated, Section 3.11's law of conserved mechanical energy, $\Delta K + \Delta U = 0$, gives the result $v_{escape} = (2Gm_1)^{\frac{1}{2}}R^{-\frac{1}{2}}$††.

5.1.5 Beyond Newton

Newton's laws (Sections 3.2-3.4 and 5.1.2) are excellent for describing much observed motion, and notably provide the understanding to launch people into space (Section 5.1.4) and get them back. Under most scenarios such laws are adequate.

But, an *absence* of limit on speed, together with the quaint Newtonian notions of absolute space and need for the stars as a practical frame of reference (Section 3.1), represent limitations that prompted further works by:
►Einstein (1905[b]) on the special theory of relativity, which addresses the limits of motion and interaction relative to any inertial frame of reference (Section 3.2).
►Einstein (1905[c]) on how mass relates to Einstein's special theory.
►Minkowski (1909) on four-coordinate (x,y,z,t) space-time as a mathematical reformulation of Einstein's special theory.
►Einstein (1916) on the general theory of relativity, which further addresses accelerating frames of reference, and the origin of gravitation.

The first postulate of Einstein's special theory of relativity: Whilst specifically making no comment on *acceleration*, and rejecting Newtonian absolutism in space and need for the stars as a practical frame of reference, Einstein postulated that the laws of physics take the same simplest form for all inertial frames of reference, where the maxim of significance is the relativity of position and velocity as referenced against any inertial frame, and the accordant lack of differentiation between inertial frames confers impossibility of any experiment in ascribing absolute position or velocity†††.

The second postulate of Einstein's special theory of relativity: This postulate is that the speed c of light in **free space** pertains to all inertial frames of reference, irrespective of the motion of its source†.

The special theory's implications with regard to inertial frames of reference: With much inspiration from his mentor Minkowski, Einstein deduced the equation $E_0 = mc^2$ of equivalence between rest energy E_0 and mass m, and, confirming the **Lorentz transforms** of space and time, further deduced changes of length and time to be attributed between frames under v of relative speed, and for such relativistic changes to become extreme as v approaches c. Accordingly:

►With c thus suggested as a universal limit of relative speed and interaction, Einstein indicated simultaneity not to be absolute for spatially separated events††.

►Einstein famously deduced the following two counter-intuitive – but observationally confirmed and potentially extreme – deviations from Newtonian physics relative to any inertial frame of reference: contracted length, and dilated (slowed) time†††.

Einstein's general theory of relativity: By including both accelerating frames of reference and gravitation, Einstein conceived the general theory of relativity in which the laws of physics take the same form for all frames of reference (whether inertial or not):

Free space is discussed in the introduction to Chapter 4.

†Suppose a space traveller, seen as moving at close to c, emits a pulse of light. Then both would be seen as moving almost together. But the space traveller still sees their pulse moving away at c.

Lorentz transforms are relativistic spatio-temporal coordinate transformations between inertial frames of reference.

††Thus such events, even if seen at one time in one frame, may be seen at different times in another.

†††An often visited example, that even Einstein (1918) considered his special theory unable to resolve, is the so-called twin paradox, which concerns how a homely twin and an excursing twin can have seemingly similar relative experiences yet, upon reunion, the excursionist has greater overall time dilation, and less aging.

But there is no paradox because the two experiences are not the same, with key attendant facts being (1) the twins having different relativities such that the homely twin sees the relativity of the excursionist, and the excursionist sees the relativity of the spatial interval of home and their turn-around point, and (2) the twins needing to reunite before each can realise the relativity of the other.

First, Einstein postulated the principle of the equivalence of gravitation and acceleration, wherein a person standing on scales at the bottom of an opaque box cannot tell whether that box is at rest on the Earth's surface or accelerating through space at about 9.8 m s^{-2}, and accordingly that experiments performed in a non-accelerating reference frame, where gravitational acceleration is equal to g, are indistinguishable from those that are performed in a reference frame that is uniformly accelerating at g.

Second, Einstein propounded that gravitation arises from the presence of mass and energy curving Minkowski's four-coordinate space-time, and that the dynamics of such curvature dictate how matter moves and evolves.

The culmination of Einstein's works†:

►Thus generalises his own special theory.

►Fully departs from Newtonian physics by dispensing with the concept of gravitational force, and thus provides a fundamentally different and unique treatment of interaction.

►Is the most successful theory of gravitation, with Table 5.3 listing its notable successes††.

<table>
<tr><td>

►Explanation of the precession of the perihelion of Mercury's orbit over time.

►Explanation of lensing of light by gravitation whereby, for example, the propagation direction from a distant astronomical body is changed, causing multiple images to be seen.

►Explanation of the wavelength of light being seen to increase – so-called red-shifting – when its propagation is subject to gravitation.

►Prediction of high-energy events inducing outward propagating ripples in space-time known as gravitational waves – later discovered at the Laser Interferometer Gravitational-Wave Observatory, California (2015).

►Prediction of *black holes* – although doubted by Einstein, but subsequently confirmed.

</td></tr>
</table>

Table 5.3: Notable successes of Einstein's general theory of relativity

---

†With particular reference to the preceeding note †††, such works:

►Notably indicate that, in Minkowski's space-time, the time experienced between two events is maximum for inertial observers – a fact which applies to the homely twin, but not necessarily the excursing one.

►Have variously been used to treat the paradox – but, as a detailed mathematical example, Muller's (2016) approach ranges over the Lorentz transforms, inertial and non-inertial frames, and simultaneity.

††Nonetheless, conundrums remain such as:

►The existence of cosmic *dark matter*.

►Current incompatibility with quantum physics.

Dark matter: Heralded by the brilliant work of Zwicky (1933) on galactic discrepancies in mass, an astonishing approximate 84% of all matter is now taken to be in some dark state that cannot be detected. While, the nature of such dark matter thus remains obscure, it is deemed necessary for there to be sufficient gravitation to accord with observed galactic motion.

A *black hole* is the end-state of a massive star – a region where both space and time are so gravitationally distorted that nothing, not even light, can escape. A large black hole may also exist at the centre of each galaxy.

5.2   Electricity

Fundamentally involving an attribute of matter known as charge (see Section 5.2.1), the physics of electricity is loosely considered here to conflate the treatments of:

► Charges in atoms†.

► Charges at rest – referred to as electrostatics.

► Charges in motion††.

5.2.1   Charge, atoms, and ions

Arguably more complex than mass (Section 2.9), the attribute of charge is more discriminating, and while (like mass) is algebraically additive, it can (unlike mass) also be negative. Some charged entities are presented in Table 5.4†††:

†Always inclusive of intra-atomic motion as a key attribute, treatment also notably involves quantum probability.

††Inclusive of intra-atomic quantum probability as well as extra-atomic classical determinism, the treatment of charges in motion notably includes both relativity (Section 5.1.5), and magnetism (see Section 5.3).

†††Charged entities have non-zero net charge.

Entity	Underlying quantisation		Net charge	
electron	as itself – it is believed to have no internal structure and thus to be fundamental		defined as $e = -\,1.602176634 \times 10^{-19}$ C, where C is the symbol for the derived SI unit of charge known as the coulomb.	
proton	taken to comprise a number of so-called gluons	$-\,2e/3$, $-\,2e/3$ and $+\,e/3$	$-\,e$	Associated note: ***Quarks*** are entities whose existence is inferred from the fleeting products of artificial high-energy particle collisions.
neutron	that bind a triplet of ***quarks*** with charges of	$e/3$, $e/3$ and $-\,2e/3$	0	
atom	entity with equal numbers of protons and electrons		0	
ion	atom having lost or gained electrons		$\pm\, n \times e$, where $n = 1,2,3, \dots$, and where + represents a loss, and – a gain	
universe	-		strongly believed to be zero	

Table 5.4: Some notable entities, and their associated quantisation and net charge

Each of Table 5.4's atoms may lose or gain electrons to exist as an ion, but ordinarily otherwise is the **stable** natural structure of:

► either one proton, or a tightly bound collection thereof, representing at least in part a so-called nucleus:

► around which are electrons of equivalent number that are relatively loosely bound at roughly increasing average distances dependent on their energy,

► but within which may also be tightly bound neutrons.

Stable entities do not spontaneously decay into lower energy states and, if not subject to external influence, may exist forever:

► Electrons and protons are widely considered stable.

► But neutrons confound: They have stability conferred through nuclear binding, but otherwise spontaneously decay within about 15 minutes into a proton, an electron, and a so-called anti-neutrino.

5.2.2 Coulomb's electrostatics

Coulomb (1785) underpinned the physics of **electrostatics** offering the law that two stationary spheres with opposite net charges (Section 5.2.1) mutually attract with a force that is proportional to both net charges, and with an inverse-square relationship with their separation.

A formulation of Coulomb's law for electrostatic particles is that the electric force $\mathbf{F}$ exerted by a first charge q_1 on a second charge q_2 is given by $\mathbf{F} = kq_1q_2r^{-2}\,\hat{\mathbf{r}}$, where k is a medium-dependent constant whose value in air is about 9.0×10^9 N m^2 C^{-2}, $\hat{\mathbf{r}}$ is a positive unit vector specifying the direction from the position of q_1 to that of q_2, and r is the intervening distance. To summarise, the electric forces associated with two electrostatic particles†:

►Are directed along the straight line joining the two particulate positions.

►Are attractive if the charges are of opposite signs, and repulsive if the same.

►Are reciprocal due to Newton's third law (Section 3.4).

►May be vectorially summed.

►Provide a complete system description only when the particles remain stationary relative to the frame of reference, hence the term electrostatic††.

Moreover, although similar in form to the law of universal gravitation (Section 5.1.2), the two laws can yield forces of remarkably different magnitude. In particular, the ratio $(kq_1q_2)/(Gm_1m_2)$ evaluates to an incredible 2×10^{39} for a proton and electron. Thus at a local level, where net charges are significant, electric forces overwhelmingly dominate†††.

5.2.3 Electric equilibrium, energy, and voltage

While electric equilibrium and zero associated potential energy (Section 3.11) imply some uniformity of charge distribution, they could not

---

The physics of *electrostatics* concerns charges at rest relative to some frame of reference (Section 2.1).

†For electrostatic bodies of charge, it may be appropriate to evaluate the vectorial sum of all applicable particulate force contributions.

††But remember that, where there is involvement of atoms and motion, relativity (Section 5.1.5) and magnetism (see Section 5.3) may also be significant.

†††Notes:
►Nonetheless, with applicability of the further attribute of mobility, large-scale values of net charge tend to zero, allowing gravitational forces to dominate.
►The mobility and possible opposing sign of charge enable dynamic shielding devices that negate the effect of approaching charge.
►But mass offers no such shielding – its nearest possible condition is that of so-called weightlessness, where the only force experienced by an object is gravitational – as usually applies to objects in space.

apply to an unrestrained uniform arrangement of like charges due to internal coulombic repulsion (Section 5.2.2). But they could apply to a uniform arrangement of $+q$ and $-q$ charges, where not only does the zero net charge act with zero large-scale external electric force, but there is also a tending to zero of local internal electric force†.

Conversely, moving any internal charge from its position of equilibrium requires counteraction of growing internal coulombic forces (Section 5.2.2) and consequential raising of the charge's electric potential energy. The scenario is usefully quantified by the concept of voltage such that if, on traversing between any two points in space, a charge q undergoes a change ΔU in electric potential energy, then there is said to be a voltage V between those two points according to the **definition** $V = \Delta U/q$††.

Furthermore, following the general tendency of systems to lose energy – such as via conversion into heat (Section 4.1) – should, between two subsequent points in space, all ΔU be lost (and there be consequential return to equilibrium), then there is an associated voltage of $-V$ referred to as a voltage drop. Conversely, should there be continuously maintained action of the voltage rises and drops, then there is provision of a new mobile-charge based equilibrium, and the operative basis of electrical circuits.

5.2.4   Electrons as cathode rays

Crookes (1879) showed that some form of charged ray can propagate between a separated pair of metallic terminals across which is a high voltage (Section 5.2.3) and between which is a strong vacuum†††.

With the metallic terminals becoming either an **anode** or **cathode** depending on the sense – a.k.a. polarity – of connection to the voltage-source, it was further found that the

†Note, generally, that charge within equilibrated systems is distributed according to mobility dictated by both the internal structure and the conditions at the boundary of the host medium.

Such a **definition** has signage that is arbitrary, but by convention. Specifically, if ΔU is positive, then:
►A positive charge q is associated with the voltage V being positive.
►A negative charge q, however, is associated with the voltage V being negative.

††Note that such voltage V:
►Has derived SI units of J C^{-1}, usually designated as V, the volt.
►Is often applied by some external source.
►Is better not to be called by the common metaphor electromotive force – voltage is not a force.

†††The work was based on a so-called Crookes' tube; an evacuated glass tube with a metallic terminal hermetically entering at each end where:
►The internal vacuum was less than 1 Pa – i.e. at least five orders of magnitude (Section 1.5) lower than atmospheric.
►A typical tube length was a few tens of cm.
►At least 10^5 V was applied between the terminals.

An **anode** terminal may supply positive charge.

A **cathode** terminal may supply negative charge.

†While Thomson became attributed as the discoverer of the electron, and electrons then became recognised as fundamental entities present in all atoms, Stoney proposed as early as 1874 for atoms to have elemental units of electricity.

The so-called *Lorentz* force is a general combined electric and magnetic formulation, often used in classical electrodynamic applications. But its electric part is simply $F = qE$.

††Notes:
►With the unknown body being electrostatic, it has an unchanging E_{ub} field.
►The charge distribution within the unknown body should not be perturbed by the mapping procedure. Thus q_{test} should be as small as possible.
►At the instant of each F_{test} measurement, q_{test} should be stationary.
►$E_{ub} = F_{test}/q_{test}$ is ideally a function only of the unknown body (and not of q_{test}) because if q_{test} is changed by some factor, F_{test} ideally changes by the same factor, leaving the ratio unchanged.
►The determined E_{ub} has the same direction as F_{test} since the q_{test} is positive.
►E_{ub} has derived SI units of both $N\ C^{-1}$ and $V\ m^{-1}$, indicating an equivalence between the magnitude of electric field and the spatial gradient of voltage (Section 5.2.3). Thus between any two positions, if there is zero field, then there is also zero spatial gradient of voltage.

mysterious rays propagated regardless of the type of metal, travelled in straight lines, and always be emitted from the cathode. Such cathode rays were thus indicated to be negatively charged, named as electrons by Stoney (1894), and proffered by Thomson (1897) as widespread, very low mass, constituents of atoms†.

However, ongoing discussion may still refer to cathode rays in the context of cathode-ray tubes. Here are some examples:

Known as thermionic emission, heating of the cathode terminal, combined with it being of durable metal such as tungsten, enables an intense sustained beam of cathode rays to be emitted. And, known as a cathode-ray gun, if the tube's anode has a central hole, many cathode rays may evade capture and exit, with a relative speed of up to about $c/10$, as an airborne beam.

In oscilloscopes and old television displays the cathode rays are retained within an enlarged tube, and a precise electromagnetic system steers them across an internal fluorescent or phosphorescent layer that is bonded to part of its inside surface. Visible emission from that layer can then result in a temporally changing image, which can safely be seen from the outside.

5.2.5 Electric field, and the Faraday cage

Electric forces (Section 5.2.2) are often expressed as so-called fields, and visualised as empirically derived vector representations known as electric field maps. Given an unknown electrostatic body, here is a possible evaluative procedure:

Measure the magnitude and direction of the associated electric force F_{test} that acts on a known particulate positive test charge q_{test} at a large number positions around the unknown body. Then, following *Lorentz* (1915), compile the electric E_{ub} field map of the unknown body defined as $E_{ub} = F_{test}/q_{test}$††.

The E_{ub} map may be depicted as a set of lines whose density indicates magnitude, and whose directions show the direction of the force experienced by the positive test charge†.

If the unknown body is of separated point-charges $+q$ and $-q$, the map is like that of Figure 5.1††.

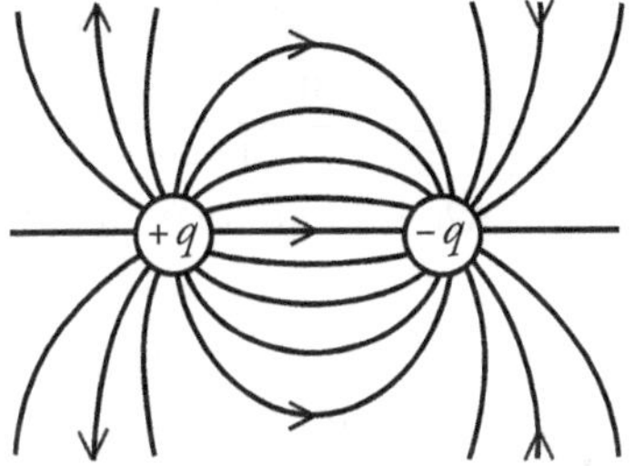

Note:
Arrows show
some
representative
directions

Figure 5.1: 2D field map for an electrostatic dipole

With the 3D symmetry of any rotation about the straight line joining the point-charges, and with a density of lines and field-magnitudes that increase towards the charge-centres, there is clearly local exemplification of coulombic attraction of the positive q_{test} to $-q$. But, in the far distance, the strength of any interaction falls away significantly faster than an inverse square law due to the dipole's zero net charge.

The E_{ub} map may then be used to calculate its associated force F exerted on an arbitrary external electrostatic point-charge Q according to $F = QE_{ub} = QF_{test}/q_{test}$†††.

But, now suppose a closed shell is introduced to the vicinity of an electric E field. Mobile charges within that shell will then redistribute in the direction of E if positive (and opposite if negative), inducing an electric field that opposes E. With sufficient redistribution of charge, equilibrium (Section 5.2.3) will be reached with zero field, and zero spatial gradient of voltage everywhere over the closed shell. The closed shell is then known as a **Faraday cage** that excludes E, as well as preventing external charge from being detected internally and vice versa.

†If the unknown body is a point-charge q, then E_{ub} would comprise a uniform set of radial lines that are directed outwards if q is positive, and inwards if q is negative.

††Notes:
►Such separation of charge is called an electric dipole, and any process causing such separation is called polarisation.
►Electric dipoles have zero net charge.

†††Notes:
►This F is in the direction of E_{ub} if Q is positive, and opposite otherwise.
►The same overall concept can be applied to each electrostatic point-charge within an external body.

Whilst a **Faraday cage** does not block magnetic fields (see Section 5.3.3):
►It can absorb or reflect approaching electric energy if the thickness of its walls exceeds the characteristic penetration depth known as the skin depth.
►It can block electromagnetic waves (Section 4.3.7) due to their containing of an electric-field component, but only if its walls have no voids larger than the propagating wavelength.

It can thus act as a radio-frequency shield or as the case of a microwave oven, if operating respectively in the radio or microwave bands of Maxwell's electromagnetic rainbow (Section 4.3.7).

5.2.6 Response of charge to an electric field

Holding charge stationary: A charge q in an electric field $\mathbf{E}$ may become stationary if the electric force $\mathbf{F} = q\mathbf{E}$ (Section 5.2.5) acting on it is counteracted by a compensatory force. Such was the scenario of Millikan (1913), who performed a classic oil-drop experiment in which the compensatory force of gravity held stationary a body q of charge, and allowed calculation of the charge of an electron:

Generating the oil drops as a fine mist caused some to acquire one or more electrons, giving a net charge q. Drops falling under gravity were viewed with a horizontally aligned microscope, an electric field $\mathbf{E}$ was applied vertically, and then $\mathbf{E}$ was varied in magnitude until a selected drop just became stationary.

Then, with reference against an inertial (Section 3.2) y-axis arbitrarily chosen to be increasing vertically downwards, and with $\mathbf{E}$ likewise designated as acting downwards, the constant-mass Newtonian second law (Section 3.3) may be applied to the drop as $qE_y + mg = 0$, giving $q = -\,mg/E_y$†.

Such q was determined by Millikan to be negative – due to E_y always being positive – and with a value, on repeated runs of the experiment, equivalent to a natural number multiplied by approximately $-\,1.592 \times 10^{-19}$ C. Such an approximate negative quantity was thus taken as the electronic charge e††.

Dynamic applications: Whilst no longer having the simplicity of an electrostatic scenario, Thomson (1897) demonstrated a beam of cathode rays to have a lateral deflection opposite to a perpendicularly applied positive electric $\mathbf{E}$ field. And, of course, even more complex movements of the beam are feasible if the applied $\mathbf{E}$ changes in time.

†Resolved in the downwards direction, the associated force components are:
► qE_y electric.
► mg gravitational near the Earth's surface (Section 3.7), where m is the mass of the drop, and g is the magnitude of the near-surface gravitational acceleration.

††The electronic charge e is now defined as $-\,1.602176634 \times 10^{-19}$ C.

5.3   Magnetism

With **lodestone** as a well-known example, Nature endows materials with **long-lived** magnetism having the distinctive properties that:

►Dependent on their macroscopic alignments, they can attract or repel one another.

►They can also become mutually interactive with a variety of other materials by inducing within them a largely action-time-limited temporary magnetism†.

Concentrating first on permanent magnetism, that of lodestone and similarly magnetic materials is fundamentally conferred through the internal structure and organisation of the constituent atoms (Section 5.2.1):

5.3.1   Atoms as magnetic media

Introduction – angular momentum, fermions, spin, and orbit: An initial appreciation of atomic magnetism is possible by first transforming Huygens' classical consideration of momentum (Section 3.8) – via radical change – into the quantum world††.

This quantum world of momentum is where new rules apply wherein the pertinent form is angular, and its values are treated as multiples of discrete, so-called quantised, amounts. Pertinent entities are so-called fermions – principally electrons, protons, and neutrons, and their constituent quarks (Section 5.2.1).

Each such fermion is considered always to carry an intrinsic quantised angular momentum referred to as spin, whose values are notable as always being of the same fixed magnitude†††.

But fermions are also considered to have additional quantised angular momentum when bound within atoms. Theoretically, each such consideration arises from the associated instantaneous assignment of space, or so-called orbital, indicating the likely range of fermionic

Lodestone is a natural form of iron oxide.

Long-lived, in relation to magnets, is often metaphorically called permanent.

†Certain metals, for example, do not interact with each other, but still have mutual attraction with a permanent magnet.

††Such transformative change is a starkly abrupt treatment of the very small that will be appreciated to conflict with known classical treatments. For further exemplification, see:
►For example, Kok (2023) for deeper introduction.
►Dirac (1928) on the quantisation of spin based angular momentum.
►Schrödinger (1926) on the quantisation of atomic orbital angular momentum.

†††Notes:
►The spin of fermions is assigned a quantisation number of ± ½. The positive value is referred to as spin-up, and the other as spin-down.
►And the size of the associated angular momenta is treated as the ± ½ quantisation number multiplied by $h/(2\pi)$.
►Fermionic spin underpins the existence, structure, and properties of the chemical elements, and thus *inter alia* helps to explain periodic-table based chemistry.
►For unbound fermions, spin helps *inter alia* to describe stellar interiors, the solar wind, and high-energy beams.

†Notes:
►Schrödinger's quantum physics subsumes ideas of particle-based wavelength and circular standing waves to specify each orbital as a unique space-dependent pattern of probability of finding an atomic fermion.
►By not commenting on the fermion's actual position, such physics holds as invalid the deterministic classical concept of orbital path.
►Conversely, instantaneous measurements of position are possible, in principle, with arbitrary precision:
►But, then, note the supplementary uncertainty principle of Heisenberg (1927) which considers angular momentum as position's conjugate variable that fundamentally cannot be simultaneously so measured. Thus, with the principle acting both ways, if one of the two conjugate variables becomes well known, the other simultaneously cannot.

Hund enunciated rules carrying the general principle that an atom's fermions inherently take levels of lowest available energy.

Pauli enunciated the so-called exclusion principle on Hund's rules that an atom's fermions must be in different quantum states – and thus, for example, each orbital can contain at most two similar fermions as long as their spins are opposite.

positions. And atoms may have numerous fermions and numerous theoretically assigned orbitals†.

Energetic ordering of an atom's fermions: **Hund** (1925) and **Pauli** (1925) helped understand atomic structure by elucidating the energetic ordering of its orbitals. With the associated spin-up designation arbitrarily associated with lower energy, discussion follows relating to electrons, protons and neutrons:

►For the peripheral electrons, the orbital of lowest energy is first accommodated by a spin-up electron, which may then become paired with a higher energy spin-down electron. And such a pairing process continues with higher energy orbitals until all the atom's electrons are accommodated. There are two broad outcomes. If the pairing is complete, the electrons contribute zero net spin to the atom. But, if an unpaired electron remains, there is a net $+ \frac{1}{2}$ spin-up contribution.

►For the protons and neutrons, an atom's nucleus is also treated according to the filling of orbitals and pairing of spins. But there are significant differences in manifestation:

First, while electrons are considered unstructured – and thus fundamental – protons and neutrons are treated as triplets of quarks (Section 5.2.1), where the triplet for protons is different to that for neutrons, and all constituent quarks are treated as fermions and hence each has a spin quantisation of $\pm \frac{1}{2}$.

Second, while it is not understood how such quark-triplets reflect the $\pm \frac{1}{2}$ net spin quantisation of protons and neutrons, there are three pairing outcomes, as outlined opposite in Table 5.5:

1	Most nuclei with even numbers of both protons and neutrons have zero net spin. This is because protons of opposite spins pair-up to give zero net spin, and the same is true for the neutrons.
2	Nuclei can have a net spin quantisation of $+\frac{1}{2}$ when there is an odd number of protons or neutrons.
3	However, there is also a new possibility of proton-neutron pairing having a spin quantisation of $+1$. This can happen, still following the enunciations of Hund and Pauli, if the pairing is in the same spin direction and the resultant paired state is of lower energy†.

Table 5.5: Possibilities for the net spin of atomic nuclei

Origin of atomic magnetism: Spin-based and orbital angular momentum may be combined as a vector sum to give a consideration of the total, or net, angular momentum. Furthermore, following Haus and Penfield (1968), such net atomic angular momentum is considered equivalent to that of a similarly axially aligned north/south pair of magnetic poles known as a magnetic dipole††.

Atoms with non-zero net angular momentum thus act as magnets. Nonetheless, orbital contributions are often small, and are even taken to be zero for atoms of the lowest (so-called ground-state) energy. The external strength of such atomic magnets, then being dominated by spin, thus depends on the final state of fermionic orbital pairing. Unpaired electrons tend to be the strongest contributors but, otherwise, nuclear contributions, although weakened by intervening electronic shielding, can be significant.

Bulk-atomic magnetism, and magnetic domains: When many atoms constitute a medium, the contribution of each to the medium's net angular momentum needs to be considered. But usually such contributions are in random directions, and tend to average out. Such bulk angular momentum is said to be quenched.

†The simplest example is the hydrogen isotope deuterium, whose nucleus (one proton and one neutron) has a net spin quantisation of $+1$.

††Notes:
► Magnetic monopoles were theoretically predicted by Dirac (1931), however, none have been discovered, and they are widely presumed not to exist.
► In the apparent absence of magnetic monopoles, the dipolar analogy of net atomic angular momentum prevails.
► Nonetheless, remember that any such analogy is a theoretical abstraction due to the non-separability of the individual poles as independent entities:

The cutting of a bar magnet into two parts, for example, simply creates two weaker bar magnets, each with their own north and south poles.

Magnetic domains, ordinarily:
► Are small – i.e. about 5×10^{-5} m in size, and only just visible under a microscope.
► Are of mutually random disposition.
► Have, in bulk, no large-scale external magnetism.

†Bulk permanent magnets:
► May be classified as ferromagnetic or ferrimagnetic, but actually comprise various metals, alloys, and rare earths.
► Can arise from a strong external magnetic field (see Section 5.3.3) together with some combination of heat and pressure.
► Can be natural – lodestone, for example, is ferrimagnetic.
► Can be made artificially.
► Can degrade naturally over lengthy periods of time.
► Can be fully demagnetised via severe environmental conditions. For example, upon reaching the so-called Curie temperature (about 1.043×10^3 K in iron), extreme thermal agitation returns the domain structure to its ordinarily non-magnetic state.

††In the most extreme ferrimagnetic case, the opposite contributions are of equal magnitude, and their mutual cancellation is complete, leading to no large-scale external magnetism at all.

†††Such electric currents, in a generalised sense, can thus be considered as embracing the determinism of the classical world, and the probabilism of the quantum one.

Furthermore, in bulk media where significant angular momentum remains – a few types of metal, alloy, and rare earth – that momentum is usually dominated by electronic spin. Clearly, unpaired electrons must exist within the atoms of such media. But the associated electronic spins must also be in extended alignment. The latter condition applies to ordered (crystalline) arrangements of atoms referred to as **magnetic domains**. With the internal unpaired electronic spins then being in bound alignment, such domains are stable and individually magnetic.

But, for there to be significant bulk magnetism, the ordinarily existing magnetic domains need to be put into mutually bound alignment, and probably also increased in size. Such a process portends the strongest forms of bulk permanent magnets, whose two main manifestations are as follows†:

Ferromagnets: If spatially uniform, continuation of the process strengthens the medium as a so-called ferromagnet, attaining saturation in the ideal state of full bound alignment.

Ferrimagnets: But, if spatially non-uniform, the final state of full bound alignment will contain domains with opposite net electronic spins. The medium – now said to be a ferrimagnet – has a strength that is always less than its ferromagnetic counterpart due to reduced net electronic spin††.

5.3.2   Electric currents as magnetic media

Pertaining to any locality where there is movement of charge relative to some frame of reference (Section 2.1), electric currents can be considered as ranging from macroscopic charged flows of arbitrary path outside atoms, to putative charged motions inside (Section 5.3.1)†††.

Indeed, in the footsteps of Newton (Section 3.1) and Coulomb (Section 5.2.2), Ampère (1826) presented the revolutionary new physics of electrodynamics by:

►Demonstrating existence of an attractive force between similarly sensed elements of electric current (repulsive if opposite), and formulating such force as proportional to both currents, and inversely proportional to their separation†.

►Demonstrating the force from a current element as magnetic via its interaction with bulk atomic magnets.

►Considering the magnetism of bulk atomic magnets as also arising from the motion of charge, specifically at the level of the particles constituting the medium.

►Asserting that the fundamental origin of all magnetism is the motion of charge.

5.3.3   Magnetic field

Introduction: Sections 5.3.1 and 5.3.2 discussed two treatments by which a magnetic medium may interact with its environment – namely via the action of a magnetic dipole, or via the related action of an electric current. Nonetheless, both actions were considered by Ampère (Section 5.3.2) as due to charged motion, and both may be mapped in terms of magnetic field. Onward discussion covers possible mapping processes and gives two key examples††:

Qualitative mapping: A simple qualitative approach to mapping a static magnetic field involves a **magnetisable** medium such as iron, which is finely filed, scattered within the vicinity, and agitated so as to accrue density and structure that reflect the pattern of the field.

Quantitative mapping: Due to the absence of probing magnetic monopoles (Section 5.3.1), the qualitative mapping of a magnetic field requires more ingenuity†††.

But consider the effect on a probing magnetic dipole which, as the basis of a magnetic compass, may immediately be used to measure the alignment of the **Earth's** magnetic field:

Indeed, if free to pivot, the dipole twists, with its north pole moving in the direction of the

†While each such current element is straight, in aggregate they can be used to build a path of any shape. Furthermore, over large scales, currents must form closed loops – as in, for example, electrical circuits (see Section 6.4) – and then, following Haus and Penfield (1968), the distant magnetic behaviour is that of a magnetic dipole (Section 5.3.1).

††Note that, although Ampère dealt only with the concept of magnetic force (Section 5.3.2), the associated magnetic field:
►Is the key new effect outside of electrostatics (Section 5.2.2).
►And that, once mapped, may be used – via analogy with the electric case (Section 5.2.5) – to calculate the magnetic force that may be exerted on a neighbouring magnetic medium.

Magnetisable is the ability to become magnetic – a state that is often only of temporary duration.

†††In practice, various technologies and analytic procedures are employed, but a basic magnetometer, for example, uses a metallic coil as a sensing element.

Notably, the **Earth** acts as a permanent magnet (Section 5.3.1) due to the convective circulation (Section 5.3.2) of its iron core. And, distinct from its geographic alignment, that of its associated magnetic field can even change over time due to the core's changing dynamics.

field and its south pole moving oppositely, until the dipole attains alignment with the field's local direction.

But, suppose the probe is also able to measure the strength of the local twisting action. The value of such so-called torque can then be combined with the probe's known dipole strength to calculate the magnitude of the local magnetic **B** field, expressed typically in terms of the derived SI unit known as the tesla (T)†.

Repeating the process at many locations allows the magnetic **B** field to be mapped with a density of lines that indicates magnitude, and appended arrows that show the direction of force that a magnetic north pole would experience.

Example 1 – map of a magnetic dipole: This has the form as in Figure 5.2††.

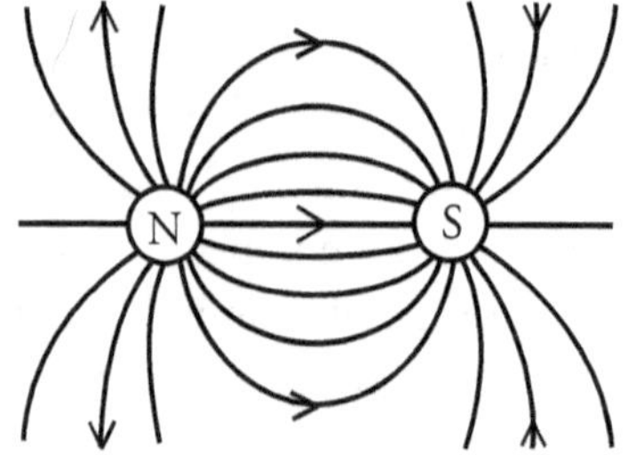

Figure 5.2: 2D field map for a static magnetic dipole – like that of a bar magnet or loop of current†††

Example 2 – magnetic map of a rectilinear electric current: Here, the field lines are circular and wrap around the axis of the current. Such lines effectively start and finish on themselves, so that notably there are no poles††††.

5.3.4 Response of current to a static magnetic field

Taking the broad view of current as any medium in which there is extra-atomic or intra-atomic charged motion (Section 5.3.2), Table 5.6, opposite, introduces for onward discussion six cases where such media may respond to an external static magnetic field (Section 5.3.3):

†Note that the probe must have minimal perturbation on the field being measured.

††Notes on Figure 5.2:
► It pertains to atomic magnets (Section 5.3.1) and electric currents around a closed loop (Section 5.3.2).
► It extends to 3D, due to symmetry, via any rotation about the dipolar axis.
► It highlights attraction between opposite poles, since a north pole would be repelled from N and attracted to S.
► Its density of lines and magnitude of field, increase with proximity to the poles.

†††But note that, as against the depicted N-S axis, there is assumed matched alignment of:
► The axis of the bar magnet.
► The axis of the loop of current (i.e. the loop would wrap around that same axis).

††††Note that, with extended coulombic action on a locally rectilinear current naturally forming a closed loop, there is an inevitable consistency between ampèrian force (Section 5.3.2) and dipolar magnetic field due e.g to:
(1) mutual attraction of similarly sensed coaxial loops via the facing of both similar current elements and opposite poles.
(2) mutual repulsion of oppositely sensed coaxial loops via the facing of both opposite current elements and like poles.

Case 1	Atomic beams
Case 2	Bulk permanent magnets (Section 5.3.1)
Case 3	Bulk so-called paramagnetic media
Case 4	Bulk so-called diamagnetic media
Case 5	Bulk resonating atomic fermions – both electronic and nuclear (Section 5.3.1)
Case 6	Electric current (Section 5.3.2)

Table 5.6: Cases for onward discussion – media that may respond to an external static magnetic field

Case 1 – atomic beams: At the time of an historic experiment by Stern and Gerlach (1922), there was no conception of electronic spin (Section 5.3.1) and no *classical* expectation for a magnetic field to have a directionally preferred effect on a propagating atomised beam. Nonetheless, the experiment's outcome was that a beam of silver atoms, passing through a strongly inhomogeneous magnetic field, split into two, tantalisingly suggesting the silver atoms to have some unidentified property:

Later, Uhlenbeck and Goudsmit (1926) provided an explanation in terms of electronic spin (Section 5.3.1): Because each atom of silver has 47 electrons, after pairing, one electron is *left over*, leaving a net spin of + ½. But there would also be a significant number of atoms with a higher-energy net spin of – ½. And the use of an inhomogeneous magnetic field would ensure a variation of force along each atom's magnetic dipole and a consequent up-or-down deflection, dependent on the sign of net spin, thus splitting the atomic beam into two.

Stern and Gerlach were first in the history of science to demonstrate, albeit unwittingly, the splitting of quantum states.

Case 2 – bulk permanent magnets: As per Section 5.3.3's discussion on the twisting of dipolar magnetic probes, bulk permanent magnets respond to an external field with their north poles moving in the direction of the field, and their south poles moving oppositely†.

For example, Larmor's (1897) *classical* treatment on how a magnetic field affects an atom's electrons would predict, at most, a modest general broadening of the beam.

With onward reference to Cases 3 and 4, such a *left-over* electron is indicative of a paramagnetic medium. But silver has anomalously weak paramagnetism, and is usually classified as diamagnetic.

†Notes on system stability and the popular myth of free magnetic energy:
► Systems of separated opposite poles have the instability of significant stored energy – their opposite poles would naturally move towards each other, with increasing rapidity until collision, to dissipate the stored energy as, say, kinetic energy or heat.
► Conversely, systems of separated like poles – with an assumed inhibition to twisting – would dissipate their energy via their poles moving apart, and offer the possibility of magnetically-sustained levitation.
► But, for the practical case of two arbitrarily orientated but unrestrained magnetic dipoles, the natural tendency is as follows: First, some stored energy is dissipated by their twisting into mutual N-S and S-N alignment. And the remaining dissipation is via mutual N-S and S-N motion until collision.

†Paramagnetic media include iron, aluminium, magnesium, manganese, platinum, titanium, and tungsten.

††The diamagnetic levitation of a frog by Berry and Geim (1997), for example, required about 16 T of magnetic field – i.e. even stronger than is used, say, in many of the practical applications of fermionic resonance (see Case 5).

Spectroscopy was introduced by Case 4 of Table 4.7 of Section 4.3.7.

(Aside: A complementary basis of evaluating light, pioneered by the University of Liverpool, is via the property of colour – for example, initial inventive work by Henderson (1988) exploits chromatic analysis via the ratiometric processing of two values of intensity (Section 4.3.3) measured over two different subsets of the overall spectrum. And, as a pertinent example, the electromagnetically robust implementation of Scully *et al.* (1994) combines traditional pulse oximetry with both fibre-optic transmission and differentially-absorptive sensory transduction to measure blood oxygenation and pulse rate of magnetic resonance patients.)

Due to its close quantum analogy, such **precession** of net spin is often called Larmor precession, even though Larmor's (1897) works concern classical orbital precession, and predate quantum physics.

Case 3 – bulk so-called paramagnetic media: Such media are attracted to regions of increased field magnitude due the field temporarily inducing alignment of their unpaired electronic spins. But practical applications require the absence of Case 2's aligned/enlarged magnetic domains because ferromagnetic behaviour is orders of magnitude greater†.

Case 4 – bulk so-called diamagnetic media: Such media are repelled from regions of increased field magnitude due the field temporarily inducing alignment of their electronic orbital motions. All media potentially apply, but the effect is especially weak, so that practical applications require a strong field, and the absence of Case 2 and Case 3 behaviours††.

Case 5 – bulk resonating atomic fermions: Finding numerous **spectroscopic** applications, and extending across electrons and nuclei, resonation of fermionic net spins within bulk atomic media (Section 5.3.1) concerns atomic net spins: (1) that mutually align with the axis of an external magnetic field, (2) which are kicked into a new off-axis alignment via the medium's atoms absorbing low-amplitude electromagnetic waves, (3) whose new alignment then rotates, or **precesses**, around the axis of the external field, (4) whose precessional frequency depends on both the field's magnitude and the medium's type of atoms, (5) whose precession is resonantly maintained via the frequency of the electromagnetic waves being matched to the precessional frequency, and (6) whose associated excited atoms subsequently relax via emission of new electromagnetic waves at the same precessional frequency.

Typically enabled by strong magnetic fields and cryogenically cooled superconducting technology, and coupled with subsequent spectroscopic analysis, the overall process offers non-destructive, selective investigation of atoms, and finds uses across the physical sciences and medicine where practical electronic and nuclear implementations are discussed as follows†:

►Electronic implementations exploit the resonant excitation of magnetically aligned net spins associated with unpaired electrons in bulk paramagnetic media – often called electronic paramagnetic resonance (EPR). With resonances typically up to a few hundred GHz, the acquisition and study of EPR spectra can be a highly effective means of understanding the properties, dynamics, and environment of any physical state of the relatively few stable instances of such paramagnetic media††.

►Nuclear implementations exploit the resonant excitation of magnetically aligned net spins of bulk atomic nuclei – often called nuclear magnetic resonance (NMR). With resonances typically in the hundreds of MHz, acquired NMR spectra are used not only to elucidate the structure, chemistry and kinetics of atoms and molecules, but also to construct 3D imagery†††:

If the magnitude of the magnetic field is spatially non-uniform, then the frequency of the resonance of a particular type of nucleus depends on position within the field. The spatial discrimination provides the imaging response, and with a resolution that increases with the magnitude of the field's gradient. Sophisticated control of the field and electromagnetic waves, relative to the sample, generates an array of 2D images from front to back, offering 3D analysis.

In the practice of **medicine**, NMR spectra are typically provided by the hydrogen nuclei in water molecules. Thus, while not suited to dry body-parts such as the periphery of bones, such spectra are routinely used to construct anatomical images of *inter alia* bone marrow, the abdomen, brain, lungs, muscles, tendons, ligaments and blood vessels. And, offering a

†Notes on practically implemented systems:
►Magnetic field magnitudes vary from a few hundred mT to over 20 T.
►Although applications range over atomic and molecular analysis, and even 3D imaging, they are all fundamentally based on using spectroscopic frequency and strength to determine, respectively, atomic type and quantity.

††Note that most such media are unsuitable due to energetic favourability of oxidising their environment to acquire electrons to fill their electronic orbitals.

†††Notes on NMR:
►Each atomic nucleus must have a non-zero net spin, such as when proton pairing or neutron pairing leaves a net spin of + ½, or when proton-neutron pairing leaves a net spin of + 1 (Section 5.3.1).
►It is a weak effect and is further subject to electronic shielding around the nucleus.
►Also to avoid its signal being swamped by EPR, it requires the absence of unpaired electrons.

For further introduction to NMR *medicine* see, for example, Keevil *et al.* (2024).

†Such so-called magnetic resonance imaging is safe, and its basic usage is not invasive (although contrast-enhancing agents may be taken internally for improved resolution).

††Notes:
► F_B is the magnetic part of Section 5.2.5's Lorentz force.
► F_B is perpendicular to both v and B due to the vector cross product, $v \times B$.
► The maximum of F_B is $q|v||B|$ when v and B are mutually perpendicular.
► If v is unconstrained, it deviates, but F_B remains perpendicular, resulting in no work done (Section 3.12) and no change of q's kinetic energy (Section 3.11).
► Associated deviations are generally much larger than in Case 1's quantum splitting of atomic beams.
► If v is constrained – say within a wire – F_B may do work on the constraint.
► F_B is consistent with Ampère's works (Section 5.3.2) by describing the action on a moving q in one wire due to the B of another.

†††Note that the product qV must be positive, as fulfilled by q and V both being negative.

††††Notes:
► With Lorentz recognised for extraordinary theoretical contribution to magnetism with a joint 1902 Nobel Prize, the Lorentz force, $F_E + F_B$, offers a general entry point to treating classical electrodynamics.
► For further introduction to such electrodynamics see, for example, Griffiths (2023).

typical spatial resolution of about 2 mm, the imaging detail is sufficient to expose injuries, tumours, and other abnormalities†.

Case 6 – electric current: Following Lorentz (1915), electric current responds to an external magnetic **B** field as $F_B = qv \times B$, where F_B is the associated magnetic force acting on each constituent charge q moving at velocity **v** relative to an inertial frame of reference (Section 3.2)††.

Thus, if there is no current, **v** and F_B are both zero, and a stationary charge remains stationary. But, if there is a current, **v** and F_B are both non-zero, and **v** will tend to deviate. Key examples are unconstrained beams of electrons (Section 5.2.4) and electric currents (Section 5.3.2) constrained within wires.

And, for the former example, an electric field (Section 5.2.5) also featured in a famous experiment by Thomson (1897) to quantify the charge to mass ratio q/m of the constituent electrons, where, relative to an inertial frame of reference, a beam of electrons from a cathode-ray tube (Section 5.2.4) was contrived have zero deviation when subjected to perpendicular, matched but opposite, magnetic F_B and electric F_E forces:

With charge q and mass m, each electron that leaves the tube's cathode is taken to lose qV of electric potential energy (Section 5.2.3) and, via its conversion, acquire speed $v = |v|$ and $\frac{1}{2}mv^2$ of kinetic energy (Section 3.11). Furthermore, following Section 3.11, is fulfilment of the energy conservation condition $- qV + \frac{1}{2}mv^2 = 0$†††.

Now, for each electron to have zero deviation, and thus have constant $|v|$ relative to an inertial frame of reference, the applicable net force F_{net} must be zero (Section 3.2). But F_{net} is the so-called Lorentz force $F_E + F_B$. Hence $F_E = qE$ and $F_B = qv \times B$ must be applied such that $qE + qv \times B = 0$††††.

For a large $q\mathbf{v} \times \mathbf{B}$, $\mathbf{B}$ is implemented perpendicular to $\mathbf{v}$, and so rearranging and taking the modulus-squared gives $|\mathbf{v}|^2|\mathbf{B}|^2 = |\mathbf{E}|^2$, which may be written as $v^2 = (E/B)^2$. Finally, with v^2 substituted into $qV = \frac{1}{2}mv^2$, the electronic q/m ratio becomes $q/m = \frac{1}{2}V^{-1}(E/B)^2$.

Thomson used various techniques to evaluate V, E, and B. And thence calculated the electronic q/m to be -1.76×10^{11} C kg^{-1}†.

5.3.5   Response of charge to a changing magnetic field

While a static magnetic field is known to affect a moving charge (Section 5.3.4), a changing magnetic field may act on a static charge to induce an electric current. Indeed, Faraday's famous **law of induction** (1832) is that a changing magnetic field causes a so-called electromotive force which, more appropriately identified as voltage (Section 5.2.3), induces electric current within **conductive media**. Two notable associated phenomena are eddy currents and the skin effect:

Eddy currents: First, assuming the existence of closed-loop conductive paths, the induced voltage will drive localised circulations of mobile charges known as eddy currents††.

Skin effect: But, wait, won't the induced eddy currents have their own magnetic fields? Yes, and their direction will, following **Lenz** (1834), oppose the external one. Thus, for a conductive medium with an induced changing current, there is an associated changing magnetic field whose direction is such as to cancel the cause of the induction.

For the specific geometry of a wire, the net effect is that current is cancelled in the interior, but actually enhanced, due to asymmetric conditions, at the periphery. Such a phenomenon is called the **skin effect**, and is often associated with repeated reversing of electric current, known as alternating current.

†Notes:
► The electronic q/m is now accepted as $-1.758\ 820\ 010\ 76(53) \times 10^{11}$ C kg^{-1}.
► The electronic mass m then follows from the known $q = e$ (Section 5.2.6).

Faraday's **law of induction** is key to understanding the operation of electrical equipment such as generators, motors, and transformers.

Conductive media have charge that is free to flow.

††Note that, if the medium resists these circulations, the eddy energy may be dissipated as heat — a key effect in inductive cookware, and in drop-tower breaking at amusement parks.

Lenz's law states that induced current has a direction that opposes the change that caused it.

Skin effect: So that, for example, a changing electric field (Section 5.2.3) applied along the length of a wire may initiate a changing electric current:
► That has a changing magnetic field (Section 5.3.7).
► That induces additional opposing circulating currents.
► That makes mobile charges tend to migrate to the surface, leaving the interior devoid of mobile charge and with negligible net field (Section 5.2.3).

So-called *Ampère's law:* Ampère (Section 5.3.3) notably never dealt with the concept of magnetic field. Nonetheless, the modern field-based rendition of his force-based works – that is universally presented and used today – is still called Ampère's law.

The *displacement current* of Maxwell is fundamentally significant:
►It implies a mutual embrace between changing electric and magnetic fields that allows their co-existence as a self-sustaining electromagnetic *field* that may propagate far from its originating accelerating charge. And, known as an electromagnetic wave, it is the same wave that, from Section 4.3.7, propagates at speed c in free space.
►Its manifestation as Maxwell's electromagnetic waves – or light – mediates force between electric charge, and completes the fundamental linkage between electricity and magnetism.
►It must be considered if the frequency is high enough to make it significant compared to electric current, or if electromagnetic radiation is deemed to be of interest.

Hitherto, *fields* have been used as a mathematical contrivance to quantify physical interaction. But the wave of an electromagnetic field is evident mediation. In fact, the modern physical approach uses quantised fields to treat most space-time (Section 5.1.5) borne interactions.

5.4   Electromagnetic unification

Introduction: Although neither approach is sufficient – with the treatment of atoms lacking relativity, and that of Ampère's electric currents also lacking quantum physics – Sections 5.2 and 5.3 indicate a deep connection between electricity and magnetism:

Classical electrodynamics: The introduced Lorentz force, $\mathbf{F}_E + \mathbf{F}_B = q\mathbf{E} + q\mathbf{v} \times \mathbf{B}$, underlies both electrical and magnetic aspects of the motion of charge.

Classical unification of fields by Maxwell: The discussions phenomenologically connected charge and field – that charge has an electric field, and is affected by an external one; and that electric current has a magnetic field, and is affected by an external one. If, relative to some frame of reference (Section 2.1), there is acceleration of charge (i.e. there is a change of current), then there will be an associated change of both electric and magnetic fields. Appearing complete, such physics was established through years of work, with notable contributions by Ampère (1826) and Faraday (1832).

But Maxwell (1865) realised that the so-called **Ampère's law** making magnetic field concomitant with electric current, needed an additional term to ensure concomitance also with time-varying electric field without the presence of current: Consider, for example, a capacitor which can support the broader existence of changing current even though the gap between its plates is a physical break that cannot allow the traverse of charge. The additional term to Ampère's law, known as Maxwell's **displacement current**, allows the changing current to be unaffected by the physical breaks of the capacitor, and to exist within the greater circuit beyond the capacitor's plates.

Furthermore, by theorising magnetic field concomitance with time-varying electric field, just as there is **Faradayesque** electric field concomitance with time-varying magnetic field, Maxwell (1865) established one of physics' most significant landmarks – the distillation of the heritage on electricity and magnetism, and his new works on mutually embracing fields and the existence of light, into a complete theory of electromagnetic unification†.

And, although still named after Maxwell, Heaviside (1889) reduced Maxwell's theory to just four equations, easing practical classical treatments of charge, electromagnetic fields, and light, suited to non-quantum aspects of *inter alia* chemistry, electric circuits, magnetism, and optoelectronic technology††.

Furthermore, having innate consistency with relativity, Maxwell's theory:

►Provided inspiration to Einstein to develop his special theory (Section 5.1.5).

►Highlights perception of the electric and magnetic constituents of the electromagnetic field as being frame dependent, such that it may be purely electric, or purely magnetic, from a particular frame, but from others may be in some combination of the two†††.

►Highlights magnetism as arising even from the slow electronic drift speeds, typically a few mm s^{-1}, in electrical circuits††††.

Quantisation: Since particulate charges and atoms owe their stable existence and properties to quantisation, while magnetism may owe its existence also to relativity, the interactions of charge and light thus need a relativistic theory of quantum electrodynamics. Such QED was introduced by Dirac (1928), completed by others in the late 1940s, described by co-inventor and master educator Feynman (1990), and, through confirming exquisitely precise measurements of the properties of particulate charges, has been deemed one of the most successful theories in the history of science.

Faradayesque electric field: Maxwell treated Faraday's electromotive force (Section 5.3.5) as if it were an electric field.

†Notably existing and manifesting under ordinary environmental conditions, Maxwell's electromagnetic unification:
►Puts the embracing fields of electricity and magnetism on an equal footing as a single electromagnetic field.
►Accepts the associated electromagnetic wave as a real self-sustaining (mediating) entity, which continues to propagate independent of the originating charge, and can induce electric current.

††Note that Heaviside's four-equation approach is typical of today's classical treatments of electromagnetism, and may be studied further in, for example, Griffiths (2023).

†††Notes:
►The relative significance of the field's two constituents is thus just an artefact of the chosen frame of reference.
►Purely magnetic fields may be associated with environments of zero net charge, and thus zero electric field.
►Purely electric fields may be associated with environments of zero net movement of charge, and thus zero magnetic field.

††††From its own frame, however, a charge has no motion and no associated magnetic field.

For further descriptive introduction to the **weak** and **strong** interactions see for example, Dodd and Gripaios (2020).

†The weak interaction helps atomic nuclei (Section 5.2.1) attain a stable mix of protons and neutrons.

Notes on **bosons:**
►If of large mass, they tend to have shorter lives and shorter mediating ranges.
►The W is charged, massive, and has a spin of ± 1. And its uncharged chum, the Z, mediates other forms of weak interaction.

Neutrinos are fermionic and somewhat like electrons (Section 5.2.1), but are unbound and without charge. They are also abundant, but difficult to detect by rarely interacting with their environment.

Anti-particles are the **antimatter** equivalents to their normal counterparts.

Antimatter: If a particle and its anti-particle are close enough they annihilate, converting their total mass into gamma-ray energy.

QCD is based principally on massless spin ± 1 bosons called gluons that directly bind quarks (Section 5.2.1), indirectly bind nuclei via the internal exchange of **mesons**, and have enough binding energy to account for about 99% of the mass of ordinary matter.

A **meson** is a short-lived quark/anti-quark pair whose ground-state spin is 0 or ± 1.

5.5   Weak interaction

The **weak** interaction is sub-nuclear, and, following initial theorisation by Fermi (1934), notably controls the two transmutations outlined in Table 5.7†:

1	An energetic proton transmutes to a neutron, emitting a mediating entity called a W **boson**, which almost immediately decays into a **neutrino** and an **anti**-electron.
2	An energetic neutron transmutes to a proton, emitting a mediating anti-W boson, which almost immediately decays into an anti-neutrino and an electron.
Notes:	►Anti-electrons and electrons are called beta particles; thus 1 and 2 are called beta decay. ►Anti-electrons are also called positrons.

Table 5.7: Weak-interaction based transmutations

The weak interaction manifests in stars, where energetic fusions may produce atomic nuclei with an unstable mix of neutrons and protons.

5.6   Strong interaction

The **strong** interaction is sub-nuclear – akin to Section 5.5's weak interaction – but is key to nuclear existence. Indeed, it is strong enough, at such scales, both to overcome electromagnetic repulsion between like charges – even amongst groups of many protons – and to bind the nuclear protons and neutrons together:

Later called quantum chromodynamics, or **QCD**, its mechanism involves boson-mediated binding of sub-nuclear particles, and explained by Fritzsch *et al.* (1973) as being due to a new quantum attribute dubbed colour – such as the colour of gluons and quarks (Section 5.2.1) responsible for the existence of protons and neutrons, and the colour of so-called **mesons** also involved in the existence of atomic nuclei.

The strong interaction manifests in stars, where energetic fusions produce unstably large atomic nuclei. Each such unstable nucleus may eject part thereof, likely an alpha particle (i.e. a helium nucleus). Known as alpha decay, such a process repeats, alongside possible beta decay (Section 5.5), until a stable atomic nucleus remains with a diameter of no more than about 10^{-14} m.

5.7   Final unification

While Maxwell's classical electromagnetic unification (Section 5.4) exists under ordinary Earth-like conditions, higher temperature offers the plausibility of the other interactions merging with equal strength as one, and hence the feasibility of a comprehensive single theory of unification. Indeed, to validate such unification, artificially attained high temperature is a useful approach†:

Electromagnetic and weak unification: Glashow *et al.* (1979) were recognised for their conceiving of the electroweak theory – a high-temperature generalisation of QED that unifies the electromagnetic and weak treatments (Sections 5.4 and 5.5), and which has been validated using particle accelerators to attain the unifying temperature and confirm the existence of the theory's mediating W and Z bosons.

Strong: QCD (Section 5.6) empirically weakens at higher temperature. And, if such a process is continued, QCD's strength would eventually reach that of the electroweak interaction, indicating the feasibility of its inclusion within a grand unified theory††.

Gravitational: Unifying gravitation within a theory of everything would require conception of a viable quantum description and, due to a likely permanent impossibility of attaining the unifying temperature, would be totally reliant on indirect forms of validation.

5.8   Questionnaire

†Albeit with possible economic peaking of capability, particle accelerators are hitherto the validators of choice, where detection of the products of energetic charged particulate collisions – usually of protons or electrons – also helps to confirm interactive processes and fundamental structure of matter.

Indeed, complemented by Lewis' (1926) proposal of the photon as a unique atom-like carrier of light, here is a chronology of some key/latest discoveries:

▸1979: The gluon as the principal mediator of the strong interaction.
▸1983: The W and Z bosons as mediators of the weak interaction.
▸1995: The top quark.
▸2000: The tau neutrino.
▸2012: The *Higgs* boson.

The *Higgs* boson is massive, short-lived, and has zero spin. It is also taken to be an excitation of the so-called Higgs field that is theorised to pervade all of space-time, to impart fundamental particles – such as electrons and quarks – with mass, and to account for about 1% of the mass of ordinary matter.

††But, there is no generally accepted grand theory, and the likely unification temperature is, moreover, far outside particle-accelerator capability, indicating the need for indirect forms of validation.

5Q1   Select a false statement about Brahe:
a   He believed in a form of Eudoxus' kinematic motion
b   He lost recognition for his astronomical data
c   He disbelieved Copernicus' heliocentricity
d   He established inverse-square-law gravitation

5Q2   Pick a true statement:
a   Planetary motion around the Sun sweeps out area at a variable rate
b   The shape of planetary orbits is elliptical
c   Planets move fastest when they are most distant from the Sun
d   Temporal period and average radius are in direct proportion for an orbiting planet

5Q3   Consider gravitational force $Gm_1m_2r^{-2}$ as equivalent to m_1a, where the unit of m
is kg, the unit of r is m, and the units of a are m s^{-2}. What, then, are the units
of G?
a $m^3\,kg^{-1}\,s^{-2}$
b $m^{-1}\,kg^{-1}\,s^{-2}$
c $m^{-1}\,kg^3\,s^2$
d $m^{-3}\,kg^1\,s^2$

5Q4   In practical application of the relation $U = -\,Gm_1m_2r^{-1}$ for gravitational potential
energy, where G is a positive constant, m_1 and m_2 are masses, and r is a distance,
which of the following should be taken as false:
a   Zero r distance is physically meaningless
b dU/dr is positive
c U has a consistently defined zero as r tends to ∞
d $Gm_1m_2r^{-1}$ evaluates as negative

5Q5   In some universe, the relation $v = (1 \times 10^3 \times R^{-1}\,m^3\,s^{-2})^{1/2} = 1 \times 10^1$ m s^{-1} holds
for the speed v of a body needed to escape a planet of radius R. What, then,
is R?
a 1×10^{-1} m
b 1×10^0 m
c 1×10^1 m
d 1×10^2 m

Page 132 answers: 25c   26c   27b   28a   29c

5Q6   Select a true statement about Newtonian gravitation:
a   Spinning bodies are inertial frames of reference
b   Gravitational force on one body due to another decreases upon the intervening introduction by a third
c   Newton's third law does not apply to astronomical bodies due to the lack of physical contact
d   All the other statements are false

5Q7   Select a false statement about Newtonian gravitation:
a   It is premised on absolute motion
b   The force between gravitating bodies is directed between their centres of mass
c   The acceleration of a body increases as it moves towards another
d   All the other statements are false

5Q8   Which option does not follow from Einstein's work on gravity:
a   The general theory of relativity
b   The principle of equivalence
c   The physics of quantum gravity
d   The physics of curved space-time

5Q9   Which option has no classical association with Coulomb's electrostatic force?
a   An inverse-square relationship
b   Charge
c   Direction
d   Neutrons

5Q10 The derived SI units of voltage, defined as energy divided by charge, are:
a $J\,C$
b $J^{-1}\,C$
c $J\,C^{-1}$
d $J^{-1}\,C^{-1}$

5Q11 Cathode rays are:
a   Photons
b   Electrons
c   Positrons
d   Protons

5Q12 Thermionic emission typically involves:
a   Room temperature operation
b   Emission of ions
c   Dense atmosphere
d   None of the other options

Page 128 answers: 1d   2b   3a   4d   5c
Page 129 answers: 6d   7d   8c   9d   10c   11b   12d

5Q13 Which of the following is not relevant to the operation of an oscilloscope?
a   Electromagnetic interaction
b   Photoelectric emission
c   Luminescence
d   High-voltage acceleration

5Q14 An ideal spherical Faraday cage has an electric field of magnitude E just outside
      its periphery and an electric field of zero at its centre. What, then, is the
      magnitude of the electric field mid-way between the periphery and centre?
a   Zero
b $E/2$
c E
d   Not known from the given information

5Q15 The equivalent derived SI units, $N\,C^{-1}$ and $V\,m^{-1}$, represent:
a   Magnetic field
b   Energy
c   Electric field
d   Voltage

5Q16 Fermionic spin:
a   Is a Newtonian rotation
b   Has no participation in stellar reactions
c   May contribute to subatomic momentum
d   Has a quantisation number of ± 1

5Q17 In consideration of an electric charge and a magnet, pick an incorrect statement:
a   Their effects can both be mapped in terms of fields
b   They both have a natural unipolar manifestation
c   Even if stationary, the physics of relativity may still have relevance
d   The treatment of the latter is based on the movement of the former

5Q18 Which of the following is incorrect regarding the theorisation of a subatomic
      orbital:
a   It is region of subatomic space
b   It must contain a subatomic particle
c   Possible occupancy comprises electrons, protons, and neutrons
d   It provides for consistency with Heisenberg's uncertainty principle

5Q19 Which descriptor conflicts with the treatment of orbitals:
a   Exclusion
b   Preferential filling of highest available energy levels
c   Internal pairing
d   Limited occupancy

5Q20 Significant magnetic behaviour is not associated with:
a   A circulating current
b   Domains of aligned spin
c   A symmetric ferrimagnet
d   A magnetic dipole

5Q21 Suppose an electron is in uniform motion along the z-axis of a 3D-set of
       Cartesian axes. If a magnetic field is then applied aligned with the x-axis, which
       of the following is true?
a   The electron's velocity remains constant
b   The electron experiences a force aligned with the x-axis
c   The electron experiences a force aligned with the y-axis
d   The electron experiences a force aligned with the z-axis

5Q22 Molecular physics may be studied via subatomic spin that is resonantly
       excited by:
a   Radio waves
b   Ultrasound
c   X-rays
d   Piezoelectricity

5Q23 For typical applications of nuclear magnetic resonance, the associated precession
       process does not:
a   Involve a so-called Larmor frequency
b   Relate to the hydrogen atoms in water molecules
c   Involve a rotation around an applied magnetic field
d   Rely on random axes of nuclear spin

5Q24 The process of magnetic resonance imaging cannot:
a   Create an array of 2 dimensional images
b   Image the outer part of bones
c   Map out blood vessels
d   Detect abnormalities in the brain

Page 130 answers: 13b   14a   15c   16c   17b   18b
Page 131 answers: 19b   20c   21c   22a   23d   24b

5Q25 How many of the following four applied fields can bring a static charge into motion:
(i) A static electric field.
(ii) A changing electric field.
(iii) A static magnetic field.
(iv) A changing magnetic field.

a ≤ 1
b 2
c 3
d 4

5Q26 With the view-point that Lenz's law is strictly classical, how many of the following three options can it help explain:
(i) Eddy currents.
(ii) The skin effect.
(iii) Diamagnetism.

a 0
b 1
c 2
d 3

5Q27 The electromagnetic interaction provides no fundamental basis for describing which of the following?
a Light
b The states of liquids and solids
c Interactions with lodestone
d Chemical reactions

5Q28 Select an incorrect statement on the treatments of unification:
a Proton/neutron transmutations emit gluons
b The Higgs boson is a quantum excitation
c There are no quarks in an electron
d Gravitation defies quantum description

5Q29 Select a false statement
a Gluons account for most of the mass of ordinary matter
b Electrodynamics – whether classical or quantum – may involve protons
c The space-time field known as Higgs is the aether of light propagation
d Particle accelerators will likely never directly validate a theory of everything

Chapter 6   Electronics and Photonics

6.1   Electric conduction

For the constituent atoms (Section 5.2.1) of any medium, the electronic energies (Section 5.3.1) belong to some distribution. And, within this distribution, the electrons that are most energetic – potentially **outermost** – may, under the right conditions, pass from one atom to the next throughout the medium – an effect known as conduction†.

The right conditions for a medium's support of conduction include there being strong interactions between neighbouring atoms, and outermost electrons attaining an **allowed** level of energy not attained by any other electron. Consider a gaseous chemical elemental body progressively condensed into a solid††:

As a gas, the atoms are mostly far apart and rarely interact. All outermost electrons are taken to have a common energy and there are no available nearby levels. Conduction in gasses is thus negligible under normal conditions†††.

However, at the onset of condensation into a solid, the atoms become close enough for the outermost electrons between each to interact strongly. But Pauli's principle (Section 5.3.1) precludes such interacting electrons from sharing the same energy, and so the common gaseous energy broadens into a band. Called the valence band, initially all its energy levels are taken, but, as the condensation and band-broadening continue, the energies of the

The **outermost** electron of an atom is that which, at any instant, is to be found furthest from the nucleus. An atom's most energetic electrons will be outermost more frequently than the others.

†Note that the term conduction refers to the movement, relative to some frame of reference (Section 2.1), of any form of charged entity, not just electrons.

Allowed level of energy: Note that the structure of atoms and the allowed electronic energy levels of interacting atoms follow the quantum rules of Hund and Pauli (Section 5.3.1). Associated electric conduction is thus a quantum effect.

††Liquids, in this context, are similar to solids. However, liquids are also free to flow (Section 4.2). So, even in the absence of mobile electrons, liquids can conduct via the movement of ions (Section 5.2.1).

†††Abnormal conditions, such as lightning, however, are very different. Lightning is a high-energy event in which the atoms of a gas are rendered as a hot sea of ions and unbound electrons. With little impediment to either, both easily move and contribute to conduction.

Electron-volt: This unit of energy is often used in atomic physics due the low values of energy typically being applicable. A likely range is $[0,10]$eV, where the e in the eV unit represents the charge of an electron.

Thus, since energy is the product of charge and voltage (Section 5.2.3), conversion between the eV and the derived SI joule is such that 1 eV is $-1.602\,176\,634 \times 10^{-19}$ J.

†Arbitrary but by convention, the signage built into the $I = q/t$ definition means that the motion of positive charge is associated with positive electric current.

Furthermore, as conceived by Franklin (1751), and given the name conventional current, such movement of positive charge:
►Provides a treatment that is intuitive and self-consistent. Specifically, from Section 5.2.3, it would arise in scenarios where a positive voltage applies.
►Has become the de facto descriptive standard.
►Conversely, real movement of negative charge is equivalent to – and hence treated as – an oppositely directed conventional current.

most energetic electrons become closer to the next allowable – but initially empty – band of energies called the conduction band. Often quantified in an energy unit known as the *electron-volt*, the final closeness between the facing edges of the valance and conduction bands, known as a bandgap, generally determines the conductivity, and form, of the resultant solid, broadly whether it is insulating or metallic:

►Insulating solids feature bandgaps that typically exceed 10 eV. Ambient energy is generally insufficient to excite valence electrons across such large bandgaps. Thus, none of the conduction-band's levels are taken, the valence band remains full, and there is negligible conductivity. Furthermore, raising the ambient energy to induce a 10 eV electronic excitation would probably first cause irreversible breakdown of the medium. Insulating solids are thus generally never viable as conductors.

►Metallic solids feature overlapping of the valence and conduction bands. The most energetic electrons are thus presented with plenty of available energy levels, and accordingly metallic solids are generally excellent conductors.

6.2   Electric current

In conductive media (Section 6.1), the voltage associated with non-uniform charge distribution (Section 5.2.3) allows the movement of charge. Furthermore, whenever charge moves relative to some frame of reference (Section 2.1), it is known as electric current. Suppose charge q is seen to flow past a point in time t, then the associated current I is defined as $I = q/t$†.

Such current I has derived SI units $C\,s^{-1}$, usually written as A, the SI base unit known as the amp. Accordingly, at any point in space where there is 1 A of current, 1 C of charge passes every second.

6.3   Electrical supply

Basic forms of electrical supply involve the electrical grid, and cells:

Electrical grid: Delivered to homes and businesses through the electrical grid, humankind enjoys a consumerist life-style driven by numerous sources of energy. Table 6.1 lists some key sources of this energy, where the goal, ultimately, is for it to be converted into electric energy. With the particular exception of solar cells, which offer direct conversion, practical sources often require numerous energy conversions. In a steam turbine, for example, the source energy is converted (1) into heat, then (2) into kinetic energy via the expansion of water into steam moving a massive turbine, and (3) into electric energy via an electrical circuit.

For efficient long-distance nation-wide distribution, the grid transmits the electric energy under two conditions. First, its current (Section 6.2) has its direction changed regularly with time, known as alternating current (AC). Second, that AC is driven at high voltage (Section 5.2.3), typically 330 kV to 500 kV.

The grid's voltage is far too high for acceptable domestic use. For the moderate safety of end-users, transformer substations are used to reduce the voltage to about 240 V or less (dependent on the country) before being routed into the home. And further reductions in voltage may be necessary to suit individual appliances.

Cells: In addition to a possible need for reduced voltage, the grid's AC is not suitable for appliances which require electric current in only one direction, known as direct current (DC). With some further introduction in Table 6.2 overleaf, such DC may be obtained either via rectification of the grid's AC, or directly from a device known as a cell:

Source: Features
Nuclear fission: Long-life technology; but costly start-up, costly decommissioning, and radioactive waste.
Burning of coal and oil: Large fossil fuel reserves; but non-renewable, only about 36% efficient, and greenhouse/toxic emission.
Incineration of waste: Renewable, and reduction of landfill; but greenhouse/toxic emission.
Falling water: Renewable, non-polluting operation efficient, reliable, and short (< 5 minute) start-up time; but costly commissioning.
Wind turbines: Renewable, non-polluting operation, and about 60% efficient; but needs ideally constant wind speed of about 30 km s^{-1}.
Sea waves: Renewable, efficient, and non-polluting operation.
Sea tides: Renewable, and non-polluting operation; but costly/challenging commissioning.
Heat of Earth's crust at about 300 C: Renewable; but may aggravate earthquakes, needs drill depths to 20 km, and subject to heat-induced corrosion via salts and sulphurous gasses.
Solar cells: Renewable, and non-polluting operation; but only about 20% efficient.

Table 6.1: Sources of energy for the electrical grid

pocket calculator	5 mA
torch light from a white light emitting diode	30 mA
6×10^{18} electrons s^{-1}	1 A
car headlight	4 A
Note 1: The DC from cells is notably underpinned by advances in modern technology – such as in energy capacity and rechargeability – that allow the operation of automobiles and other massive equipment.	
Note 2: DC is an inefficient means of transmitting energy, and so is not suited to long distances.	

Table 6.2: DC approximate examples, and notes

†The process notably does not create charge, it simply redistributes charge – the net charge of the cell remains zero.

††With the ability to elevate the potential energy of charge, a cell is an example of a so-called active component.

A cell is based on a conductive solution between two pieces of different metals called electrodes. With concurrent release of energy, the electrodes support different ionic (Section 5.2.1) reactions with the adjacent solution, and a consequential driving of the solution's ions into a non-uniform distribution, where one electrode gains net positive charge and is called an anode, and the other gains net negative charge and is called a cathode†.

The cell must do an increasing amount of work (Section 3.1.2) against Coulomb's electrostatic repulsion (Section 5.2.2) to add further charges to each electrode. And such a process tends to impart the electrodes with increasing magnitudes of both potential energy and intervening voltage (Section 5.2.3)††.

Nonetheless, the elevated energy and voltage would both tend to dissipate if the growing coulombic repulsion is able to drive the charge distributions back to uniformity through some external conductive path – specifically via the connection of a conductive and continuous external circuit.

6.4   Circuits, polarity, and batteries

Following Section 6.3, a cell that is in a state of electrical isolation is under an equilibrium whereby its ionic reactive action balances the coulombic repulsion from its electrodes. And its charges have no conductive path to regain uniformity of distribution, and hence ideally retain their potential energy and voltage.

But, upon the connection of a conductive and continuous external circuit, the charges respond to the coulombic repulsion by moving through that circuit towards the opposite electrode. And, in doing so, they lose their potential energy and voltage, and regain uniformity of distribution. The cell, however, continues to do the opposite by struggling to restore the non-uniform charge distribution between the electrodes, and accordingly a new equilibrium is established†.

The flow of charge has various manifestations, such as in the movement of positive or negative ions within conductive solutions, and the *movement* of electrons in metallic wires. Whichever applies, the general practice is to treat them as ***Franklin's*** conventional current (Section 6.2).

Now consider, for example, the following scenario – a circuit that may support current in either direction, and a connected cell that drives the circuit's current and has a nominal voltage V which, following Franklin's convention, is always quoted as positive:
►Then, conventional current leaves the cell's anode (Section 6.3), passes through the circuit, and returns to the cell's cathode (Section 6.3)††.
►The direction of the conventional current in the circuit depends on the circuit's connective orientation to the anode and cathode of the cell. Inverting the connection – or polarity – means that the circuit experiences reversal of the current. Circuits may be sensitive to the direction of current; thus distinguishing between the cell's anode and cathode is essential to correct connection and operation.

Furthermore, connecting a metallic wire from the anode of one cell to the cathode of another creates a device called a battery. A battery can contain any number of cells ≥ 2, and may have a variety of accessible electrodes†††.

6.5   Electric energy and power

Contrasting with exceptional (say $c/10$) electronic speeds from a cathode-ray gun (Section 5.2.4), that in typical wired circuits is only a few mm s^{-1}. Thus, with minimal kinetic energy, the electronic activity in typical circuits is dominated by potential energy:

†However, as soon as the continuity of the external circuit, anywhere, is broken – e.g. by the opening of a switch – the flow of charge everywhere ceases, and the cell returns to its isolated state.

And even the *movement* of abstract positive entities within semiconductors known as holes (see Section 6.10).

On ***Franklin's*** conventional current, it is important to remember the following:
Always being of positive charge, it is not necessarily a true current, but simply a conceptualised portrayal of current in which:
►Magnitude reflects reality.
►But that either (1) its direction reflects a real net flow of positive charge, or (2) its opposite direction reflects a real net flow of negative charge.

††Of course, if the circuit is metallic, the real current is electronic, and is in the opposite direction.

†††Notes:
►Between any pair of such electrodes, the intervening voltages combine additively (see e.g. Section 6.6).
►Thus, dependent on the chosen pair, a variety of net voltages may be available.
►Note that, if like electrodes are connected, the opposing sense/polarity would cause the voltage of one cell to combine with the negation of the other. And, in the extreme case of both cells being of voltage V, the net voltage would be zero.

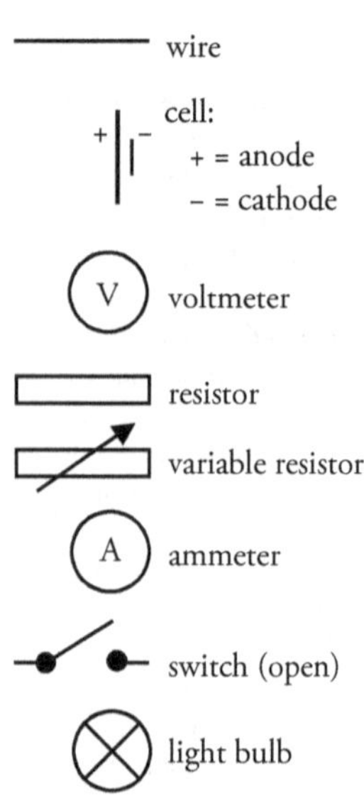

Figure 6.1: Some component symbols

Considering Franklin's conventional current (Section 6.2), each positive charge q that leaves the anode of a cell (Section 6.3) has a positive electric potential energy ΔU given by $\Delta U = qV$ (Section 5.2.3), where V is the considered-positive voltage of the cell. Passive components in a conductive and continuous external circuit may then progressively dissipate ΔU. And the fully spent charge arrives at the cell's cathode, has its lost ΔU replaced by the cell, and the cycle repeats. The cell thus acts as a continuous energy pump for charge.

The ratio q_{tot}/t of the total conventional charge q_{tot} leaving the cell in time t represents the supply I of electric current. Accordingly, there is an associated positive supply ΔU_{tot} of energy given by $\Delta U_{tot} = q_{tot}V = IVt$†.

Furthermore, electric power P is the temporal rate $\Delta U_{tot}/t$ (Section 3.13). It thus also follows that there is an associated positive supply P of power given by $P = IV$.

Note that electricity companies combine power and time to specify total supplied energy. Their energy unit is the so-called kilowatt-hour, meaning one kilowatt of power supplied continuously for one hour.

6.6   Circuit componentry and Ohm/Kirchhoff based analysis

With some symbols shown in Figure 6.1, various components may be used in a circuit. But the resistor is key since its property of resistance is essential to all circuits, whether AC or DC (Section 6.3). Resistance irreversibly converts electric energy into heat, and prevents catastrophically high values of current. Ideally, such resistive constraint is independent of frequency. Moreover, practical circuits may also have the properties of capacitance and inductance††.

In general, analyses may proceed via the so-called lumped-circuit model, where†:

►Resistance, capacitance, and inductance are taken to reside within discrete components known respectively as resistors, capacitors and inductors.

►The wiring of the circuit is assumed to be perfectly conductive (i.e. without resistance, capacitance, or inductance).

►Currents and voltages (Sections 6.2 and 5.2.3) are taken to be spatially independent of the wiring of the circuit. And, to ensure that charge is conserved, current is taken not to change within each component. Thus, components inter-connected solely as a daisy-chain, for example, are taken to carry the same current.

►The concept of equivalent circuit may be used to replace the property of an arbitrary part of the circuit with a single equivalent component, thus easing calculation of that part's input current, while subsequent analyses may determine the internal currents and voltages.

►Faraday-induced current (Section 5.3.9) is assumed to be insignificant.

►Frequency is assumed to be low enough to avoid wave-like propagation of electric energy (Section 5.4).

Ongoing analysis: Focussing on circuits that are **purely resistive**, and noting further constraints on the fly, such as **steady-state** DC operation, now consider the laws of Ohm (1827) and Kirchhoff (1845):

Ohm's empirical law, and concept of resistance: A component which is found, under steady-state DC operation, to have current I proportional to applied voltage V, is said to follow the empirical **Ohm's law** $V = IR$, where plotting V against I is a straight line passing through the origin with positive constant gradient R.

†For further introduction to the lumped-circuit model see, for example, Agarwal and Lang (2005).

Purely resistive circuits do not have significant capacitance and inductance.

In **steady-state** DC operation:
►Voltages and currents are constant.
►Ideally inductance has no significance, and inductors can be ignored.
►Capacitance is critical. Any branch of a circuit that has a capacitor will ideally carry no current.

Notes on the applicability of **Ohm's law:**
►It may not be valid to invoke the lumped-circuit model's assumption of perfectly conductive wiring.
►Compliant components are said to be ohmic, and have power dissipation (Section 6.5) written as: $P = IV = I^2R = V^2/R$.
►Compliance in purely resistive circuits ideally applies even in cases of changing/alternating voltage.
►An equivalent compliance can also apply to capacitive and inductive circuits following a reformulation of the $V = IR$ equation – see, for example, Agarwal and Lang (2005).
►There will be no ohmic compliance (resistive or otherwise) if significant non-linearities exist due, for example, to (1) the presence of large voltage, or (2) the operating environment inducing a significant change of resistance.

†It is, however, to be remembered that Ohm's law:
- Is purely empirical.
- Has numerous exceptions such as in the non-linearities of insulators, semiconductors, and filament bulbs:

In filament bulbs, for example, an increase of voltage causes a rise of temperature due to increased heat dissipation, and this in turn causes increased resistance.

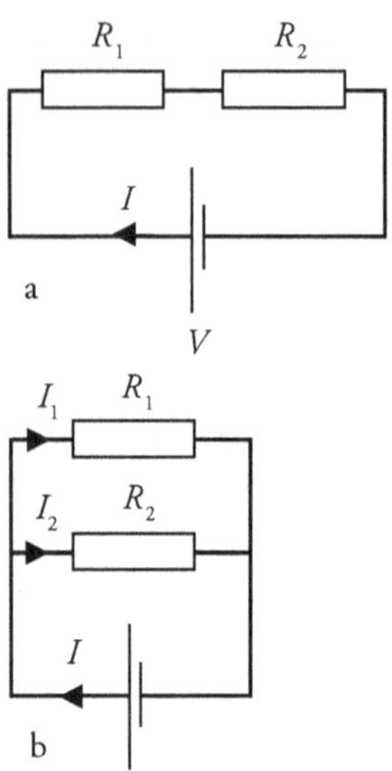

Figure 6.2: Circuits with series (a) and parallel (b) topologies

Furthermore, R is known as the component's resistance, and has derived SI unit of ohms, symbol Ω†.

Kirchhoff's current law: For the circuit diagrams of Figure 6.2, consider that conventional current I (Section 6.2) leaves the cell, and that a node is anywhere that multiple wires join. Kirchhoff's current law then invokes conservation of charge at each such node stating that, regardless of the number of connected wires, there is an exact equivalence between the total entering and total exiting currents:

- Figure 6.2(a): All points of the wire are nodes, such that there is one input and one output. With the output current thus equalling the input current, I clearly remains as I through to the start of R_1. And I also leaves R_1 following the lumped-circuit model. Via the same arguments, I also leaves R_2 and ultimately returns, in its entirety, to the cell. Said to have a series topology, the single conductive loop of Figure 6.2(a) is thus modelled everywhere to carry the same current I – as is consistent with the conservation of charge.

- Figure 6.2(b): With the additional labelling of I_1 and I_2, there is also a three-wire node to the left of R_2, where Kirchhoff's current law indicates that $I = I_1 + I_2$. The second three-wire node to the right of R_2 is redundant due to providing the same equation. The three-wire nodes enforce a ladder-like structure, where the uprights are wires, and each rung also accommodates a component. Had there been only two component-rungs, the result would be the familiar series topology. But now there are three rungs. Whenever there are three or more component-rungs (1) the associated topology is said to be parallel, and (2) the voltage across each, according to the lumped-circuit model, is the same.

Kirchhoff's voltage law: Kirchhoff's voltage law states that the **sum** of the voltages around any closed conductive loop must equal zero – the principle being that, for one circuit of the loop, and regardless of starting point, there are exactly matching aggregates of voltage rises and drops (Section 5.2.3) – as is consistent with the conservation of energy since each charge always gains and loses the same amount.

Applicable loops are defined by their constituent parameters – for example:

►One loop and one parametric set (V, I, R_1, R_2) apply to Figure 6.2(a).

►Three loops and three parametric sets (V, I, I_1, R_1), (V, I, I_2, R_2), and (I_1, R_1, I_2, R_2) apply to Figure 6.2(b).

Application of Ohm and Kirchhoff's laws: Whilst Ohm's law describes voltage/current relationships for simple topologies, its integration with Kirchhoff's laws, with careful consideration to **directional sense** and sign, permits the analysis of circuits of arbitrary complexity††.

For example, the combined approach will now be used to establish rules for the summation of resistances in series and parallel:

Summing of two resistances in series: The circuit in Figure 6.2(a) carries current I everywhere. Thus, Kirchhoff's voltage law with a clockwise loop gives $V - IR_1 - IR_2 = 0$, or $V = I(R_1 + R_2)$. Similarly, $V - IR_E = 0$ or $V = IR_E$ when the two resistors are replaced by equivalent resistance R_E.

Inspection of the two equations for V shows that $R_E = R_1 + R_2$, which is the rule for summing two resistances in series.

Summing of two resistances in parallel: Kirchhoff's current law gives $I = I_1 + I_2$ at the three-wire nodes of Figure 6.2(b). Also, using the voltage law, and a clockwise loop comprising V, I_1, and R_1, gives $V - I_1R_1 = 0$. In the same way, $V - I_2R_2 = 0$. And, then,

Such a **sum**, for example, justifies Section 6.4's claim of additively combined voltages in batteries.

On **directional sense** and sign, note initially that:
►If, within some loop, the Kirchhoff voltage of an active component, such as a cell, is considered as positive, then that of dissipated passive ones, such as resistors, must be considered as negative.

††In general:
►Draw the circuit, including a component wherever an electrical property arises, and apply, to each, a unique symbol – e.g. resistance R.
►For each current at each node, apply a unique symbol, choose an arbitrary sense, and label with an arrow.
►For each closed loop, choose an arbitrary sense, and label with an arrow.
►For the voltage across each component, apply unique symbolism via the following conventional-current inspired rules:
(1) $+ V$ for a cell of nominal voltage V if the sense of the loop is from the anode to the cathode (otherwise $- V$).
(2) $- IR$ for a resistance R if the loop and I have the same sense (otherwise $+ IR$).
(3) See e.g. Agarwal and Lang (2005) otherwise.
►Sufficiently apply Kirchhoff's laws to the independent nodes and loops to generate the same number of independent equations as unknowns.
►Solve for the unknowns.
►Check the answers.

eliminating I_1 and I_2 from $I = I_1 + I_2$ gives $I = V/R_1 + V/R_2 = V(1/R_1 + 1/R_2)$.

The voltage law also gives $V - IR_E = 0$, or $I = V(1/R_E)$, when the two resistors are replaced by their equivalent resistance R_E.

Inspection of the two equations for I shows that $1/R_E = 1/R_1 + 1/R_2$, which is the rule for summing two resistances in parallel.

6.7   Electrical measurement

Instrumentation for electrical measurement requires careful selection and use. Just two examples are introduced here – so-called ammeters and voltmeters†:

Used for in-situ measurements of electric current, ammeters are connected in series with the component of interest and minimally perturb that current to be measured by having low internal resistance, which contributes negligible series resistance.

Voltmeters are used for both isolated and in-situ measurements of voltage. In both cases, they are connected in parallel with the component of interest, and minimally perturb the voltage to be measured by having high internal resistance, which causes minimal current to be drained.

6.8   Blackbodies

To some degree, all matter emits light. But the emission's spectral dependence evaded full explanation prior to the establishment of the treatment of so-called blackbodies. Whilst approximating certain real objects such as incandescent light bulbs and stars, a blackbody is a theoretical idealised body that:
► Absorbs all incoming light, but emits light only over a certain spectral range:
► Is termed black due to both the 100% absorption (and consequent zero reflection,

†With the contemporary trend towards digital multifunctional capability, an arbitrary instrument for electrical measurement may:
► Be analogue or digital.
► Concern multiple parameters.
► Concern various connection topologies. For example, connection could be (1) to an isolated component, or (2) in series or parallel (Section 6.6) with an in-situ component within an operating circuit.

transmission, and scattering), and the lack of significant visible emission below about 800 K.

►Whose emission spectrum is not only strongly temperature dependent, but also starts at some short wavelength, rises sharply to a peak of intensity – where Wien (1893) explained the associated wavelength to vary inversely with temperature – and subsequently returns slowly to zero at long wavelength.

But a blackbody's full emission spectrum and overall temperature dependence were fully explained by Planck (1901) via a law based on the assumption that excited atoms constituting the blackbody could vibrate only with quantised energies. Planck's law, and his quantisation of blackbody vibrations, were great triumphs in physics that initiated modern quantum theory†.

6.9   Photoelectric effect; photonic energy, detection, and counting

Known as the photoelectric effect, Lenard (1902) observed that, when ultraviolet light is incident on a metallic surface that surface may emit electrons into the surrounding space††.

Einstein (1905[a]) explained Lenard's photoelectric effect by:

►Taking the energy quantisation, that Planck assumed for a blackbody's atomic vibrations (Section 6.8), also to apply to the incident light.

►Postulating such **quantisation of light** to be of energy E given by $E = hf$, where h is Planck's constant.

►Hypothesising that a fixed amount of energy Φ, known as work function, is needed for an atom of the surface to release an electron.

►Taking the remaining energy $hf - \Phi$ to become the kinetic energy of the released photoelectron.

Quantification of h and Φ: By virtue of their kinetic energy, and largely by chance, some photoelectrons may collide with a nearby second metallic surface. And that surface's efficiency of

†Such quantum theory is based on physical quantities, such as energy, having a limit to their smallest amount – or so-called quantum – of existence.

††Whilst, classically, the kinetic energy of the emitted electrons would depend on the light's intensity and any frequency could be used if sufficiently intense, Lenard's observations had surprising contrary associations:
►The light's frequency must be above a certain threshold for any electrons to be emitted – hence the need for ultraviolet. And then:
►Increasing the frequency increases the kinetic energy of the emitted electrons, and:
►Increasing the intensity increases the number of the emitted electrons.

Quantisation of light: So now light is explained in terms of both waves (Section 5.4) and quanta. The wave treatment supports some phenomena; the quantum treatment supports others. So is light a wave or a quantum? Could it even be neither of these?

One may be reminded of Magritte's *The Treachery of Images*, which is the rendering of a pipe captioned by 'Ceci n'est pas une pipe.' The fact is that waves, quanta, or whatever, are just words for physical treatments, and that physicists use the treatment that best represents their knowledge. Whilst physicists may act with ontological intent, Nature retains the protective shroud of human perception.

collection could be increased by connecting, to the two surfaces, an external circuit with a series source of steady-state voltage (Section 6.6).

Alternatively, consider the scenario of Table 6.3, where the external voltage is adjusted to make the current in the external circuit just become zero:

1	The emitted electrons need to be attracted back to the photoelectric surface via that surface being connected to the anode (Section 6.3) of the voltage source. The associated positive voltage, say V, then supplies, to each electron, the negative electric potential energy of $\Delta U = eV$ (Section 5.2.3).
2	Such ΔU may be considered as work W done to stop each photoelectron. Hence, from the work-energy theorem (Section 3.12), $W = \Delta U = \Delta K$, giving $eV = - (hf - \Phi)$.
3	But, written as $- eV = hf - \Phi$, provides for more intuitive graphing.

Table 6.3: Scenario of stopping a photoelectric emission

In practice, I is measured with a series ammeter (Section 6.7), V is increased until I just becomes zero, and then V is measured with a parallel voltmeter (Section 6.7). And the process is repeated for various frequencies f of light. Then a plot (Section 1.16) of the positive quantity $- eV$ against f yields a straight line whose gradient equals h, and whose $- eV$ intercept equals $- \Phi$†.

Photons, and photonic energy: Lewis (1926) named Einstein's light quanta as photons. The energy of each such photon is thus $E = hf$††.

The photonic E varies with frequency, and is thus largest for gamma rays and smallest for radio waves. Some examples are given in Table 6.4 where, for a few choices of free-space wavelength $\lambda_0 = c/f$ (Section 4.3.7's Table 4.13), $E = hf = h\lambda_0/c$ is given in derived units of eV (Section 6.1) and J.

†Note that h is a universal constant, but Φ varies with the type of photoelectric metal.

††For a fixed-frequency body of n photons, each of energy E, the total energy E_n and power P_n are simply given respectively by $E_n = nE$ and $P_n = nE/\Delta t$, where Δt is the associated amount of time.

Free-space electromagnetic wavelength and band	eV	J
1×10^{-5} m mid infrared	1×10^{-1}	2×10^{-20}
1×10^{-6} m near infrared	1	2×10^{-19}
1×10^{-7} m ultraviolet	1×10^{1}	2×10^{-18}

Table 6.4: Some examples of photonic energy

Photon detection and counting: Despite the small energies of Table 6.4, it is possible to detect all associated photons. But most applications of photon counting concern the near infrared and higher energy bands†.

While the detector's speed of response relative to the photonic rate of arrival is an important related consideration, applications of photon detection and counting rely on the light level being so low that statistically only one photon is available at the detector at any one time. And, therein, sensitivity of the detector to low light levels is key. Generally a multiplicative detection process is required where one photon ultimately liberates many electrons††.

The traditional and still state-of-the-art multiplicative detection technology is the photomultiplier, where photons enter one end of an evacuated tube, and each acts on a photoelectric surface potentially liberating one electron. And, upon subsequent acceleration by several hundred volts, the liberated electron may energetically strike an electrode called a dynode, liberating about four more. And, upon their acceleration and the striking of a further dynode, the process repeats. If each dynode liberates N output electrons for each input one, and there are d dynodes, the total multiplicative gain is N^d. If, for example, $N = 4$ and $d = 10$, then more than a million electrons are released upon each photoemission, and the associated peak current, then developed by an external circuit, is sufficient to be detected†††.

†Notes:
►Ambient energies of up to, say, 1 eV are thermally abundant under typical conditions. Such thermal noise usually makes ordinary detection systems unsuitable, unless cryogenically cooled.
►But, with technology appropriate to the selected photonic energy, applications spanning astronomy, metallurgy, and medicine have found major success, with the mapping of the human genome being notably spectacular.

††This includes the action of so-called avalanche photodiodes and photomultiplier tubes.
Ordinary photodetectors do not multiply, and are generally too noisy.

†††Photomultiplier developments, past and future:
►Original constructions featured glass tubes that were bulky, fragile, and sensitive to shock and vibration.
►But, in the interests of *inter alia* increased environmental robustness, and reduced signal noise, there is now a drive towards miniature monolithic construction. These so-called channel photomultipliers operate akin to their bulkier predecessors, but with their secondary electrons derived from internal collisions with the wall of a curved, semiconductive vacuum channel.
►See Section 6.10, next, for some physics of semiconductors.

6.10 Semiconductors

The technological ability to fabricate complex circuitry by tailoring the local conductivity of highly-pure semiconducting crystal lattices, and the associated invention of the so-called p-n-p transistor in 1948 initiated the modern electronics industry:

Intrinsic semiconductors: In pure form, semiconducting material is referred to as intrinsic. Such material has an electronic energy distribution that is similar to those of insulators (Section 6.1), but with a bandgap that is typically an order of magnitude smaller. For example, the bandgap of pure germanium is about 0.7 eV and that of pure silicon is about 1.1 eV.

Ambient conditions – such as of heat, light, and voltage – readily excite valence electrons across such bandgaps. And the increased number of electrons in the conduction band raises the conductivity of the material.

But each such excited electron also leaves behind a newly vacant site in the valence band referred to as a hole. The hole of such an electron-hole pair is a site of electronic deficiency, representing a net positive charge. Furthermore, if the hole is free to move, it will – akin to Franklin's notion of conventional current (Section 6.2) – also contribute to the conductivity of the material.

Intrinsic semiconductors have various uses: Germanium was first to be demonstrated and is still used in amplitude-modulated (AM) radio receivers (see Section 6.11). Cadmium sulphide is used as so-called **photoresistors**, and silicon has become the mainstay of the electronics industry:

Concepts of carriers and dopants: In intrinsic semiconductors, the mobile electrons and holes are equal in number. But semiconductors can be created with an imbalance of mobile electrons and holes. Whichever is the dominant is called

In the operation of **photoresistors**, the energy $E = hf$ of incident photons (Section 6.9) exceeds the semiconductor's bandgap, and excites electrons across it, leading to increased conductivity. With the illuminating intensity then being encoded in terms of reduced resistance (Section 6.6), such devices – a.k.a. light dependent resistors – are available for wavelengths ranging from the ultraviolet to the infrared.

the majority carrier, and the other is called the minority carrier.

Majority and minority carriers are created by replacing a regular sub-arrangement of atoms within an intrinsic lattice with dopant atoms. Such doping tailors the local conductivity and allows the creation of devices with complex functionality. Relative to the **host** intrinsic semiconductor, the choice of dopant is critical.

As per the terminology of Section 6.1, now discussed are two different types of dopant atom that create so-called n-type and p-type semiconducting material†:

Arsenic-based n-type material: Arsenic atoms have one more valence electron compared to silicon atoms. Doping into an intrinsic silicon lattice then creates a so-called donor energy level just below the conduction band. As illustrated in Figure 6.3, electrons from the donor level are easily excited into the conduction band, resulting in mobile negatively charged majority carriers††.

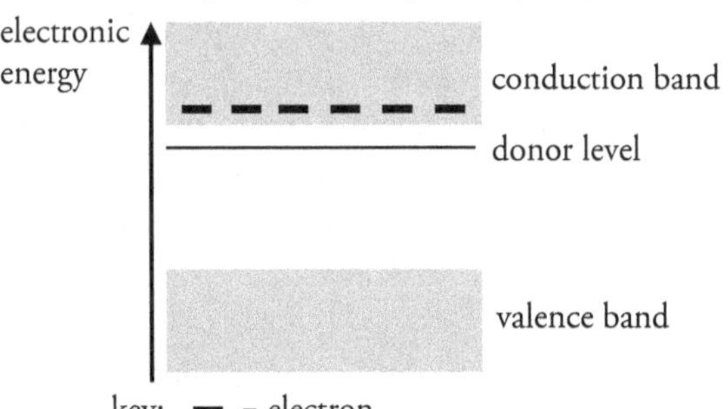

Figure 6.3: Electronic energies in n-type material

Such n-type semiconductors have much higher conductivity than the intrinsic silicon host.

Gallium-based p-type material: Gallium atoms have one less valence electron compared to silicon atoms. Doping into an intrinsic silicon lattice then creates a so-called acceptor energy level just above the valence band. As illustrated in Figure 6.4, overleaf, the acceptor level takes up electrons that are easily excited from the valence

Given its overall importance, ongoing discussion assumes the **host** to be silicon.

†Notes:
► The n of n-type means negative.
► The p of p-type means positive.

††Notes on associated positive charges:
► Thermal energy at room temperature is sufficient for close to 100% donation. Thus, although the arsenic atoms are rendered as positive ions, they are now part of a uniform and stable silicon-like bonding structure with no free energy sites and no associated conductivity.
► Mobile holes, conversely, can be left in the valence band after its electrons are excited into the conduction band. But this process is far less likely since much more energy is required than for excitations from the donor level.
► Holes are thus the minority carriers.

band, leaving behind mobile holes as positively charged majority carriers†.

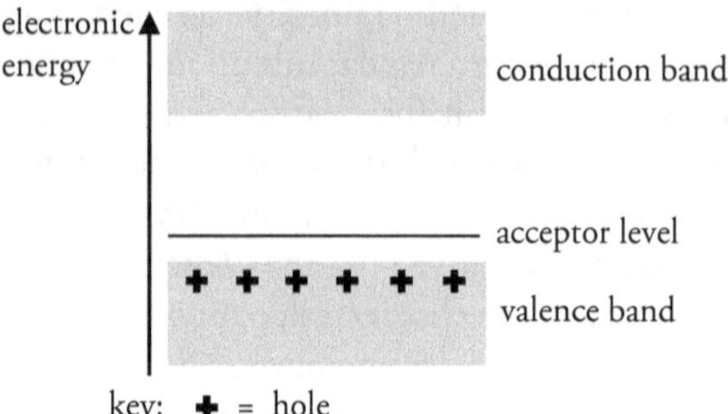

Figure 6.4: Electronic energies in p-type material

Such p-type semiconductors have much higher conductivity than the intrinsic silicon host.

The p-n junction: If there is a contacting interface – or junction – between p-type and n-type materials, some n-type electrons move across and recombine with the p-type holes. This leaves a layer of material that extends either side of the junction with no mobile charges called a depletion layer. The depleted p-type material has net negative charge, and the depleted n-type material has net positive charge. The changed charge distribution means there is a voltage (Section 5.2.3) across the junction. This so-called barrier voltage stops the crossing of further electrons, and limits the width of the depletion layer††.

Various semiconductor devices exploit p-n junctions and depletion layers:

Diodes: A p-n junction passes current in only one direction, and hence acts as a diode. Applying an external voltage to try to force current in the reverse direction (up to a limit) does not work because it increases the barrier voltage†††.

Photodiodes: Assuming the photonic energies of incident light exceed the bandgaps of a p-n junction's depletion layer, electron-hole pairs are generated, wherein the electron and hole of each, under the influence of the barrier voltage, will migrate to opposite sides of the junction. The associated movement of charge, known as photocurrent, is proportional to the incident intensity, and affords the device with a convenient means of detecting light.

Transistors: With revolutionary ubiquitous application that replaces most vacuum tube technology, and with the essential feature of offering some change in output for a given input, transistors comprise a family of devices of diverse configurations and characteristics†.

Two key examples are the so-called bipolar and field-effect transistors††:

►Bipolar transistors have three alternating doped, and adjacent, semiconductor layers, p-n-p or n-p-n, operating essentially as two contacting back-to-back p-n junctions. Invented by Shockley (1948), the essential feature of such devices is that small currents applied to the central layer can produce large variations in current between the other two†††.

►In field-effect transistors, conductivity along a doped channel is controlled for primary use as fast on-off (high-low) switches††††.

Charge-coupled devices: The photosensitivity of a depletion region may be combined with a mechanism of trapping and subsequent reading of the photo-generated charge carriers. Tightly packed arrays of such charge-coupled devices are notably used in astronomical imaging with exposure times of up to about a minute.

Impact of the semiconductor industry: As per Table 6.5, the semiconductor industry has replaced most competing technology, and offers next generation developments in many fields such as astronomy, metallurgy, and biomedicine.

1	Intense light sources and sensitive detectors.
2	Mobile telephones.
3	Computational microprocessors.
4	Assorted consumer, control, and security electronics.
5	Data storage.

Table 6.5: Selected scope of the semiconductor industry

†For more introduction see, for example, Agarwal and Lang (2005).

††Some initial comparisons:
►A field-effect transistor is a unipolar device whose operation is based on *either* electrons or holes. But the operation of a bipolar transistor is based on *both* electrons and holes.
►Field-effect transistors are driven by voltage. But bipolar transistors are driven by current.
►Field-effect transistors tend to be smaller and faster.
►Field-effect transistors are now the most commonly used type of transistor.

†††Bipolar transistors can switch current, but their primary use is amplification, where each typically offers a current gain of up to × 100. Their configuration is such that the central layer is called the base, and the two outer layers are called the emitter and collector.

††††Such field-effect transistors have found major application in microprocessors and other computational equipment requiring many switching elements. Their configuration is such that the conductive channel extends between so-called source and drain terminals, and a perpendicularly applied voltage, via a so-called gate terminal, controls adjacent depletion geometry and hence changes the channel's width and conductivity.

6.11 Communication

While the act of communication may exploit various energy *transformations*, the transmission in typical modern systems is electromagnetic (Section 5.4). Moreover, as introduced in Table 6.6, the applicable range of wavelengths is huge, extending from kilometres for radio to microns for the near infrared.

Frequency bands (Hz) × [0.3, 3]		Wavelength bands (m) × [0.1, 1]		Continuous waves, possibly also with continuous carrier-modulated encoding of analogue and digital signals, for:	
radio	10^5	10^4		over the horizon	navigation, and maritime radio
	10^6	10^3			navigation, aviation radio, and **AM** radio
	10^7	10^2			worldwide shortwave radio
	10^8	10^1		line of sight	**VHF** television, and **FM** radio
	10^9	10^0	*microwaves*		**UHF** television, global positioning, Wi-Fi, and mobile phone communication
	10^{10}	10^{-1}			Wi-Fi, and satellite communication
	10^{11}	10^{-2}			satellite communication, and astronomy

Note: Wavelengths are free-space following frequency f as the quantity c/f (Table 4.3).

near infrared	Much shorter free-space wavelengths (m)		For astronomical detection, as well as pulsed waves for digitally encoded communication that is:
	1.55, 1.31	$× 10^{-6}$	►line-of-sight through free-space (Section 4.3.7) ►through optical fibres

Table 6.6: Categorisation of electromagnetic bands for transmission/communication

Furthermore, dependent on configuration, such systems must support high data-rate transmissions through the atmosphere, outer space, wires, or optical fibres:

Transmissions in the atmosphere and outer space: The atmosphere has properties crucial to the support of electromagnetic transmission, but these were unknown to Marconi, and his pioneering 1901 demonstration of radio waves across the Atlantic was expected to fail. Nonetheless, Marconi fortuitously succeeded by using waves of a low enough frequency for the *ionised* upper atmosphere to refract them back towards the ground. But many applications, today, involve higher-frequency line-of-sight transmissions that would propagate onwards, undeviated, into space. Such transmissions may be returned via satellites.

Table 6.7 provides a practical summary:

Implementation	Purpose
▸Ground-to-ground, at low (over-the-horizon) frequencies	Terrestrial communications
▸Ground-to-space-to-ground, at high (line-of-sight) frequencies	Communications via satellites
▸Space-to-ground, at high (line-of-sight) frequencies	Radio, infrared, and even higher frequency astronomy

Table 6.7: Summary of electromagnetic capability

Transmissions in wires and optical fibres: Conductive wires are widely used locally, but **glass optical fibres** are preferred for extended distances. Electromagnetic transmission through such fibres contrasts strikingly with radio by typically being in the near infrared and pulsed†.

The fibres also usually have a step profile of refractive index (Section 4.3.7, Figure 4.11) in which there is core glass of index n_1 coated with cladding glass of slightly lower index n_2. A simple picture of in-fibre propagation is that, when n_1 is greater than n_2, the fibre supports total internal reflection upon each glancing incidence at the core/cladding interface††.

Also, if a range of internal propagation angles is supported – as applies to so-called multimode fibres – there will be a variety of in-fibre propagation lengths. And the resultant variation in propagation times will have the undesired effect of spreading an input pulse in time, limiting the rate at which repeated pulses can be unambiguously transmitted.

But the dispersion in time can be minimised by reducing the core diameter until only a single propagative mode is supported. The resultant so-called **singlemode fibre** is thus the modern solution to high data-rate fibre-optic transmission.

Glass optical fibres have mechanical flexibility due to their diameter being only 125×10^{-6} m, and offer *inter alia* improved transmission distance, security, and interference relative to conductive wires.

†Notes:
▸Pulsed transmission is a succession of high/low intensities of light.
▸The frequency of near infrared exceeds that of radio by many orders of magnitude.

††For fibres where such a simple ray-based picture applies:
▸The core diameter is large compared to the propagating wavelength.
▸Snell's law (Figure 4.11) indicates that, if the angle of incidence at the entry face is greater than $\sin^{-1}(n_2/n_1)$, the light will be continually reflected from side to side during its onward in-fibre propagation.
▸There is a variety of in-fibre propagation angles relative to the fibre's axis, indicating numerous modes of propagation to be supported.
▸Their collective name is multimode fibre.

The **singlemode fibre** is the antithesis to the multimode fibre (as per †† above), where the small core diameter not only supports just one mode, but also enforces a wave-like form of propagation where the concepts of ray propagation, and total internal reflection no longer apply – see, for example, Hecht (2015).

AM carriers are notably susceptible to amplitude noise picked up from ambient sources.

FM carriers are less affected by noise since perturbing a wave's frequency is difficult.

Notes on **pulsing:**
►If the on/off states are of minimised duration, there can be more pulses per unit time.
►Of historical interest is the early telegraphic code, based on a dot and dash alphabet, successfully used by Marconi and known as Morse code, but that Vail (1838), with seemingly little appetite for the world's applause, is quietly remembered as inventor.

†For example, suppose the ADC has 16-bits, then it can sample the analogue electrical signal with a resolution of one part in 2^{16}, giving the ability to distinguish 65 536 different electrical strengths.

††Notably varying with the type and implementation of system, such bandwidth:
►Is deemed to be twice the maximum source frequency for an AM system.
►May be 8 MHz for an obsolete analogue television channel.
►May be 40 MHz for a high definition digital television channel.
►May be sufficient to support hundreds of digital television channels via *inter alia* increasingly sophisticated schemes of encoding, compression, and multiplexing.

Encoding: Encompassing both analogue and digital techniques, the encoding of signals to be communicated involves some form of modulation:

Purely analogue systems typically involve the encoding of analogue source signals as amplitude or frequency modulations, **AM** or **FM**, of a uniform radio wave called a carrier. The carrier's central frequency defines the channel of communication, and frequency-dependent tuning and decoding hardware selects the desired channel, and extracts the original signals.

The modulation in purely digital systems is via **pulsing** – the sustained succession of states that are either high or low (on or off): Such states may exist electromagnetically as the emission of a pulsed laser diode. And they may also exist electrically as the output from, say, a digital camera. But any analogue electric signal may be digitised via an integrated circuit known as an analogue to digital converter (ADC), wherein the fidelity of the process may be improved by:
►Raising the sampling resolution with an ADC that has more bits – an ADC with *n*-bits, for example, has 2^n different numbers available for any given sampling†.
►Raising the sampling rate with an ADC of greater speed.

Hybrid approaches are common wherein, for example, digital TV signals are encoded via complex schemes of controlling the amplitude, phase, and frequency of carrier waves.

Regardless of the chosen form of encoding, a key characteristic is the range of constituent frequencies – or so-called bandwidth. Such bandwidth reflects quality, and tends to be higher in digital systems due to choosing a typically much higher central frequency††.

Generation and detection: Such processes depend on the transmission medium and chosen technique of encoding:

Analogue techniques fundamentally stem from Section 5.4: To generate radio waves for atmospheric transmission, electrons are forced to oscillate – i.e. accelerate – back and forth within a conductive wire. That wire then acts as an antenna which radiates radio waves into the neighbouring space. The frequency of the radiated waves is that of the electronic oscillations. Acting in reverse, antennas may also be used for detection. This is where the sinusoidal electric field associated with an incoming radio wave induces oscillation of the antenna's electrons, causing an alternating current at the same frequency.

Purely digital techniques typically exploit pulsed near infrared light, where laser diodes are used for emission, and photodiodes are used for detection (Section 6.10, subsections diodes and photodiodes)†.

The digital future: While antenna based systems are fundamentally based on the analogue nature of waves, the modern preference is either as their digital hybridisation or, instead, as the pure digitisation of pulsed near-infrared laser light. With some benefits of the latter given in Table 6.8, purely digitised communication sees applications ranging from extended terrestrial distances over optical fibre to satellite based distances over free space.

1	Terrestrial and space-based communications are facilitated via the use of high-power laser diodes.
2	Terrestrial singlemode fibre-optic installations offer low-loss, divergence-free transmission.
3	The digital encoding and protocols of networks and channels improve information security, making eavesdropping more difficult.
4	Digitised optical transmission reduces susceptibility to interference.
5	Bandwidths are high due to the high central frequencies associated with the near infrared††.

Table 6.8: Some advantages of digital communication

†Notably, laser diodes are capable of intense directional emission, making them suitable for:
► Easy coupling into singlemode optical fibres, and (non-amplified) fibre-optic transmissions of at least 100 km (although, to allow for splitting of the signal, practical local systems may be specified at 20 km).
► Free-space satellite communications.

††Notes on bandwidth:
► That of laser diode technology currently exceeds 1 GHz.
► And installed purely digital systems can ideally achieve a matching *data rate* that exceeds 1 Gbit s^{-1}.

Notes on *data rate:*
► A bit is taken as the unit of digitisation.
► The matching 1 Gbit s^{-1} capability is attained by currently installed full-fibre and free-space systems.
► But any installed system that has some conductive wire in its network may have an overall limit of, say, only 40 Mbit s^{-1}.
► Nonetheless, optical fibre itself is not a practical limitation.
► And the next target in the evolution of both full-fibre and free-space systems is to upgrade the laser diode and photodetector technologies to attain in excess of 10 Gbit s^{-1}.

6.12 Electromagnetic emissions used in medicine

Techniques numbered 2 to 4 of Table 6.9 are discussed here†:

1	Visible (and nearby) light introduced as asides: ►In optical coherence tomography (Section 4.3.6). ►In pulse oximetry (Section 5.3.4).
2	Visible (and nearby) light in fibre-optic endoscopy.
3	X-rays in medical therapy and diagnostic imaging.
4	Gamma rays in diagnostic imaging.

Table 6.9: Some medical uses of electromagnetic emission

Fibre-optic endoscopy: As a highly versatile imaging technique that is configurable for real-time ***examination*** of many body-parts via a microscope or monitor, endoscopy makes use of a flexible multi-functional cable whose main element is a bundle of optical fibres for both illumination and a tightly packed subset thereof for gathering and transmitting images††.

One end of the endoscope is inserted into the body, and manoeuvred to the body-part of interest. And the end-face of each imaging fibre then gathers an average intensity and colour from the local element of the body-part. The other end of the endoscope remains outside the body, and faithfully preserves the image via its fibre-ends being of similar disposition to the internal ones. The bundle of imaging fibres is said to be coherent. Endoscopic imagery, that is both detailed and bright, needs operation at high spatial resolution and high optical power:
►High spatial resolution implies that the core (Section 6.11) of each imaging fibre should be of small diameter d, since each core simply provides an average illumination, with no detail†††.
►High optical power, conversely, implies a large value of d††††.

But the trade-off with resolution can be mitigated noting that power also increases with the fibre's so-called numerical aperture – see, for example, Hecht (2015). Since this is defined as $(n^2_{core} - n^2_{cladding})^{1/2}$ – where n is refractive index (Section 4.3.7) – images may thus be brightened, within engineering limits, by increasing the difference between n_{core} and $n_{cladding}$†.

X-ray therapy and diagnostic imaging: Although high-intensity X-rays are used in the therapeutic destruction of tumours, low-intensity X-rays are used in the imaging of tumours, broken bones, and other types of abnormality††.

In diagnostic applications, an image is created from the spatial variation of absorption of X-rays across bones, air pockets, fat, soft tissue, and other body-parts. And detail within the absorptive signal may be improved by introducing contrast-enhancing media, with high X-ray absorption, into the body-parts of interest – e.g. barium or bismuth within the digestive system; and iodine within the cardiovascular system, kidney, and brain.

Traditional implementations involve exposure of body parts to a single broad beam of X-rays followed by capture of the transmitted profile on a photographic plate for later examination by a clinician†††.

But systems whose imaging is both faster and of higher resolution combine geometric scanning with multi-element semiconductor (Section 6.10) detection††††:

Indeed, the profound 1970's advance, where X-ray detection is combined with computed tomography, uses (1) an annular diagnostic head to pass X-rays as a slice through the patient, and (2) a set of closely spaced radially-aligned ***detectors***, on the other side, to capture the emerging absorptive signal. The head's detectors typically number a thousand or more for quick building of images, and be of 0.5 mm ***size*** for high spatial resolution. Computer based processing of the detector outputs combined with rotation of the diagnostic

†Notes:
►In silica-based fibres, the engineering limit is that of internal mechanical stress caused by the difference in refractive index.
►A large numerical aperture is consistent with a large range of in-fibre propagation angles, which also implies a significantly multimode fibre (Section 6.11).

††Notes:
►Typical systems produce X-rays as the manifestation of energy released by the rapid deceleration of energetic electrons striking a massive solid target.
►The biological harm that is still possible with diagnostic X-rays is often considered to be outweighed by the potential benefits.

†††Note that the captured profile essentially compresses 3D information within the patient into a 2D image.

††††Such an approach, nonetheless, uses higher doses of X-rays, significantly restricting the number of allowable procedures over a given patient's lifetime.

Such ***detectors*** notably overcome insensitivity of semiconductors to X-rays via each being coupled to scintillating crystal, which first converts the X-rays into flashes of visible light.

However, such ***size*** is seeing a newer trend towards a two-fold reduction for yet higher resolution.

†While much diagnosis involves computational processing, and tomography involves sliced imagery:
► The term 'computed tomographic (or CT) scanning' nearly always refers to X-rays.
► X-rays may be avoided altogether e.g. via ultrasound (Section 4.3.6), or magnetic resonance (Section 5.3.4), or both.

The main attraction in the use of *gamma rays* is that they can penetrate up to about 10 cm of solid media.
(Aside: In contrast, the beta particles of Section 5.5 may penetrate to a few mm, and the alpha particles of Section 5.6 to a about 50 microns.)

Metabolic activities, that are typically examined, encompass *inter alia*:
► The metabolism of oxygen.
► The activity of tumours.
► The functioning of the brain, such as in vision, speech, and schizophrenia.
► The flow of blood.

Detection: Like with X-rays, the detection of gamma rays is tricky, and practical schemes also first use scintillating crystal.

Regardless of its type of emission (gamma rays, beta particles, or alpha particles), such spontaneous atomic *disintegration* is referred to as radioactivity.

Example of *half-life:* For a sample with a typical half-life of 6 h, the radioactivity, over a day, will drop by $24/6 = 4$ half-lives, equivalent to a factor of $2^4 = 16$.

head builds a detailed 2D image of the slice of anatomy; and then some combination of multiple such heads and axial translation leads to full 3D imagery.

The two methods may be combined, where (following an injury for example) a single X-ray exposure is used for an initial examination, and then a computed tomographic scan is used for detailed anatomical study†.

Gamma-ray diagnostics: Although usually combined with computed tomography or even magnetic resonance (Section 5.3.4) for greater spatial resolution, *gamma-ray* based diagnostic systems of basic form may resolve 15-mm-sized regions, but all have the key new benefit of highlighting *metabolic* activity. Originating from specialised chemical (radiotracer) compounds designed to be concentrated by the body in a functionally dependent manner within its parts and pathways, the gamma rays propagate in straight lines, escape the body, and then are subject to *detection*. Notably featuring a combination of the processes of decay and annihilation, here are two typical schemes whereby the radiotracers originate gamma rays:
► Decay only: Here the radiotracer's atoms suffer random spontaneous *disintegration* into smaller ones – a process which also emits gamma rays. Each such decay is quantified by the derived SI unit of radioactivity the becquerel (Bq) defined as one decay per second, and has a duration quantified by *half-life* defined as the time for a sample's radioactivity to drop by a factor of two. In the interests of both patient safety and medical efficacy, the radiotracers should be designed for minimal radioactivity, half-life, and physiological impact, as well as no toxicity and sub-24-hour bodily excretion. A typical example is technetium-99m.

A basic detection arrangement, that compresses all depth information within the radiotracer's 3D distribution into a 2D image (akin to traditional X-ray detection) involves a so-called gamma camera – a device which uses angle-restricting (collimating) technology, for the efficient localised collection of gamma rays, in combination with scintillation and photomultiplier tubes (Section 6.9) for high detection sensitivity†.

But advanced implementations use single-photon detections combined with sliced tomographic imagery. Practical schemes first produce a detailed 2D image of a slice of metabolism via a rotating annular diagnostic head with one or more gamma cameras – each with an angularly disposed array of photomultiplier tubes – and then produce full 3D imagery via axial translation of the head††.

►Decay and annihilation: Here, and as per the physics of Section 5.5, each atomic decay of the radiotracer emits a positron, which then quickly annihilates with a nearby electron such that the combined positron/electron mass m manifests, via Section 5.1.5's rest energy $E_0 = mc^2$, as a counter-propagating pair of gamma photons. And a ring of many scintillator/photomultiplier detectors around the patient, combined with computer based signal **processing** detects the photon pairings with high efficiency, and correlates them in time to produce a detailed 2D image of a slice of metabolism. And combination with axial translation leads to full 3D imagery. Facilitated by the use of specialised radiotracers with very low radioactivity and very short half-life, such so-called positron-emission tomography is the state of the art of gamma-ray based metabolic imaging, with 3D spatial resolutions reaching around 5 mm†††.

6.13 Questionnaire

†Notes:
►The scintillation is via a large wafer-shaped crystal, which is aligned with the plane of collimation. And, then, the associated flashes of visible light are captured by a 2D bank of 30 to 90 photomultiplier tubes orientated in the same plane.
►Such gamma cameras are widely used in metabolic imaging.

††Notes:
►Single-photon detections are enabled by suitably reducing the concentration of the radiotracer, and images are constructed via sophisticated signal processing algorithms.
►Single-photon gamma-camera technology is widely used in metabolic imaging.

Such a **processing** method is collimator-free and notably overcomes:
►The inability of traditional optics to focus gamma-ray emissions.
►The difficulty of determining the direction of gamma-ray propagation.

†††Notes:
►The half-life of the specialised radiotracers may be as short as a few minutes, usually requiring in-hospital fabrication to support the ensuing necessarily fast deployment.
►There is, however, limited system deployment due to cost and technical constraint.

6Q1   Within how many of the following scenarios is there net movement of charge:
    1) A cathode ray beam
    2) A bolt of lightning
    3) An isolated battery
    4) A closed electrical circuit
a ≤ 1
b   2
c   3
d   4

6Q2   Which phrase is not closely associated with good conduction:
a   Pauli's prohibition on sharing the same energy
b   Interaction of neighbouring atoms
c   Available energy levels
d   Widely separated energy bands

6Q3   The derived SI units of electric current are:
a $C\,s^{-1}$
b $C\,s$
c $A\,s^{-1}$
d $A\,s$

6Q4   Current sustained by a metallic wire is:
a   Ionic
b   Of a speed akin to cathode rays
c   Conventional
d   Electronic

6Q5   For generating electricity, which of the following is most likely to be an advantage?
a   High investment cost
b   Release of greenhouse gasses
c   Availability of renewable resources
d   Electromagnetic interference

6Q6   For generating electricity, which of the following is most likely to be a disadvantage?
a   Long equipment lifetime
b   High conversion efficiency into the final energy form
c   Short start-up time
d   Creation of landfill

Page 164 answers: 39a   40a   41b   42a   43c   44b

6Q7   Select the correct option regarding these two questions on cells:
      1) Does the loss of internal energy lead to a loss of voltage?
      2) Does their output current tend to zero if their voltage tends zero?
a   1) Yes. 2) Yes.
b   1) Yes. 2) No.
c   1) No. 2) Yes.
d   1) No. 2) No.

6Q8   Select a false statement about a cell:
a   It has zero net charge
b   It both creates and resists coulombic repulsion
c   Conservation laws imply that any exiting energy must return
d   If isolated, its voltage ideally remains constant

6Q9   Select a false statement about a battery:
a   It may contain three electrodes
b   Its internal conduction is typically via mobile electrons
c   Its energy is derived from chemical reactions
d   Its voltage can be externally dropped via resistive components

6Q10 The derived SI units of resistance, defined as voltage divided by current, are:
a $V\,A$
b $V^{-1}\,A$
c $V\,A^{-1}$
d $V^{-1}\,A^{-1}$

6Q11 Select a false statement regarding typical circuit analysis:
a   Circuit nodes conserve charge
b   Series components carry the same current
c   A closed conductive loop dissipates all supplied electric potential energy
d   Adding another resistance in parallel increases a topology's overall resistance

6Q12 The power dissipation of a component associated with 0.50 A and 2.0 V is:
a   0.25 W
b   1.0 W
c   2.5 W
d   4.0 W

6Q13 Which statement is wrong? Ammeters are measuring instruments which:
a   Are used in series
b   Are now typically of digital operation
c   Are applied to isolated components
d   Are configured for weak parametric interaction

Page 158 answers: 1a   2d   3a   4d   5c   6d
Page 159 answers: 7a   8c   9b   10c   11d   12b   13c

6Q14 The particle model of light:
a   Is premised on interference
b   Explains photoelectricity
c   Explains blackbodies
d   Is not premised on photons

6Q15 Given that a system is initially undergoing photoelectric emission, the rate of
ejection of electrons would likely increase if:
a   There is increased frequency of illumination
b   The kinetic energy of the ejected electrons was to decrease
c   There is increased intensity of illumination
d   The photoelectric work function was to increase

6Q16 If a first dynode generates four output electrons for each input one, and there is a
subsequent chain of two similar dynodes, the overall electronic gain would be:
a   12
b   16
c   64
d   81

6Q17 On a photomultiplier used for photon-counting, select a false statement:
a   It has a vacuum channel
b   Its underlying process occurs at high speed
c   Its underlying process is based on blackbody emission
d   It may have a semiconductive channel

6Q18 Select a false statement about voltage:
a   It exists across a uniformly doped semiconductor if in an isolated state
b   It concerns electric potential energy
c   It exists between two different metals within the same conductive solution
d   It will persist for longer across an insulator than across a conductor

6Q19 Which of the following is not true of intrinsic semiconductors?
a   Their conductivity is generally better than that of insulators
b   Ambient conditions may increase the mobility of their charge
c   They may arise from the growth of pure crystal lattices
d   They are treated as having overlapped bands of energy

6Q20 Which of the following helps intrinsic semiconductors to conduct?
a   Purity
b   Narrow electronic energy bands
c   A minimal band gap
d   Cooling

6Q21 Which of the following does not help intrinsic semiconductors to conduct?
a   Application of an external voltage
b   Introduction of holes
c   Darkness
d   Introduction of dopants

6Q22 Select the correct option regarding these two questions:
      1) Can a bunch of 3×10^{-19} J photons be detected with a 5×10^{-19} J bandgap?
      2) Are electrons the majority carriers of p-type semiconductors?
a   1) Yes. 2) Yes.
b   1) Yes. 2) No.
c   1) No. 2) Yes.
d   1) No. 2) No.

6Q23 Select a false statement about a pn-junction:
a   Its creation involves the movement of charge
b   It contains both p-type and n-type material
c   It is created as two contacting pieces of intrinsic semiconductor
d   It has an internal voltage

6Q24 A single pn-junction cannot be a:
a   Photodiode
b   Conductive element
c   Switch
d   Non-conductive element

6Q25 Select a false statement about a semiconductor's depletion layer?
a   It is a region with almost no dopants
b   Its geometric width varies with applied external voltage
c   It is a region with almost no mobile charges
d   It is associated with the concept of barrier voltage

6Q26 Long distance ground-to-ground communication via microwaves is generally
      achieved:
a   Through glass optical fibres
b   Via propagation through the lower atmosphere
c   Be being bounced off satellites
d   Via refraction from the ionosphere

162   Physics' Assimilation and Purpose

Page 160 answers: 14b   15c   16c   17c   18a   19d
Page 161 answers: 20c   21c   22d   23c   24c   25a   26c

6Q27 Choose a false statement about fibre-optic transmission:
a   The refractive index of the core exceeds that of the cladding
b   A large number of propagative modes minimises dispersion
c   Simple treatments of propagation involve the concept of reflection
d   A small core size is an ideal configuration for communication

6Q28 What resolution can a 5-bit analogue to digital converter achieve?
a   1 part in 8
b   1 part in 14
c   1 part in 18
d   1 part in 32

6Q29 How many of the following statements are true?
    1) In the practice of communication, the central frequency of amplitude
    modulation is generally greater than that of frequency modulation.
    2) Amplitude modulations are generally more susceptible to interference than
    frequency modulations.
    3) Semiconductor lasers are widely used as sources for fibre-optic
    communication.
a   0
b   1
c   2
d   3

6Q30 Regarding high-definition television, how many of the following phrases apply?
    1) Phase modulation. 2) Digital encoding. 3) The use of a carrier.
a   0
b   1
c   2
d   3

6Q31 The principal reason for configuring a fibre-optic bundle to be coherent is:
a   To produce interference
b   To transmit images
c   To polarise light
d   To totally internally reflect

6Q32 The practice of endoscopy encompasses how many of the following activities?
1) Washing. 2) Cutting. 3) Grasping. 4) Stitching.
a   1
b   2
c   3
d   4

6Q33 Which statement is not appropriate to optical fibres used for high-resolution
endoscopic imaging:
a   They should have a thin cladding
b   They should have a small numerical aperture
c   They should be tightly packed
d   They should have a small core diameter

6Q34 Which of the following is not part of X-ray medicine?
a   Destruction of tumours
b   Introduction of radioactive materials into the body
c   Imaging of the digestive and cardiovascular systems
d   Computed tomography

6Q35 Select the fundamental basis of X-ray diagnostics:
a   Resonance
b   Interference
c   Absorption
d   Scintillation

6Q36 Select the most accurate description of radioactivity:
a   An emission of radio waves
b   A deterministic process
c   A nuclear precession
d   An amount of becquerels

6Q37 If a radioactive sample has a half-life of 1 hour, how long will it take for the
radioactivity to drop by a factor of four?
a   An eighth of an hour
b   A quarter of an hour
c   2 hours
d   4 hours

6Q38 Which of the following has the deepest penetration depth in anatomical media?
a   Alpha particles
b   Beta particles
c   Gamma rays
d   Visible light

Page 162 answers: 27b   28d   29c   30d   31b
Page 163 answers: 32d   33b   34b   35c   36d   37c   38c

6Q39 Radioactive material used in diagnostic imaging is:
a Physiologically concentrated
b Inevitably of high toxicity
c Selected for a long half-life
d Naturally occurring

6Q40 The main emission from subatomic annihilation is of:
a Gamma rays
b X-rays
c Radio waves
d Visible light

6Q41 Medical systems of positron-emission tomography do not:
a Offer tracking of physiological processes
b Rely on a single gamma camera
c Exploit a process known as annihilation
d Exploit interactions with electrons

6Q42 Piezoelectric transducers are used in the practice of:
a Ultrasound scanning
b Computed tomographic scanning
c Endoscopy
d Body scanning via nuclear magnetic resonance

6Q43 Regarding the practice of non-diagnostic forms of medicine, how many of the
      following are used?
      1) Ultrasound. 2) Magnetic resonance. 3) X-rays.
a 0
b 1
c 2
d 3

6Q44 Which of the following techniques of diagnostic imaging always involves putting
      foreign matter into the body?
a Ultrasound scanning
b Endoscopy
c Computed tomographic scanning
d Magnetic resonance imaging

Chapter 7   Space and Time

7.1   Nature of space

Space enjoys a kaleidoscope of treatments ranging over the Newtonian, Einsteinian, and quantum worlds. On a terrestrial footing it is the host for ourselves and familiar everyday objects. Further afield – dotted by satellites, planets, and stars – is outer space of almost incomprehensible proportion. The space between stars is also an exceptional vacuum and is thus an excellent approximation to the idealised concept of free space (Section 4.3.7). Indeed, inter-stellar space has, on average, only about one atom (Section 5.2.1) per cubic centimetre†.

Nonetheless, the localised denseness of inter-stellar atoms is one **key** to cosmology whose outward manifestations range from formation of the local power-houses – the stars – to the ongoing evolution of the universe itself††.

Space also acts as the universe's recycling centre using the debris from failed bodies to generate new ones, and wherein the ultimate in denseness – and associated temperature and energy – is the so-called **black hole**, the largest examples of which are purported to reside at **galactic** centres.

†But such denseness is actually far from constant, ranging from about 10^6 – as in the best artificial vacuum – down to as little as 10^{-1}.

Other such **keys** apply too, such as the mysterious entities of dark matter (Section 5.1.5), and dark energy (see Section 7.8).

††Associated understanding is enhanced by:
► Cosmologists, who theorise on the origin and evolution of the universe.
► Astronomers, who observe the universe's constituents through the detection and measurement of their emitted light – a notably passive activity that contrasts starkly with the controlled experiments of conventional empiricists.
► Further reading, such as provided by Morison (2008).

Black holes have such extreme gravitation that nothing – not even light – can escape. Moreover, they continue to grow due to continually trapping gravitationally attracted nearby matter and energy.

A **galaxy** is a localised but vast body of matter and energy, with billions of stars, bound by its own gravity.

Astronomical data is notably often reported in non-SI units. E.g:
►The light-year is the distance in free space (Section 1.6) travelled by light in one year.
►The astronomical unit, at about 1.50×10^{11} m, is the average radius of the Earth's orbit of the Sun.
►The parsec is about 3.26 light-years, 2.06×10^5 astronomical units, and 3.08×10^{16} m.
►The arcsecond is a unit of angle, where 2π radians:
= 360 degrees
= 360×60 arcminutes
= $360 \times 60 \times 60$ arcseconds.

†Notes on detection:
►Specialist technologies are required for X-rays and gamma rays – as alluded to in Section 6.12.
►Otherwise, semiconductor (Section 6.10) technologies are mainly now used.

††Notes:
►Radio photons are far weaker than those shown.
►While the atmosphere is transparent to the visible, partial or full absorption applies to the other bands.

7.2 Principles of astronomy

The earliest *astronomical* observations were limited to the most intense bodies visible to the naked eye. By the 1600s, much dimmer bodies could be seen with the invention of the telescope. The photographic plate was invented in the 1800s, allowing recording of the telescopic images. And Figure 7.1 shows recent advances in detecting spectral regions beyond the visible†:

Date	Band	Comparative wavelength
1930	radio	longest
1960	infrared	longer than visible
1960	ultraviolet	shorter than visible
1970	X-ray	short
1990	gamma ray	shortest

Table 7.1: Recent advances in detecting astronomical bands

On such observations, note that:
►They are all electromagnetic (Section 5.4).
►From Section 6.11's Table 6.6, the shortest radio (and microwave) wavelength is 1 mm.
►And the wavelength λ decreases thereafter.
►Hence, via Section 6.9's relation $E = hf = hv/\lambda$, electromagnetic frequency f, and photonic energy E both increase towards the gamma rays.
►Moreover, as illustrated in Table 7.2, photons with the highest energies come from the most energetic astronomical bodies††.

Astronomical bodies of increasing energy	Maximum photon energy (eV)	Name of associated electromagnetic band	
molecular clouds	1×10^{-3}	millimetre	Note: names refer to the associated wavelength.
so-called cosmic dust comprising particulate matter up to about 100 microns	4×10^{-2}	submillimetre	
cool stars	2	infrared	
Sun-like stars	4	visible	
very hot stars	1×10^3	ultraviolet	
exploding end-states of massive stars, known as supernovae	1×10^6	X-ray	
galactic centres / black holes	$\to \infty$	gamma ray	

Table 7.2: Photonic energies from some astronomical bodies

Also note that outer space is immense. Thus considering, for example, the extreme estimated distance of 1×10^{26} m to the furthest galaxies and the potentially large propagation times of Table 7.3, the light that arrives at Earth can be extremely weak:

from the Moon	1 second
from the Sun	8 minutes
from Pluto	5 hours
from **Proxima Centauri**	4 years
from our galactic centre	3×10^4 years
from the furthest galaxies	1×10^{10} years
Note that most outer space is considered to be a perfect vacuum (Section 7.1), and hence the speed v of electromagnetic propagation is the fastest possible, defined as $v = c = 299\,392\,458$ m s^{-1}†.	

Table 7.3: Times of electromagnetic flight to the Earth

Such matters, and more, present extreme challenges to astronomers. Not only is most observation limited to the study of stars due to the dimness of distant bodies, but their essential instrument, the **telescope**, must have sufficient:

► Sensitivity to low levels of light.

► Resolution to small angles of subtension.

► Robustness to environmental effects – such as of gravity, temperature, and the atmosphere:

7.2.1   Sensitivity, and its atmospheric seeing

Given uniformly distributed incoming light, the sensitivity of a telescope (Section 7.2) is proportional to the area of its light-gathering mirror. Thus, for two telescopes, taking the ratio of their light-gathering areas provides a comparison of their sensitivities††.

But the level of light that reaches a telescope (1) fundamentally depends on the intensity and distance of the source, and (2) may depend on attenuation by the atmosphere†††.

Intensity and effect of distance: Suppose power P_s emits from A of surface area. Then, as an average measure, the emitted intensity I_s is

Proxima Centauri is the next star beyond the Sun.

†The quantity c is discussed under 'electromagnetic propagation and speed' in Section 4.3.7.

A basic such **telescope** has two key parts:
► A large parabolic mirror that collects and focusses the astronomical light.
► A device that detects and records the focused image: With the modern preference being electronic, the photographic plate is replaced with various technologies – the basic key one being a tightly packed array of charge-coupled devices (Section 6.10).

††For example, the radius of the mirrors of Hawaii's two so-called Keck telescopes is 5 m, and the radius of the active part of the human eye is about 4 mm. Compared to the human eye, the sensitivity of the Keck telescopes is thus $(\pi \times 5^2)/(\pi \times (4 \times 10^{-3})^2) = 2 \times 10^6$ times greater.

The astronomers' desire to see dimmer bodies located deeper into space drives a constant need for bigger telescopes.

†††Notes:
► Only point (1) applies if the telescope is operated from space.
► Point (2) also applies if the telescope is located on the Earth's surface.
► Any observation through the Earth's atmosphere is referred to generically as atmospheric seeing.

defined as $I_s = P_s/A_s$, which, for a star of, say, radius r_s becomes $I_s = P_s/(4\pi r_s^2)$.

Similarly, the average intensity I_d in the vicinity of a detector is defined as $I_d = P_d/A_d$, where P_d is the power at the detector, and A_d is the surface area of the detector. Referred to as an apparent intensity, I_d generally differs from I_s, where not only is there dependence on emission uniformity, but significant reductions are likely due to divergence and attenuation:

For the specific example of spherically uniform emission and divergence, and no attenuation, (1) the average **intensity** I_d at some detection distance D becomes $I_d = P_s/(4\pi D^2)$, and (2) taking equivalence to P_d/A_d, rearranging for P_s, and substituting into $I_s = P_s/(4\pi r_s^2)$ yields the star's surface intensity I_s:

► directly as $I_s = P_d D^2/(A_d r_s^2)$.

► or as the ratio $I_s/I_{sun} = P_d D^2/(I_{sun} A_d r_s^2)$ relative to the Sun, which is the astronomers' preferred form known as luminosity†.

Attenuation arising from atmospheric seeing: Attenuation by the atmosphere reduces the sensitivity of detection, and principally involves absorption and scattering (Section 4.3.7). Due to all associated attenuation mechanisms, the Earth's atmosphere acts as a protective barrier against many spectral regions, including gamma rays, X-rays, most ultraviolet, and much infrared.

Conversely, spectral regions that retain high transparency include the visible, some small windows of infrared, and radio, leaving these with the best opportunities for sensitive ground-based astronomical detection.

7.2.2   Resolution, and its atmospheric seeing

Generic considerations: The angular resolution of a telescope concerns the ability to see distinctly two point sources that are close together in angle – the smaller the resolvable angle, the greater the resolution. For a given telescope, the resolution is best in space. But, when incoming light suffers the turbulence of atmospheric seeing (Section 7.2.1), focussed images become distorted via the two broad categories of unwanted effect outlined in Table 7.4†:

Defocus	Momentary movement of the image either in front of or behind the quiescent focal plane.
Blur	Momentary sideways movement of the image.

Table 7.4: Imaging deficiencies due to turbulence

Such imaging deficiencies result in reduced angular resolution. Nonetheless, the reduction can be mitigated by locating the telescope high up a mountain, noting that only about 10% of the atmosphere is at an altitude of over 10 km.

Impact on the determination of position, motion and distance: A body's position in space is determined from the telescope's precise setting of direction needed to collect its emission. Motion perpendicular to that direction is then assessed via changes in position over time. And the body's distance may be measurable by the surveyor's method of trigonometric parallax:

The method involves detecting the body's emission from two ends of a local baseline orientated perpendicularly to the body's position in space. Then, if the baseline is of length b, and the two viewing positions subtend an angle of θ radians at the body, the distance D to the body follows geometrically as the approximate relation $D \cong b/\theta$. For astronomical bodies, such as the stars, the goal is to determine large values of D. Thus, b needs to be big, which is typically achieved as the diameter of the Earth's orbit of the Sun by observing the body for a whole year. And θ needs to be small, which is achieved by using a telescope with a high angular resolution.

Nonetheless, the benefit of high altitude operation is limited, and turbulence-afflicted (non-radio) signals may be resolved to only 1 arcsecond under good conditions but, otherwise, likely worse than 20 arcseconds††.

†As often observed by the naked eye, such effects make starlight twinkle – i.e. to change quickly in brightness or even colour.

††Note that the resolution of radio telescopes is fundamentally far worse, as discussed next.

†Notes:
►Conversely, in space, atmospheric seeing no longer applies, and the former visible-light based Hipparcos telescope covered tens of thousands of the nearest stars, aided by an angular resolution approaching 0.001 arcseconds.
►For stars further afield, distances may be estimated using a combination of indirect methods that include comparison with known nearer stars.

††Note that other considerations apply too such as:
►The construction of the light-gathering mirror being of near-perfect geometric form.
►Maintaining that geometric form during operation.
►Preventing stray light from reaching the detector.

†††Notes:
►Thus, for example, if the gathering of light involves radio rather than visible, a much larger mirror is needed for the same resolution.
►Rayleigh's criterion is an arbitrary conception of diffraction-limited resolvability, but it is effective, and widely used.
►The curious may wish to examine the similarity of the criterion's formula with $(d/1.22)\sin\theta \cong \lambda$ of Table 4.17's Case 2 for the first dark fringe of diffractive superposition from a small circular hole (albeit with differently defined d and θ parameters).

Ground-based telescopes, accordingly, have determined the distances of only a few of the nearest stars†.

Theory: Whilst potentially impacted by atmospheric seeing, angular resolution is always subject to diffractive superposition – a fundamental propagative effect that Table 4.17's Case 2 indicates to illuminate areas of image that geometrically are expected to be dark††:

In particular, when imaging a point source, like that of a distant star, the expected bright spot-like image spreads out and becomes surrounded by a series of dark and bright concentric rings known as Airy's rings. The imaging of two stars produces two bright central spots and two sets of Airy's rings. If the stars are sufficiently close that their diffractive images overlap and appear as one, they cannot separately be resolved.

To assess the likely resolvability of two point sources, Rayleigh (1879) adopted the criterion that the central spot of one diffractive image must be at least as far away as the first dark ring of the other, and accordingly deduced their smallest resolvable diffraction-limited angular separation θ (in radians) to be given by the approximate formula, $\theta \cong 1.22\lambda/d$, where d is the diameter of the detector, and λ is the propagating wavelength. Thus, for high angular resolution, the light-gathering mirror needs a large diameter d, and be gathering light of a short wavelength λ†††.

Impact on imaging: The perhaps at-best 1 arcsecond resolution of turbulence-afflicted visible and infrared signals, and the regardless far worse resolution at radio's long wavelengths both starkly compare with diffraction-limited opportunities in space. For example, the orbiting Hubble telescope gathers diffraction-limited images in the visible with an angular resolution of 0.05 arcseconds.

7.2.3 Mosaic mirrors, and active optics

If a telescope's light-gathering mirror is of 4 m diameter, its mass may be 15×10^3 kg requiring a particularly strong and rigid support structure. Mirrors of say > 6 m are impractical since they distort excessively under gravity. A solution is their formation as a multi-facetted light-weight mosaic. Such facets may have a thickness of only about 20 cm, allowing real-time **deformation** via an array of actuators to correct for distortions caused by tilting or a change of temperature. Known as active optics, the method is typically used in all medium to large sized telescopes to maintain the geometric accuracy of their light-gathering mirrors†.

7.2.4 Adaptive optics for diffraction-limited imaging

Schemes known as adaptive optics remediate turbulence-afflicted loss of angular resolution (Section 7.2.2) through broadly involving (1) electronic cameras for monitoring fluctuations in an image, (2) fast computers for constantly re-calculating that image's centre, and (3) some form of corrective action. The corrective action for radio telescopes is largely electronic via the use of computational algorithms. But in the infrared and more recently in the visible, it is mechanical. In Hawaii's two Keck telescopes, for example, feedback to actuators fixed to small mirrors near the telescope's focus gives up to 20 nm of deformation every millisecond for automatic re-centring of the image††.

7.2.5 Aperture synthesis for increased imaging resolution

Correlating the outputs from more than one telescope – known as aperture synthesis – is an alternative approach to using larger diameters of mirror (Section 7.2.2) for high-quality imaging, where angular resolution is now dependent on the telescopes' separation:

Such **deformation** notably needs only to be slow, with a frequency of about 0.1 Hz.

†For example, Hawaii's two Keck telescopes both have a 10 m light-gathering mirror formed as a mosaic of 36 two-metre facets. And, in both, all such facets enjoy computer-controlled active optics to form part of a parabolic light-gathering surface accurate to 50 nm.

††Notes:
▸Operating in the infrared, the adaptive optics of the two Keck telescopes gives a ten-fold improvement in angular resolution. The result, at about 0.04 arcseconds, is close to the diffraction limit.
▸Adaptive optics should not be confused with active optics because it is conceived and applied differently, and has the distinguishing feature of high operating frequency – hundreds of hertz are required to react to fluctuating turbulence.

†One such implementation is the so-called Very Long Baseline Array (VLBA), USA. See, for example, Napier (1994).

††The short wavelengths associated with the visible are of particular interest due to their intrinsically high diffraction-limited resolution. Early work on signal correlation was based on optical interferometry, typically using fixed fibre-optic links between telescopes.

The newer trend is towards direct electrical correlation, similar to that used in the infrared. Dravins *et al.* (2015), for example, reported a scheme of photomultiplier based photon-correlation that, by also circumventing atmospheric turbulence, gave diffraction-limited resolution in the visible.

†††Binary stars may be close enough to exchange material between their atmospheres, or sufficiently far apart for their mutual orbit to take hundreds of years. But most have orbital periods that range from a few days to a few months, and have separations that are less than 1 astronomical unit (Section 7.2).

††††Smale (2020), for example, showed that $m_1/m_2 = r_2/r_1$, where r_1 and r_2 are the individual maximum distances to the common centre of mass. Thus, in principle, a value for m_1/m_2 follows from measurements of r_1 and r_2. (Note that $r_1 + r_2 = r$.)

Implementation is established at radio wavelengths, where correlated electrical phase between the outputs of telescopes separated across, or even between, continents offsets the long wavelength to give an angular resolution of 0.001 arcseconds, or even better†.

For matching capability in the visible, maintaining small differences of phase over long distances, and the residual limitations of atmospheric seeing (Sections 7.2.1 and 7.2.2), are exciting challenges††.

7.3   Stellar mass

Stellar mass is a key, but difficult, parameter to assess. Fortunately, binary systems of stars are as common as single stars, and they allow an initial approach to the problem: The two stars in each binary are closely bound to each another by mutual gravitation, and each orbits around their mutual barycentre (Section 5.1.2)†††.

Associated with Kepler's the law of periods (Section 5.1.1), Smale (2020) derived the total binary mass as $m_1 + m_2 = 4\pi^2 r^3 G^{-1} T^{-2}$, where m_1 and m_2 are the masses of the individual stars, r is their maximum separation, G is the gravitational constant (Section 5.1.2), and T is the period of the mutual orbit. Accordingly, measurements of r and T allow the calculation of $m_1 + m_2$. The individual masses, m_1 and m_2, then follow upon derivation of an independent second equation, such as that for the mass ratio m_1/m_2††††.

For individual stars, another trick is needed: A relationship between mass m and luminosity l (Section 7.2.1), first announced by Halm (1911), is now taken to be of the approximate power-law form, $l \propto m^{3.5}$ for most stars in early life. Taking, for example, the known 2×10^{30} kg mass of the Sun (Section 1.4), the constant of proportionality follows, and other stellar masses can be calculated given l.

7.4   Stellar surface temperature

Assuming the **emitted spectrum** from a star to be that of a blackbody, the surface temperature may be assessed by applying Wien's law (Section 6.8). But such a spectrum may be superposed by **absorption lines** caused by absorption by ionised (Section 5.2.1) gasses within the stellar atmosphere; thus an **analysis of colour**, which averages out the spectral differences, may provide a more accurate approach.

Overall, the surface temperature is assessed as approximately 0.6×10^4 K for the Sun, and $[0.3, 3] \times 10^4$ K for the other stars.

7.5   Stellar surface composition

An analysis by **Payne** (1925), on how the Sun's absorption lines (Section 7.4) depend on ionisation at a given temperature, led her to determine the abundance and temperature of the superficial elements. The results presented in her doctorate were startling and revolutionary. The Sun was revealed to have more hydrogen and helium than any other element – and in the case of hydrogen by many orders of magnitude.

With hydrogen thus indicated to dominate the stars, she also hinted at it being by far the most abundant element in the universe. She was right on both counts, providing insight that would revolutionise both astronomy and cosmological modelling†.

7.6   Stellar birth, evolution, and death

The stars, owing to their energy, abundance, and ubiquity, hold special importance in cosmology:

Across regions of space hundreds of light-years (Section 7.2) in size, within features known as galactic spiral arms, are molecular clouds mostly of hydrogen but also of some heavier elements, compounds, and dust. Such clouds, on average, may have a molecular denseness of only 10^2 per cubic centimetre, and

A star's **emitted spectrum** can only be from near its surface since this may freely propagate into space while any deeper emission is fully absorbed/scattered beforehand.

Each **absorption line** within a given spectrum results from the presence of a particular chemical element, and manifests as absence over some short spectral range.

The **analysis of colour**, following the aside of Section 5.3.4, may involve ratiometric processing of two values of intensity measured over two different subsets of the overall spectrum.

Payne's work has come to be recognised as the definitive explanation of:
►The connection between a star's superficial spectral detail and both chemical composition and temperature.
►The domination of the Sun's atmosphere by hydrogen.

†And yet she was initially overlooked, if not actively worse, by the contemporary male-dominated scientific orthodoxy that the Sun's elemental composition should be similar to that of the Earth.

a temperature of only 10 K but, nonetheless, constitute the regions of interstellar space from which stars are born:

Responding to its own gravitation, each cloud collapses towards its core and gains rotational velocity. If a common centre is not sustained, collapse will continue towards a number of separate cores with slower rotational velocities. Rising pressure within each core means a rise of temperature. And the presence of charged particles produces a magnetic field (Section 5.3.6) which favours collapse along the axis of rotation as a planetary-forming disk.

When the core has a temperature that exceeds about 1.0×10^7 K, it supports fusion of its hydrogen where the reaction products, helium and neutrinos (Section 5.5), are slightly less massive than the reactants. The lost mass m appears as radiant heat E_0 according to Section 5.1.5's equation of rest energy $E_0 = mc^2$†.

The cloud core has thus become a self-sustaining star, outputting the energy by which the local solar system, including any constituent planets, can live††.

7.6.1   The Hertzsprung-Russell diagram

Revealing interesting patterns when each star is plotted as a point, and having a central locus comprising all hydrogen-fusing stars dubbed the main sequence, the Hertzsprung-Russell diagram is a profound 2D representation of the birth, life, and death of stars. Exemplification is provided opposite via:

▶Figure 7.1, which properly shows the diagram's non-linear horizontal axis of surface temperature, its non-linear vertical axis of luminosity (Section 7.2.1), and its connection with stellar mass, but which simplifies its points as loci.

▶Table 7.4, which shows both the supporting data, and new data highlighting the fundamental connection between a star's mass and its duration on the main sequence†††.

†Thus a small amount of mass can generate a lot of energy. In fact, stars lose a small proportion of their mass over life, typically about 20%. A star's initial mass is thus of major interest for two reasons:
▶It can be taken, to a reasonable approximation, as the star's mass over life.
▶It is the key driver towards the star's own evolution.

††Neglecting any absorption lines (Section 7.4), such stars emit approximately as blackbodies (Section 6.8).

†††Note that the duration t of a star being on the main sequence is that of its fusing of hydrogen, and is thus proportional to the star's amount of hydrogen divided by the star's rate of using its hydrogen. It follows that $t \propto m/l$, where m is the star's mass, and l is its luminosity.

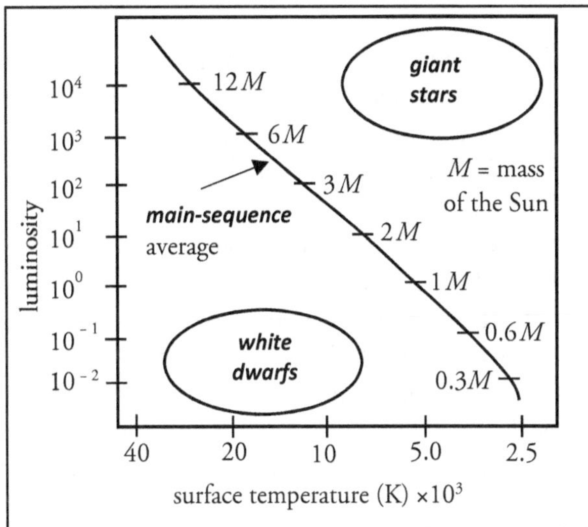

Figure 7.1: Idealised Hertzsprung-Russell diagram showing approximate/average loci (rather than points)†

Mass	Surface temperature ($\times 10^3$ K)	Luminosity, l	Duration, t (years)
$0.3\,M$	3	10^{-2}	2×10^{11}
$0.6\,M$	4	10^{-1}	8×10^{10}
$1\,M$	6	1	1×10^{10}
$2\,M$	8	10^1	1×10^9
$3\,M$	12	10^2	3×10^8
$6\,M$	18	10^3	6×10^7
$12\,M$	28	10^4	6×10^6
Note: M = mass of the Sun (about 2×10^{30} kg)			

Table 7.5: Some approximate main-sequence data†

7.6.2 Fusing of hydrogen, and first red giant

Dependent on core temperature, the birth of a star (Section 7.6) is marked by two main potential pathways for the fusion of hydrogen into helium:

At about 1.0×10^7 K, hydrogen nuclei fuse by **direct** proton-proton reactions. But, at about 2.0×10^7 K, faster fusion can dominate catalysed via the so-called **CNO-cycle**, where carbon converts first into nitrogen, then into oxygen and back into carbon again.

†Notes on the Hertzsprung-Russell diagram and its supportive data:

►Its **main-sequence** stars have the largest recorded abundance, and, by fusing hydrogen, are considered alive. Furthermore, the associated rate of fusion is relatively slow so that its **duration** t covers most of their lifetimes. In particular, the constant of proportionality for the relation $t \propto m/l$ follows from known main-sequence stars, and t for the others can be calculated given their values of m and l.

►Its **giant stars** are also alive by fusing elements beyond hydrogen; they are relatively luminous and making increasingly heavy elements.

►Its **white dwarf** stars, however, are dead; they have fully spent their fusionable fuel, are no longer producing heat, and are slowly cooling.

The **direct** pathway dominates in the Sun because its core temperature is only about 1.5×10^7 K.

The **CNO-cycle** dominates in stars of greater than 1.5 solar masses, and whose cores originally contain some carbon.

Upon the establishment of either pathway, the release of energy pauses the core's gravitational collapse, and the star attains stable values of temperature and luminosity.

However, as the core becomes exhausted of hydrogen, it is left as dense and (temporarily) inert helium. The fine balance between the output of energy and gravitation is broken, and gravitational collapse of the core resumes. The star moves off the main sequence, and enters into a shorter period of old age. Rising temperature caused by the collapsing core causes the remaining outer hydrogen to fuse – a process known as shell burning – causing the star to swell, as a so-called **red giant**, to typically many times its original size.

7.6.3   Fusing of helium, and second red giant

When the contracting core of Section 7.6.2 reaches about 1×10^8 K, its helium starts to fuse to form carbon. There may be an initial violent release of energy known as a helium flash, but the output quickly settles down as a relatively short second phase of life, again with stable values of temperature and luminosity.

Eventually the core's helium becomes exhausted. The core resumes gravitational collapse, and its rising temperature initiates helium shell burning and a second red-giant expansion (Section 7.6.2). What happens from here depends critically on the star's mass††:

7.6.4   Death of light stars

In stars of less than about eight solar masses, the core (Section 7.6.3) remains too cold to fuse its carbon. The core's collapse and the shell's expansion both proceed but, with no more fusion-generated heat, the star dies leaving its outer layers in nearby space as a so-called **planetary nebula** – an intricately structured volume of hot diffuse gas.

When the Sun fuses its hydrogen shell, and becomes a *red giant*, it will vaporise Venus and possibly also the Earth.

††If massive enough to generate sufficient core temperature, ever-faster cycles of fuel exhaustion will ensue, with the core generating successively heavier elements.

Planetary nebula: Beware that this unfortunate historic term has nothing to do with planets.

The contracting core is resisted by growing electron pressure, and reaches stability with white-hot temperature, but Earth-like size and about 10^9 kg m^{-3} density. The so-called white dwarf behaves like a blackbody (Section 6.8), and slowly cools by emitting light energy to become a less luminous brown dwarf†.

7.6.5   Death of heavy stars

Stars of greater than about eight solar masses continue to burn, first fusing their carbon (Section 7.6.3) into neon. And, if sufficiently massive, will continue to undergo cycles of fuel exhaustion, each with its attendant core-collapse and red-giant phase. But the cycles must stop after fusing silicon because the fusing of its product, iron, is endothermic††.

Rather than the relatively sedate deathly formation of a light-star's planetary nebula, an iron-cored star ends its life in a process so explosive, and marked by processes so different, that it is given the special name, a supernova:

The abrupt rise of temperature caused by the supernova's rapidly collapsing core synthesises new elements even heavier than iron and violently explodes a large proportion of the star's outer part into space. While the temperature of the remaining core rockets to about 5×10^9 K, energetic gamma rays break down the iron nuclei by a process called photodisintegration, and electrons and protons combine to form neutrons and neutrinos (Section 5.5).

Thus, as the remaining core becomes dominated by neutrons, a huge quantity of elemental matter is exploded into space that represents the composition of the Earth, and other likely life-sustaining planets†††.

If the supernova's remaining core has a mass of less than about three solar masses, neutron pressure is sufficient to resist further collapse, and stability is achieved at a diameter of

†Numerous brown dwarfs have been discovered. But ultimately cooled black dwarfs are taken not yet to exist because the required cooling duration would exceed the currently modelled cosmology of the universe.

††So:
►What originates atoms heavier than iron, and hence the elemental compositions for Earth-like planets?
►What are the implications to the universe of a progressive shift from hydrogen to heavier elements?

†††Biological life, as known to humans, is possible only due to (parts of) the universe already having aged through at least one generation of stars. The known complex chemistry and biology of the universe is sustained through heavy stars giving up their life.

†Black holes have no confirmed mechanisms of emission, and are thus difficult to detect. However, their existence can still be inferred because:
►Their gravitation influences the motion of nearby bodies, and is sufficiently severe even to deviate the propagation of nearby light – an effect known as gravitational lensing.
►Inwardly gravitating nearby material, heated by its extreme acceleration, emits X-rays which, if not also captured, propagate outward into space.

Static universe: Einstein's initial conception was of universal uniformity of space, and independence of time.

††Note that physical laws supporting time's directional independence, and possible reversal, conflict with:
►The weak interaction (Section 5.5) known to have time-direction dependence.
►Quantum physics' probabilistic nature of description and measurement.
►The apparent onward arrow of thermodynamics that probabilistically drives systems towards equilibrium.

†††All such conflicts conflate with further questions such as is time:
►Quantised?
►The cause of the thermodynamic arrow?

††††Further substance behind such points can at least be found in, for example, Muller (2006).

a few tens of km, and a density of about 10^{17} kg m^{-3}. Now called a neutron star, the core rotates with a period typically between 4 s and 0.002 s. And, if such rotation results in the emission of detectable electromagnetic pulses, the neutron star is known as a pulsar.

But if the remaining core exceeds about three solar masses it will continue its collapse beyond the neutron phase to form a black hole (Section 7.1) – an entity whose extreme gravitation distorts the local space-time (Section 5.1.5) so severely that not even light can escape†.

7.7   Nature of time

Against an uncertain scientific standing, such as introduced in Table 7.6, the human condition would attribute time with contrary, albeit enigmatic, significance. Time as imprinted on the human psyche is inexorably onward, passes interminably slowly for the keenly alert youth but in a flash for the old, carries the inevitability of decay and death, and attracts an intense desire for deeper understanding and debate.

1	Its eternal but ever-changing condition of the now betwixt past and future has confounded intellectuals from Aristotle to Einstein, and beyond.
2	It evolves the universe towards an equilibrium of matter and energy, but why not just energy, and why so little antimatter?
3	It, according to Einstein's initial modelling of a **static universe** is, in a sense, outside that universe.
4	It bears some directional conflict with, otherwise, equally capable historical and evolutionary classical determinism††,†††.
5	It has an absolute basis in current theories of quantum physics that conflicts with its Einsteinian relativity (Section 5.1.5)†††.
6	Could it, for example, have a cosmological origin? Or, is it merely outside of physicality, impossible to be understood by physics?

Table 7.6: Some scientific awkwardnesses of time††††

Indeed, according to Minkowski and Einstein (Section 5.1.5), time is no more significant than a fourth dimension, and simply to be regarded as a descriptor of change, not as of itself, but within the relativistic framework of space-time, wherein changes of time are inextricably linked to changes of space, and vice versa. Also, according to Einstein, the dependent intervals of time are seen not only to vary between different frames of reference, but also to dilate significantly for entities moving at close to c – the latter, for example, being verified by Frisch and Smith's (1963) measurement of increased half-life for fast-moving muons†.

But there is no such benefit for the tardy. Inanimate and artificial bodies will decay; biological systems and even stars will die. Ageing, wherein time is progressive and irreversible, would appear a natural paradigm supported even by the thermodynamic concept of increasing entropy††.

Cosmologically, time is fundamental. Black holes (Section 7.1) are pertinent cases. Due to extreme gravitation, Einstein's general theory of relativity (Section 5.1.5) indicates that black holes slow time – even tending to zero – relative to the very surroundings that they inexorably proceed to consume. And, on the scale of the universe, the origin, eternity, and even cessation of time are open concerns of supreme cosmological significance:

†Representing a massive short-lived form of electron, a muon may be created when a high energy atomic fragment from space – a.k.a. a cosmic ray – interacts with the nucleus of an oxygen or nitrogen atom in the upper atmosphere.

††With the concept of increasing entropy introduced by Clausius (1865), and later enunciated as the second law of thermodynamics, there is an apparent inevitability for the universe to experience progressive disorder – or chaos – where there is ever-increasing equilibrium and ever-decreasing energy available for work.

7.8   Eternity and the universe

In considering time on the scale of the universe, it should first be asked whether such time has an origin. No would be the answer according to Einstein's early thinking; and, for example, Bondi, Gold, and Hoyle (1948) who theorised an eternally expanding universe of constant density.

†Although pejoratively named the big bang by Hoyle, the term has nonetheless entered our lexicon.

††Notes:
► Modelling of the big bang originates from work by Alpher, Bethe, and Gamow (1948) on the origin of the chemical elements.
► The modelling pertains solely to the expansion of space, and is taken to carry ordinary matter unchanged within it.
► The modelling also concerns progressively decreasing average material density, and is thus contrary to the early assertions of Bondi, Gold, and Hoyle.
► Significantly colder than even the universe's 10 K molecular clouds, the 3 K cosmic microwave background has a photon energy of about 7×10^{-4} eV and a wavelength of about 2 mm. (Section 7.2's Table 7.2 provides an interesting comparison.)

†††Note that, had gravity been the sole controlling effect, expansion should be slowing down.

Cosmological constant: This quantity, conversely, is now seeing a renaissance in the treatment of the mysterious dark energy.

That space, itself, is expanding is widely accepted following the observational discovery by Hubble (1929) that the galaxies in space are receding from each other according to their Doppler red-shifts (Sections 4.3.2 and 5.1.5), and specifically that their outward speeds are proportional to their distance.

The continued expansion of space implies that some time ago there could have been singularity of existence, and that the universe, as is currently known, derived as some hot expansive event†.

Such a big bang, even today, should leave a remnant after-glow of microwave energy coming from all directions in space. And such a remnant – and hence also the big bang – was confirmed through measurements by Penzias and Wilson (1965) on excess antenna temperatures. Comprising photons consistent with the emission from a 3 K blackbody (Section 6.8), such microwaves are extremely weak, and are known as the 3 K cosmic microwave background. As 3 K is consistent with the modelled cooling associated with about 14 billion years of expansion since the big bang, the universe is taken to about 14 billion years old††.

Intriguingly, Reiss *et al.* (1998) observed the expansion of space to be proceeding at an accelerating rate. This startling discovery means that something other than gravity is controlling the expansion, and in a positive sense. Coined dark energy by Turner (1998), there has since been no definitive progress towards establishing its true nature or potential evolution†††.

So will the universe continue to expand and persist forever? Einstein originally conceived (but later rejected) a quantity in his general theory of relativity known as the **cosmological constant**. In fact, with the constant's appropriate value, the general theory provides support for the accelerated expansion of space.

However, the constant's value originally chosen by Einstein for a static universe, actually leads the general theory to predict instability, and hence inevitable contraction. That space, despite its dark energy, could eventually reach some maximum size and then contract is of philosophical intrigue. The universe could then ultimately disappear in an annihilating big crunch, or even continue life as cyclical crunches and bangs.

Whatever the truth, there are undoubtedly more ramifications to Nature than currently revealed, and **fundamental** physics remains to be established.

7.9   Questionnaire

Fundamental physics and its route towards universal explanation is pitted against wonderful unresolved cosmological questions, such as:

► Is there a theory of everything that includes unification of the strong interaction and gravitation (Section 5.7).

► What is the true fabric of the universe [1]?

► Is black-hole based consumption of matter and energy (Section 7.1) an inevitable one-way ticket; or could they, for example, evaporate via so-called Hawking (2011) radiation?

► How will expansion evolve, and will there ever be collapse?

► Could time ever reverse, and entropy (Section 7.7) ever decrease?

► Is the present observation merely of a part of some continuous whole, or is it of just one example of numerous such entities within the entirety of the universe?

---

[1] With current estimates of about 27% dark matter (Section 5.1.5) and 68% dark energy, it is humbling that ordinary matter (including ourselves) is taken to represent only about 5% of the present-day universe.

7Q1   Which option that lists astronomical sources by increasing maximum energy:
a   Cosmic microwave background. Cosmic dust. Molecular clouds.
b   Cosmic dust. Molecular clouds. Living stars.
c   Molecular clouds. Super novae. Cosmic dust.
d   Super novae. Cosmic microwave background. Living stars.

7Q2   The highest-energy electromagnetic band associated with black holes is:
a   Gamma ray
b   Infrared
c   Radio
d   Visible

7Q3   To one significant figure what, in SI base units, is a light-year?
a 9×10^{15}
b 9×10^{12}
c 9×10^{18}
d 1×10^{1}

7Q4   Exactly how many arcseconds are in a circle?
a   360
b   21 600
c   129 600
d   1 296 000

7Q5   How many radians, to 3 significant figures, are in an arcsecond?
a 0.290×10^{-3}
b 0.291×10^{-3}
c 4.84×10^{-6}
d 4.85×10^{-6}

7Q6   How many of the following three items are of relevance to angular resolution?
        1) Wavelength. 2) Airy's rings. 3) Rayleigh's criterion.
a   0
b   1
c   2
d   3

7Q7   Choose the option that covers main regions of atmospheric transparency:
a   Gamma ray and radio
b   Ultraviolet and microwave
c   Visible and infrared
d   Millimetre and submillimetre

Page 186 answers: 28c   29c   30b   31d   32a   33d   34a

7Q8   How many of the following three statements are true?
  1) The lowest electromagnetic frequencies are of radio waves.
  2) Photonic energy increases with electromagnetic wavelength.
  3) Electromagnetic propagation is slower in media of higher refractive index.
a   0
b   1
c   2
d   3

7Q9   The sensitivity of a the light-gathering mirror of a telescope is least likely to be affected by:
a   The intensity of the source body
b   The distance of the source body
c   The turbulence of the atmosphere
d   The size of the mirror

7Q10 The most important option for seeing distinctly two close stars is:
a   A high sensitivity of detection
b   A high level of optical diffraction
c   High quality imaging optics
d   A high level of atmospheric absorption

7Q11 Which option about a body's apparent intensity is true?
a   It is an emitted intensity
b   It is a detected intensity
c   Its determination requires knowledge of the body's surface area
d   Its determination requires knowledge of the body's distance

7Q12 If there is a constant intensity of illumination over a large area, and if there is a doubling of the radius of the telescope used to detect it, what happens to the detected power?
a   It stays the same
b   It increases by a factor of 2
c   It increases by a factor of 4
d   It changes by some other factor

7Q13 How many of the following are significantly gained by using large telescope?
  1) Overcoming of atmospheric turbulence.
  2) Observing of dim bodies.
  3) Resolving of bodies close together in angle.
a   0
b   1
c   2
d   3

184   Physics' Assimilation and Purpose

Page 182 answers: 1a   2a   3a   4d   5d   6d   7c
Page 183 answers: 8c   9c   10c   11b   12c   13c

7Q14 The least applicable option on determining stellar distance is:
a   Baseline parallax
b   Ground based detection of X-rays
c   Diffraction-limited optics
d   Comparative studies of nearby stars

7Q15 The best practical means of correcting atmospheric turbulence is:
a   Using multiple telescopes
b   Continually changing the entire shape of a light-gathering mirror
c   Using fast electronics
d   Composing a light-gathering mirror from multiple parts

7Q16 Considering 1) visible and 2) radio, the number of adaptive-optics and
        aperture-synthesis technologies used in mainstream ground-based astronomy is:
a   1) 1.   2) 1.
b   1) $\geq$ 1.   2) 1.
c   1) 1.   2) $\geq$ 1.
d   1) 2.   2) 2

7Q17 Luminosity:
a   Is an apparent intensity
b   Has derived SI units of $J\ s^{-1}\ m^{-2}$
c   Is proportional to the Sun's intensity
d   Has a functional dependence on distance

7Q18 Which of the following statements about a star's emission is false?
a   It can provide information on chemical composition
b   It is of relatively short wavelength in early life
c   Its physics closely follows the theory of blackbodies
d   Its colour depends on atmospheric temperature

7Q19 An initial observation of a cosmic body is sufficient to determine its:
a   Apparent intensity
b   Distance
c   Motion
d   Mass

7Q20 Following detection, which is the most important in calculating luminosity?
a   Its size
b   Its age
c   Its distance
d   Its mass

7Q21 Select a false statement about a molecular cloud that is contracting:
a   It has a decreasing rotational velocity
b   It is driven by gravity
c   It has a rising temperature
d   It can divide into a number of smaller clouds

7Q22 Significant concentration of charged particles in a molecular cloud is likely to
        cause:
a   Significant production of neutrons
b   The cloud to expand
c   Geometric asymmetry
d   No significant difference in behaviour compared to uncharged clouds

7Q23 Which of the following statements about the birth of a star is false?
a   It starts proton-proton reactions
b   It fully resists its own gravitation
c   It starts hydrogen shell burning
d   It starts the longest stable phase of its life

7Q24 A star on the main sequence is:
a   Not creating helium
b   Not fusing hydrogen
c   Not significantly contracting
d   Doing none of the above

7Q25 Long-term energy output from stars comes mainly from:
a   Rotation
b   Gravitational potential
c   Mass
d   Photodisintegration

7Q26 Which of the following statements about stellar life is false?
a   Its duration is greater for stars that are more massive
b   Its progress can be determined via the abundance of heavy elements
c   Its evolution can be appreciated via the Hertzsprung-Russell diagram
d   Its onset of old age is marked by the fusing of helium

7Q27 What is the CNO-cycle?
a   A process of fusing helium
b   A process of catalysis
c   A process involving copper
d   An astronomical rotation

Page 184 answers: 14b   15c   16a   17c   18b   19a   20c
Page 185 answers: 21a   22c   23c   24c   25c   26a   27b

7Q28 Red-giant phases of stars are not associated with:
a   Shell burning
b   Fuel depletion
c   Core expansion
d   Onset of raised atmospheric temperature

7Q29 Which of the following is not associated with the death of a star like the Sun?
a   Ejection of layers of atmosphere
b   Formation of a white dwarf
c   A remnant core that substantially contains iron
d   A remnant core that behaves like a blackbody

7Q30 The death of a star that is much more massive than the Sun would not result in:
a   A pulsar
b   A white dwarf
c   A black hole
d   A neutron star

7Q31 Which of the following is not associated with a supernova?
a   Creation of neutrinos
b   Breaking down of iron nuclei
c   Exhausted exothermic nuclear fuel
d   Explosion of the core

7Q32 Which phrase does not apply to pulsars?
a   Significant rhythmic variation in size
b   Significant rate of rotation
c   Sizes of a few tens of km
d   Composition of neutrons

7Q33 Which of the following options does not support the theory of the big bang?
a   Existence of 3 K cosmic microwaves
b   Bodies in space possessing red-shifted spectra
c   Hubble's work
d   Belief that the universe is of eternally constant density

7Q34 Which of the following options is not a feature of black holes?
a   Hastening of time relative to elsewhere
b   Induced X-ray emission
c   Theoretical evaporation
d   Bending of light

Date	Name	Contribution
*c.*530BC	Pythagoras	Pythagoras' theorem of mathematics (although already known to ancient Babylonians a thousand years earlier).
*c.*505BC	Heraclitus	Origination and philosophy of the concept of energy.
*c.*380BC	Eudoxus	Modelling of a geocentric universe.
*c.*300BC	Euclid	Euclid's optics, In (as first publication): La Prospettiva di Evclide, Fiorenza, 1573 (The perspective of Euclid; law of reflection).
*c.*250BC	Archimedes	Principle of buoyancy.
*c.*1016	Ibn al-Haytham	Kitāb al-Manāẓir, As (first publication): Opticae Thesaurus Alhazeni Arabis, Basel, Eusebius Episcopius, 1572 (Book of optics; principles of optics and experimentation, influencer of Bacon).
1543	N. Copernicus	De Revolutionibus Orbium Coelestium, Nuremberg (On the revolutions of the heavenly spheres; advocate of heliocentricity).
1588	T. Brahe	De Mundi Aetherei Recentioribus Phaenomenis Liber Secundus, Uraniborg, Hven, Ch. 8 (Second book about recent phenomena in the celestial world; outline of geoheliocentric model of universe – precision pre-telescope measurements of planetary position were completed by 1597).
1609	J. Kepler	Astronomia Nova, Heidelberg (New astronomy; first and second laws of planetary motion determined from Brahe's data).
1610	G. Galilei	Sidereus Nuncius, Venitiis (Starry messenger; founding of telescope based astronomy).
1619	J. Kepler	Harmonices Mundi Libri V, Linz (The harmony of the world; third law of planetary motion determined from Brahe's data).
1620	F. Bacon	Novum Organum, J. Ravesteinii & Elsevier, Amsterdam (A new logic; first modern formulation of the scientific method).

1621	W. Snell	Law of refraction, In (as first publication): Discours de la méthode pour bien conduire sa raison et chercher la vérité dans les sciences, R. Descartes, Leyde: Jan Maire, 1637 (Discourse on the method to conduct one's reason well, and seek the truth in the sciences; Discourse on method, with credit to Snell).
1638	G. Galilei	Discorsi e Dimostrazioni Matematiche, Intorno à due Nuove Scienze, Leida, Appresso gli Elsevirii (Dialogues concerning two new sciences; exemplification of the scientific method).
1663	B. Pascal	Traitez de l'Equilibre des Liqueurs, Paris (Treatise on the equilibrium of liquids; principle that a change of pressure applied to an ideal fluid is transmitted undiminished to all parts of its volume and surface).
1669	C. Huygens	*A Summary Account of the Laws of Motion, communicated by Mr. Christian Hugens in a Letter to the R. Society, and since printed in French in the Iournal des Scavans of March 18, 1669 st. n.*, Philosophical Transactions, Vol. 4, 925-928 (Conservation of momentum).
1678	R. Hooke	Lectures de Potentia Restitutiva, or Of Spring Explaining the Power of Springing Bodies, John Martyn (Hooke's law).
1687	I. Newton	Philosophiae Naturalis Principia Mathematica, Londini (Mathematical principles of natural philosophy; the Principia).
1690	C. Huygens	Traité de la Lumière, Chez Pierre Vander Aa, Marchand Libraire, A Leide (Treatise on light; Huygens' principle).
1727	P. Bouger	Essai d'Optique sur la Gradation de la Lumière, Paris (Optical treatise on the gradation of light; descriptive law of intensity transmitted by absorbing media).
1738	D. Bernoulli	Hydrodynamica, Argentorati (Hydrodyamics; equation of ideal fluids).
1751	B. Franklin	Experiments and observations on electricity, London: Printed and sold by E. Cave, at St. John's Gate.

1755	D. Bernoulli	Réfléxions et Eclaircissemens sur les Nouvelles Vibrations des Cordes Exposees dans les Mémoires de l'Académie de 1747 & 1748, In: Histoire de l'Académie Royale des Sciences et Belles Lettres, Berlin, Vol. 9, 147-172 (On new vibrations in strings; principle of superposition).
1785	C.A. Coulomb	Second Mémoire sur l'Électricité et le Magnétisme, In: Histoire de l'Académie Royale des Sciences, Imprimerie Royale, Paris, 578-611 (Second dissertation on electricity and magnetism; Coulomb's law).
1802	T. Young	II. The Bakerian Lecture. *On the theory of light and colours*, Philosophical Transactions of the Royal Society, 9212-9248 (Double-slit experiment on the wave nature of light).
1807	T. Young	Lecture on Collision, and on Energy, In: A Course of Lectures on Natural Philosophy and the Mechanical Arts, William Savage for Joseph Johnson, London, Vol. 2, 51-56 (Refer to page 52 for formal introduction to energy, one of many topics published over two volumes).
1808	E.L. Malus	*Sur une proprieté de la lumière réfléchie par les corps diaphanes*, Nouveau Bulletin des Sciences par la Société Philomathique de Paris, Paris, Tome 1 (1807-1809), 266-269 (On a property of light reflected by translucent substances; Malus' law).
1822	J. Fourier	Theorie Analytique de la Chaleur, Chez Firmin Didot, père et fils, Paris (The analytic theory of heat; Fourier's law).
1826	A.M. Ampère	Memoir on the Mathematical Theory of Electrodynamic Phenomena, Uniquely Deduced from Experience, In: Mémoires de l'Académie des Sciences de l'Institut de France, Vol. 6, 175-388 (Ampère's law).
1827	G. Ohm	Die Galvanische Kette, Mathematisch Bearbeitet, T. H. Riemann, Berlin (The galvanic chain, processed mathematically; Ohm's law).

1832	M. Faraday	*Experimental researches in electricity*, Philosophical Transactions of the Royal Society, London, Vol. 122, 125-162 (Law of electromagnetic induction).
1834	H.F.E. Lenz	*Über die bestimmung der richtung der durch elektrodynamische vertheilung erregten galvanischen ströme*, Annalen der Physik, Vol. 107, 483-494 (About the determination of the direction of the galvanic currents excited by electrodynamic distribution; Lenz's law).
1838	S. Morse A. Vail	Named Morse code, invention by Vail of telegraphic encoding as a dot and dash alphabet (see supporting historical literature now held at the Smithsonian Institution Archives).
1842	C. Doppler	*Über das farbige Licht der doppelsterne und einiger anderer gestirne des himmels*, Abhandlungen der Königlichen Böhmischen Gesellschaft der Wissenschaften, Vol. 2, 465-482 (About the coloured light of the double stars and some other stars in the sky; Doppler effect).
1845	G.R. Kirchhoff	*Ueber den durchgang eines elektrischen stromes durch eine ebene, insbesondere durch eine kreisförmige*, Annalen der Physik und Chemie, Vol. 64, 497-514 (About the electric current running through a plane, especially through a circular form; fundamental current and voltage laws).
1849	H. Fizeau	Sur une Experience Relative à la Vitesse de Propagation de la Lumière, In: Comptes Rendus Hebdomadaires des Séances de l'Académie des Sciences, Bachelier, Paris, Vol. 29, 90-92 (On an experiment relating to the propagation velocity of the light).
1865	R. Clausius	*Ueber verschiedene für die anwendung bequeme formen der hauptgleichungen der mechanischen wärmetheorie*, Annalen der Physik, Vol. 201, Iss. 7, 353-400 (About various forms of the main equations of mechanical heat theory convenient for application; first and second laws of thermodynamics).

1865	J.C. Maxwell	*A dynamical theory of the electromagnetic field*, Philosophical Transactions of the Royal Society, London, Vol. 155, 459-512 (Electromagnetic unification).
1871	J.W. Strutt (Lord Rayleigh)	LVIII. *On the scattering of light by small particles*, The London, Edinburgh, and Dublin Philosophical Magazine and Journal of Science, Vol. 41, 447-454.
1879	Lord Rayleigh	XXXI. *Investigations in optics, with special reference to the spectroscope*, The London, Edinburgh, and Dublin Philosophical Magazine and Journal of Science, Vol. 8, 261-274 (Diffraction in cases of circular geometry, Rayleigh's criterion).
1879	W. Crookes	On Radiant Matter: A Lecture Delivered to the British Association for the Advancement of Science at Sheffield, E.J. Davey, London.
1887	A.A. Michelson E.W. Morley	*On the relative motion of the earth and the luminiferous ether*, American Journal of Science, Vol. 34, Iss. 203, 333-345 (Use of Michelson's interferometer).
1888	J.C. Maxwell	Matter and Motion, (As republication by): Cambridge University Press, 2010 (Up to then contemporary coverage of Newtonian physics, workable interpretation of Newton's second law).
1889	O. Heaviside	XXXIX. *On the electromagnetic effects due to the motion of electrification through a dielectric*, Philosophical Magazine, Vol. 27, Iss. 167, 324-339 (Rewriting of Maxwell's equations in modern form).
1892	H.R. Hertz	Untersuchungen Ueber Die Ausbreitung Der Elektrischen Kraft, Johann Ambrosius Barth, Leipzig (Investigations on the propagation of electric energy; experimental speed of electromagnetic waves).

1893	W.C.W.O.F.F. Wien	Eine Neue Beziehung der Strahlung Schwarzer Körper zum Zweiten Hauptsatz der Wärmetheorie, In: Sitzungsberichte der Königlich Preussischen Akademie der Wissenschaften zu Berlin, Berlin, 55-62 (A new relationship between the radiation of blackbodies and the second law of the heat theory; laws governing the radiation of heat, leading to 1911 Nobel Prize).
1894	G.J. Stoney	*Of the 'electron' or atom of electricity*, Philosophical Magazine, Series 5, Vol. 38, 418-420 (Stoney first used the term, electron, in 1891, but published on atoms having elemental units of electricity as early as 1874).
1897	J. Larmor	LXIII. *On the theory of the magnetic influence on spectra; and on the radiation from moving ions*, Philosophical Magazine, Series 5, Vol. 44, Iss. 271, 503-512 (Larmor precession).
1897	J.J. Thomson	*Cathode rays*, Philosophical Magazine, Vol. 44, 293-316 (Work on electrodynamics and magnetism leading to 1906 Nobel Prize).
1901	M. Planck	*Ueber das Gesetz der Energieverteilung im Normalspectrum*, Annalen der Physik, Vol. 309, Iss. 3, 553-563 (On the law of distribution of energy in the normal spectrum; Planck's law and theory of oscillatory energy quanta leading to 1918 Nobel Prize).
1902	P.E. Lenard	*Über die lichtelektrische wirkung*, Annalen der Physik, Vol. 8, 149-198 (About the photoelectric effect).
1905[a]	A. Einstein	*Concerning an heuristic point of view toward the emission and transformation of light*, American Journal of Physics, Vol. 33, Iss. 5, 1-16 (Explanation of photoelectric effect leading to 1921 Nobel Prize).
1905[b]	A. Einstein	*Zur elektrodynamik bewegter körper*, Annalen der Physik, Vol. 17, 891-921 (On the electrodynamics of moving bodies; the special theory of relativity).

1905[c]	A. Einstein	*Ist die Trägheit eines Körpers von seinem Energiegehalt abhängig?*, Annalen der Physik, Vol. 18, 639-641 (Does the inertia of a body depend upon its energy-content?).
1909	H. Minkowski	*Raum und Zeit*, Physikalische Zeitschrift, Vol. 10, 104-111 (Space and time; notion of four-coordinate space-time, to be used in Einstein's general theory of relativity, also see: https://www.minkowskiinstitute.org/mip/MinkowskiFreemiumMIP2012.pdf).
1911	J. Halm	*Further considerations relating to the systematic motions of the stars*, Monthly Notices of the Royal Astronomical Society, Vol. 71, Iss. 8, 610-639 (The luminosity power law of stars).
1911	E. Hertzsprung	*Uber die Verwendung Photographischer Effektiver Wellenlängen zur Bestimmung von Farbenäquivalenten*, Potsdam (On the use of photographic effective wavelengths to determine colour equivalents; Hertzsprung-Russell diagram illustrating patterns of stellar life).
1913	R.A. Millikan	*On the elementary electrical charge and the Avogadro constant*, Physical Review (American Physical Society), Vol. II, No. 2, 109-143 (Experimentation on electronic charge leading to 1923 Nobel Prize).
1915	H.A. Lorentz	The Theory of Electrons, Dover, New York (2nd edition 1952) (Theory of electrodynamics, 1902 Nobel Prize).
1916	A. Einstein	*Die grundlage der allgemeine relativitätstheorie*, Annalen der Physik, Vol. 49, Iss. 7, 769-822 (Foundation of the general theory of relativity).
1918	A. Einstein	*Dialog über Einwände gegen die relativitästheorie*, Naturwissenschaften, Vol. 6, 697-702 (Dialogue about objections to the theory of relativity; addressing of the so-called twin paradox).
1922	W. Gerlach O. Stern	*Der experimentelle nachweis der richtungsquantelung im magnetfeld*, Zeitschrift für Physik, Vol. 9, 349-352 (Experimental proof of directional quantisation in a magnetic field).

1925	F. Hund	*Zur deutung verwickelter spektren, insbesondere der elemente scandium bis nickel*, Zeitschrift für Physik, Vol. 33, 345-371 (For the interpretation of complex spectra, especially the elements scandium to nickel; rules accounting for the way the electronic states of atoms are organised).
1925	C.H. Payne	Stellar Atmospheres; a Contribution to the Observational Study of High Temperature in the Reversing Layers of Stars, Ph.D. Thesis, Radcliffe College, Cambridge, Massachusetts.
1925	W. Pauli	*Über den zusammenhang des abschlusses der elektronengruppen im atom mit der komplexstruktur der spektren*, Zeitschrift für Physik, Vol. 31, 765-783 (On the connection between the completion of electron groups in an atom and the complex structure of spectra; work on exclusion principle leading to 1945 Nobel Prize).
1926	G.E. Uhlenbeck S. Goudsmit	*Spinning Electrons and the Structure of Spectra*, Nature, Vol. 117, 264-265.
1926	G.N. Lewis	*The conservation of photons*, Nature, Vol. 118, No. 2981, 874-875 (Naming as photon the quantum of light).
1926	E.R.J.A. Schrödinger	*An undulatory theory of the mechanics of atoms and molecules*, The Physical Review, Vol. 28, No. 6, 1049-1070 (Work on quantum theory leading to 1933 Nobel Prize, joint with P.A.M. Dirac).
1927	W.K. Heisenberg	*Ueber den anschaulichen inhalt der quantentheoretischen kinematic und mechanic*, Zeitschrift für Physik, Vol. 43, 172-198 (On the perceptual content of quantum theoretical kinematics and mechanics; quantum theory and uncertainty principle, leading to 1932 Nobel Prize).
1928	P.A.M. Dirac	*The quantum theory of the electron*, Proceedings of the Royal Society A, Vol. 117, 610-624 (Work on quantum theory leading to 1933 Nobel Prize, joint with E.R.J.A. Schrödinger).

1929	E.P. Hubble	*A relation between distance and radial velocity among extra-galactic nebulae*, Proceedings of the National Academy of Sciences, Vol. 15, Iss. 3, 168-173 (Hubble red shift).
1931	P.A.M. Dirac	*Quantised singularities in the electromagnetic field*, Proceedings of the Royal Society A, Vol. 133, 60-72 (Theoretical magnetic monopole).
1933	F. Zwicky	*Die rotverschieb ung von extragalaktischen nebeln*, Helvetica Physica Acta, Vol. 6, 110-127 (The red-shift of extragalactic nebulae; postulation of dark matter).
1934	E. Fermi	*Versuch einer theorie der β-strahlen*, Zeitschrift für Physik, Vol. 88, 161-177 (Introductory theory of beta decay).
1939	R.H. Fowler E.A. Guggenheim	Statistical Thermodynamics: a Version of Statistical Mechanics for Students of Physics and Chemistry, Cambridge University Press (Zeroth law of thermodynamics).
1948	R.A. Alpher H. Bethe G. Gamow	*The origin of chemical elements*, Physical Review, Vol. 73, 803-804 (Original modelling of the concept of the big bang).
1948	W. Shockley	Filing of U.S. Patent 2 569 347: Circuit Element Utilizing Semiconductive Material, Granted 1951 (Invention of bipolar transistor).
1948	H. Bondi T. Gold	*The steady-state theory of the expanding universe*, Monthly Notices of the Royal Astronomical Society, Vol. 108, 252-270.
1948	Hoyle	*A new model for the expanding universe*, Monthly Notices of the Royal Astronomical Society, Vol. 108, 372-382.
1960	S. Von Hoerner	*Die numerische integration des n-körper-problemes für sternhaufen. I*, Zeitschrift für Astrophysik, Vol. 50, 184-214 (The numerical integration of the n-body problem for star clusters).
1963	S. Von Hoerner	*Die numerische integration des n-körper-problemes für sternhaufen. II*, Zeitschrift für Astrophysik, Vol. 57, 47-82 (The numerical integration of the n-body problem for star clusters).

1963	D. Frisch J.H. Smith	*Measurement of the relativistic time dilation using μ-mesons*, American Journal of Physics, Vol. 31, 342-355 (The μ-meson is a former name for the muon).
1968	H.A. Haus P. Penfield Jr	*Force on a current loop*, Physics Letters A, Vol. 26, Iss. 9, 412-413 (Magnetic dipole interpretation of circulating current).
1973	H. Fritzsch M. Gell-Mann H. Leutwyler	*Advantages of the color octet gluon picture*, Physics Letters B, Vol. 47, Iss. 4, 365-368 (Proposed basis of the strong interaction).
1979	S.L. Glashow M.A. Salam S. Weinberg	Nobel Prize for the electroweak theory unifying the electromagnetic and weak interactions.
1988	P.J. Henderson	Displacement detection, UK Patent Application 2197717A, Published 25 May (Inventive principle, and example underpinning research at the University of Liverpool on chromatic modulation based systems).
1990	R.P. Feynman	QED - The Strange Theory of Light and Matter, 1st edition, Penguin.
1994	P.J. Napier	The Very Long Baseline Array. In: J.G. Robertson, W.J. Tango (eds), Very High Angular Resolution Imaging, International Astronomical Union, Springer, Dordrecht, Vol. 158, 117-124 (Aperture synthesis in the infrared).
1994	P.J. Scully R. Holmes G.R. Jones	*Remote, in-vivo monitoring of blood oxygen saturation of patients using optical fibres*, In 1994 Conference on Lasers and Electro-Optics Europe, Technical Digest Series (Optica Publishing Group, 1994), paper CWI4.
1996	C. Payne-Gaposchkin	An Autobiography and Other Recollections, 2nd edition, Cambridge University Press, 227.
1997	M.V. Berry A.K. Geim	*Of flying frogs and levitrons*, European Journal of Physics, Vol.18, No.4, 307-313.
1998	A.G. Reiss (and 19 others)	*Observational evidence from supernovae for an accelerating universe and a cosmological constant*, American Astronomical Society, Vol. 116, 1009-1038.
1998	M.S. Turner	Theoretical cosmology, naming of so-called dark energy.
2004	J.R. Taylor	Classical Mechanics, University Science Books.

2005	A. Agarwal J.H. Lang	Foundations of Analog and Digital Electronic Circuits, 1st edition, Morgan Kaufmann.
2008	I. Morison	Introduction to Astronomy and Cosmology, 1st edition, Wiley.
2009	M. Gould E. Hurst	Bridging the Gap to University Mathematics, Springer.
2011	S.W. Hawking	A Brief History of Time, Bantam.
2013	F. Englert P.W. Higgs	Joint Nobel Prize for understanding the origin of subatomic mass.
2014	**Masood Hasan**	Wish, expressed as private verbal communication to his daughter (**Naveed Henderson**) and grand-daughter (**Maliha Henderson**), that the present works be published.
2014	**Naveed Henderson**[1] **Maliha Henderson**	Original of numerous private verbal relays of **Masood Hasan's** wish to the present author.
2015	D. Dravins T. Lagadec P. Nuñez	*Optical aperture synthesis with electronically connected telescopes*, Nature Communications, Vol. 6, Article 7852. (https://www.nature.com/naturecommunications).
2015	J. Hecht	Understanding Fiber Optics, 5th edition, Laser Light Press.
2016	R.A. Muller	Now – The Physics of Time, W.W. Norton & Company (The meaning of the present, with particular coverage of thermodynamic entropy, quantum entanglement, and relativity – including theory of the so-called twin paradox).
2019	La Brochure sur le SI SI Brochure	Le Système international d'unités (SI) - The International System of Units (SI) 9th edition, V3.01, August 2024, Bureau International des Poids et Mesures (An initiative towards world-wide unification of measurement, available print options: French, English, concatenated French and English).
2020	J.E. Dodd B. Gripaios	The Ideas of Particle Physics, 4th edition, Cambridge.
2020	A. Smale	*Deriving Kepler's formula for binary stars*, https://imagine.gsfc.nasa.gov/features/yba/CygX1_mass/binary/equation_derive.html.

---

[1]Naveed Henderson (née Hasan) is the daughter of the late Masood Hasan, and wife of the present author.

2021	F.L. Anderson	*Huygens' Principle geometric derivation and elimination of the wake and backward wave,* Scientific Reports, Vol. 11, Article 20257 (https://www.nature.com/scientificreports).
2022	J.R. Taylor	An Introduction to Error Analysis: The Study of Uncertainties in Physical Measurements, 3rd edition, University Science Books.
2023	D.J. Griffiths	Introduction to Electrodynamics, 5th edition, Cambridge University Press.
2023	P. Kok	A First Introduction to Quantum Physics (Undergraduate Lecture Notes in Physics), 2nd edition, Springer (For interactive figures see: https://www.pieter-kok.staff.shef.ac.uk/interactive/).
2024	S. Keevil R. Padovani S. Tabakov T. Greener C. Lewis (eds)	Introduction to Medical Physics, 1st edition, CRC Press.

Preliminary Index of Prefaced and Specialist Topics

Main Index